AF812798

Palgrave Series in Contemporary Korean Studies

Series Editors
Hyeong-ki Kwon
Department of Political Science
Seoul National University
Seoul, Korea (Republic of)

Song Chong Lee
Department of Religious Studies
Seoul National University
Seoul, Korea (Republic of)

Over the past decade, South Korea has experienced a remarkable surge in global popularity. This phenomenon is largely fueled by influential cultural forces such as K-Pop, K-Dramas, K-Beauty, and K-Cuisine, among others. In the past decade, the number of foreign universities and research institutes dedicated to Korean studies has doubled, indicating a deepening commitment to understanding Korean culture and society. Building on the current cultural momentum of interest in contemporary Korea and growing scholarly interest, this book series proposal aims to refresh, update, and, where necessary, redirect the discourse in Korean Studies. The focus is on contemporary issues and concerns, organized around seven major thematic areas: 1) Value and Identity (religion and society), 2) Politics and Economy, 3) K-Future (philosophy), 4) K-Narratives (literature), 5) Modernity and Development, 6) Contemporary K-Music, and 7) Hallyu (Korean Wave). This project is initiated by SNU to help shape global discussions about Korea. The goal is to advance contemporary Korean studies with global networks of scholars.

Yohan Yoo • Song Chong Lee
Editors

Reimagining Korea

Identity and Values in a Changing World

palgrave
macmillan

Editors
Yohan Yoo
Department of Religious Studies
Seoul National University
Seoul, Korea (Republic of)

Song Chong Lee
Department of Religious Studies
Seoul National University
Seoul, Korea (Republic of)

ISSN 3059-3549 ISSN 3059-3557 (electronic)
Palgrave Series in Contemporary Korean Studies
ISBN 978-981-96-6989-9 ISBN 978-981-96-6990-5 (eBook)
https://doi.org/10.1007/978-981-96-6990-5

© The Editor(s) (if applicable) and The Author(s), under exclusive license to Springer Nature Singapore Pte Ltd. 2025

This work is subject to copyright. All rights are solely and exclusively licensed by the Publisher, whether the whole or part of the material is concerned, specifically the rights of translation, reprinting, reuse of illustrations, recitation, broadcasting, reproduction on microfilms or in any other physical way, and transmission or information storage and retrieval, electronic adaptation, computer software, or by similar or dissimilar methodology now known or hereafter developed.
The use of general descriptive names, registered names, trademarks, service marks, etc. in this publication does not imply, even in the absence of a specific statement, that such names are exempt from the relevant protective laws and regulations and therefore free for general use.
The publisher, the authors and the editors are safe to assume that the advice and information in this book are believed to be true and accurate at the date of publication. Neither the publisher nor the authors or the editors give a warranty, expressed or implied, with respect to the material contained herein or for any errors or omissions that may have been made. The publisher remains neutral with regard to jurisdictional claims in published maps and institutional affiliations.

This Palgrave Macmillan imprint is published by the registered company Springer Nature Singapore Pte Ltd.
The registered company address is: 152 Beach Road, #21-01/04 Gateway East, Singapore 189721, Singapore

If disposing of this product, please recycle the paper.

Contents

Notes on Contributors

Merose Hwang is an associate professor in the History Department at Hiram College, a small liberal arts school in Northeast Ohio (USA). Hwang's recent research includes "*Kut* as Political Disobedience, Healing, and Resilience," *A New Outlook at Atrocities* (Palgrave Macmillan Studies on Human Rights in Asia, 2023), "The Liberatory Effects of Indigenous Ceremonies in the Aftermath of Mass Trauma," *Peace as Liberation: Visions and Praxis from Below* (Springer Nature, 2023), and "Enduring Violence and Commemoration: Korea's Cheju April 3 Incident," *Violence: An International Journal* (Sage, 2023). Hwang is currently researching Cold War civilian deaths in Northeast Asia, Maoist movements in South Asia, and decolonization praxis in education.

Hyunjoo Jung is an associate professor in the Department of City Planning at Seoul National University, Seoul, Korea. As a geographer, Jung's research revolves around urban studies, gender, and migration. Her recent research focuses on multicultural spaces of migrants and gendered urban experiences. Her recent publications include "The Impact of Educational Migration in the Transition to a Modern City: Focusing on Bukchon as the Locus of Educational Migration to Gyeongseong," *Seoul Journal of Korean Studies*, 37(1) (2024, with Yang); "Multiplicity and Path Dependency in the Modeling of Historical Routes: A Case Study of the Wonju Basin in the Central Region of the Korean Peninsula," *Professional Geographer*, 76(1) (2024, with Ko and Shim); "Perspectives and Practices of Feminist Urban Researchers," *SPACE*, 54(11) (2019); and "Making Homes Survival Places: The Experience and Practices in

Fear of Crime of Young Women Living Alone in Seoul," forthcoming in *Gender, Place & Culture* (2025, with Jang). She contributed a chapter "Ethical Issues Arising from the Fuzzy Boundary Between the Researcher and the Researched: The Case of Mental Mapping" to an edited book by Warr, Deborah et al., *Ethics and Visual Methods: Theory, Methodology and Practice* (Palgrave Macmillan, 2016).

Grace Kao is the IBM Professor of Sociology and Professor of Ethnicity, Race, and Migration (by Courtesy) at Yale University. Her work focuses on: (1) racial, ethnic, and immigrant differences in educational outcomes and transition to adulthood; (2) interracial friendships and romantic relationships; (3) sociology of music, especially K-pop and the hallyu; and (4) dating and marriage in South Korea and has published many books and articles on these topics. Her books include *Diversity and the Transition to Adulthood in America* (2022, University of California Press, with Phoebe Ho and Hyunjoon Park), *The Company We Keep: Interracial Friendships and Romantic Relationships from Adolescence to Adulthood* (2019, Russell Sage Foundation, with Kara Joyner and Kelly Stamper Balistreri), and *Education and Immigration* (2013, Polity Press, with Elizabeth Vaquera and Kimberly Goyette). She regularly teaches classes on K-pop, the hallyu, Korean wave, and race, ethnicity, and immigration. According to Google Scholar, her work has been cited more than 17,000 times. She is the previous Vice President of the American Sociological Association. She is a regular contributing columnist for *The Korea Herald*, Korea's largest English-language newspaper, where she writes about K-pop, the Korean wave, and other sociological topics.

Minah Kim is a senior research fellow at the Humanities Research Institute of Incheon National University, Incheon, Korea. Her publications include *A History of Christian Social Movement in Korea*, vol. 1–3 (co-author, The National Council of Churches in Korea, 2024), "Religious Governance as Collaboration for the Resolution of Disgust: The Case of Protestantism in South Korea," *Religions* (MDPI, 2022), "The Influence of the Protestant Evangelical Movement on the Korean Civil Movement: The Case of the Citizen's Coalition for Economic Justice (CCEJ)," *Theology and Praxis* (The Korean Society for Practical Theology, 2022), and "The Relationship between Religion and Society in the COVID-19 Era: The Case of Protestantism in South Korea," *Religions* (MDPI, 2021). Her recent research interests are the social movements of Korean religions, the history of Protestantism and democratization in Korea, religion and human rights, and religion and social disasters. In 2024, Minah Kim is teaching *Studies in Contemporary Religious Change* at Seoul National University, and *Understanding Contemporary Sociology* and *Humans, Society, and Ethics* at Incheon National University.

Soo-Ah Kim is an associate professor at Seoul National University, Department of Communication and Interdisciplinary Program in Gender Studies. Kim studied cultural studies at Seoul National University. Related to the Japanese military sexual slavery issue, Kim participated in the testimony team of testimony book, *Forcibly Taken Korean Military "Comfort Women" 4: History Rewritten through Memories* (2001). Kim's research area has mainly been popular culture with a focus on feminism, and she currently works intensively on gender aspects in the field of digital media literacy. Her publications include "The #MeToo Movement and Korean Journalism: Comments on Online News Coverage of the Trial of Former Governor Ahn Hee-jung" (2020, *Journal of Asian Sociology*, 49(4)), as well as *Logout, safely* (2021, Book, in Korean) and *Game Contents and Gender Representation* (2023, Book, in Korean).

Song Chong Lee is a professor in the Department of Religious Studies at Seoul National University, Seoul, Korea. He is the author of *Ham Sok Hon's Ssial Cosmopolitan Vision* (New York: Lexington Books, 2020). His most recent publications include "Bringing Back the Old Religiosity: Interfaith Cosmopolitan Civil Religion," *Journal of Church and State* (Oxford University Press, 2024), "The Violence of New Religious Movements and the Entrepreneurial Model: With a Focus on the Shincheonji Church of Jesus in Korea," *The Journal of Religion* 3, no. 3 (The University of Chicago Press, 2023), and "Homo-Historicus of Wilhelm Dilthey and Ham Sok Hon," *Clio: A Journal of Literature, History, and the Philosophy of History* 50, no. 2 (Indiana University-Purdue University Press, 2023). Lee's research interests focus on religion and politics, cosmopolitanism, and Korean religions.

Liora Sarfati is an anthropologist and folklore researcher specializing in Korean and Japanese cultures. Her primary research focuses on shamanic rituals in Korea, where healing and prediction are carried out through possession by gods and spirits. She also explores contemporary protest movements in Seoul, examining how cultural performance and vernacular religion intersect with social activism. Sarfati holds dual PhDs in Folklore and Ethnomusicology, and East Asian Languages and Cultures from Indiana University, Bloomington. Her expertise spans ethnography, digital humanities methodologies, and the role of cultural performance in contemporary societies. She is the author of *Contemporary Korean Shamanism: From Ritual to Digital* (Indiana University Press, 2021) and co-editor of *The Routledge Handbook of Korean Religions* (under contract). Her work has been published in various peer-reviewed journals, including *Journal of Korean Studies*, *Religions*, *Journal of Folklore Research*, *Asian Studies Review*, and *Urbanities: Journal of Urban Ethnography*.

Hae-young Seong is an associate professor in the department of religious studies at Seoul National University. He is a scholar specializing in the psychology of religion and mysticism, with particular expertise in comparative religious studies, the interplay between institutional religion and personal spirituality, and evolving trends in religiosity. He earned his PhD in Religious Studies from Rice University in 2008, after completing his MA and BA at Seoul National University. Some of his recent research covers Freudian and Abhinavaguptan concepts of desire and sublimation, as well as Suwoon Choe Je-u's religious experiences. His publications include *The Religious Experience of Suwoon Choe Je-u and Mysticism* (Seoul National University Press) and the co-authored *Religion, Now It Is Enlightenment* (Bukseongjae). He also translated *Civilization and Its Discontents* for Korean readers (Seoul National University Press).

Yohan Yoo is a professor in the Department of Religious Studies at Seoul National University, Seoul, Korea. His research adopts a comparative approach to diverse religious topics, encompassing areas such as indigenous shamanic beliefs and practices in Jeju, Korea, theory and methodology in religious studies, iconic and performative aspects of sacred texts, and intersections between myth and cotemporary literature. He is the author of *Korean Religious Texts in Iconic and Performative Rituals* (Equinox, 2024) and three books in Korean: *Myths of Our Era* (2012), *Understanding Religious Studies* (2020), and *Understanding Religious Symbolism* (2021). He also co-authored *Cosmologies of Pure Realms and the Rhetoric of Pollution* (Routledge, 2021) and co-edited *Books as Bodies and as Sacred Beings* (Equinox, 2021) with James W. Watts.

List of Figures

List of Tables

CHAPTER 1

Introduction: Reimagining Value and Identity in Contemporary Korean Cases

Yohan Yoo

1 In-betweenness in Contemporary Korea: Toward General Explanations

The chapters in this volume explore issues of value and identity as they emerge in contemporary Korea. Among the various themes that appear throughout the discussions, "in-betweenness" is one that several contributors highlight in different ways. For example, in Chap. 10, Merose Hwang argues, "Itaewoner" artists' subcultural methods of commemorating the Itaewon Disaster stem from their "in-between" or "fringe" identity. In Chap. 6, Hyeonjoo Jung describes Korea as an "ambiguous multicultural society... in such a transitional phase," emphasizing the tension between the rapid rise of transnational migration and the country's reluctance to fully embrace multiculturalism. Similarly, in Chap. 2, Grace Kao demonstrates how the global phenomenon BTS embodies an in-between state—balancing its identity as a distinctly Korean group with the

Y. Yoo (✉)
Department of Religious Studies, Seoul National University,
Seoul, Korea (Republic of)
e-mail: yohanyoo@snu.ac.kr

© The Author(s), under exclusive license to Springer Nature Singapore Pte Ltd. 2025

Y. Yoo, S. C. Lee (eds.), *Reimagining Korea*, Palgrave Series in Contemporary Korean Studies,
https://doi.org/10.1007/978-981-96-6990-5_1

need to minimize Korean elements to achieve greater success in the American market. In many ways, Contemporary Korea exists in an ambiguous, transitional, and in-between state.

This sense of in-betweenness can also be described as "a sort of bridge" (Yoo 2024, 2–3; Eliade 1982, 53). Contemporary Korea embodies this bridge-like state, positioned between and linking the West and the East, the modern and the pre-modern, and the future and the past. While South Korea now enjoys unprecedented economic and cultural prosperity, many in North Korea continue to struggle under a dictatorial regime. Even as South Korea stands at the forefront of cutting-edge technological advancements, its people still carry the collective memory of the colonial period (1910–1945). Today, Korea is recognized as one of the world's most modern nations, yet only a few generations ago, it was a colonized and impoverished country.

Korea's in-betweenness, or its position as a bridge, is closely intertwined with religion, which serves as a fundamental source of value and identity. Religion plays a central role in many chapters of this volume. Christianity, often associated with the West, and Buddhism, regarded as Korea's primary traditional religion, continue to maintain a delicate balance of influence. Even in a country at the leading edge of artificial intelligence and renewable energy advancements, Confucianism and shamanism remain deeply embedded in cultural practices and social norms.

For readers unfamiliar with Korea's religious landscape, a brief overview may be useful. Christianity remains the largest religion in South Korea, though its numbers have declined in recent years, as discussed by Hae-Young Seong in Chap. 8. According to the November 2015 census, Christians make up 27.7% of the population, with Protestants accounting for 19.7% and Catholics for 8%. Buddhism, at 15.5%, remains no less significant as Korea's primary *jeontongjonggyo* (traditional religion). Beyond formal religious affiliations, Confucianism—once the dominant ideology of the Joseon Dynasty (1392–1910)—continues to shape Korean society through ancestral rites and a social hierarchy that prioritizes elders. Shamanic practices, including rituals and divinations, have also endured for centuries and remain an integral part of contemporary spiritual life. Additionally, since the late nineteenth century, Korea has witnessed the rise of numerous new religious movements, some of which have attracted widespread followings (Yoo 2024, 2).

The concept of in-betweenness in contemporary Korea is deeply reflected in its religious landscape. As a bridge where major global religions intersect under the umbrella of Korean religions, Korea provides a distinctive setting where diverse traditions interact and shape society. Studying religion in Korea, therefore, allows scholars to examine multiple religious traditions within a single national context. This volume presents cases spanning a wide spectrum of religious traditions, including Islam, Buddhism, Protestantism, Catholicism, shamanism, and new religious movements—collectively representing nearly half of the so-called world religions alongside emerging faiths. I am confident that examining Korean religions in relation to value and identity will yield valuable insights for developing broader theories and explanations on these topics. In many ways, exploring religions in Korea is, in practice, engaging with a microcosm of global religious diversity.

Due to its in-betweenness, ambiguous state, and dynamic transitional stage, contemporary Korean cases provide an effective lens for understanding society and human experience. This is precisely why the authors of this volume focus on Korea—not merely because most of the authors happen to be Korean or have a particular interest in Korean culture, but because we recognize the "enormous cognitive power" (Smith 1982, xii) embedded in the study of contemporary Korea. I borrow this phrase from Jonathan Z. Smith, who argues that the study of Judaism possesses enormous cognitive power due to its in-between position within Western religious frameworks. He describes Judaism as "close, yet distant; similar, yet strange; 'occidental,' yet 'oriental'; commonplace, yet exotic" (xii). Smith contends that this in-betweenness makes Judaism an ideal test case for addressing critical methodological issues such as definition and comparison. Likewise, we argue that contemporary Korea, with its own complex and shifting in-between status, offers valuable insights for broader theoretical discussions, particularly drawing upon its cognitive power.

As demonstrated above, one of the most striking characteristics of contemporary Korea is its in-betweenness. I am confident that reimagining value and identity in this context will lead to broader theoretical insights, drawing upon the cognitive power that Korea's in-betweenness generates. This cognitive power allows contemporary Korean studies to serve as a valuable test case for key methodological questions across a wide range of disciplines represented in this volume, including sociology, religious studies, gender studies, and migration studies.

For this project to generate broader perspectives and theoretical insights, I also believe the chapters must be accessible to readers who may not have deep knowledge of Korean history and culture. We do not approach contemporary Korean studies "as a set of special cases and of matters so technical that only initiates can follow discussions" (Smith 1982, 19). With this in mind, the authors have sought to write each chapter not only for specialists in Korean studies but also for all those interested in contemporary society, religion, values, and identity.

2 Value and Identity in Contemporary Korea

The two interrelated terms, value and identity, are central to this volume and recur throughout its chapters. The contributing authors engage in these concepts as they are generally understood in academic discourse. In this section, I will briefly outline their meanings and significance.

David Graeber introduces the concept of value as employed in three academic disciplines. First, in the sociological sense, value refers to "what is ultimately good, proper, or desirable in human life." Second, in the economic sense, it denotes "the degree to which objects are desired, particularly, as measured by how much others are willing to give up to get them." Third, in the linguistic sense, value can "be most simply glossed as meaningful differences" (Graeber 2001, 1–2).

The Korean sociologist Hong-Jung Kim synthesizes these three dimensions of value and defines it as "what is distinguished from others, pursued as an object of desire that is justified and validated," or more simply, "a distinguishable object of valid desire" (Kim 2024, 241). Kim further differentiates between the two meanings of "social value." In the first sense, the adjective "social" does not refer to the specific content of a value but rather to the collective characteristics of the process by which a value is formed. In this sense, social value is what is agreed upon, recognized, approved, and ratified by the majority of a society's members (242). In the second sense, "social" does not signify the process by which a value is shaped but rather its content. Social values in this sense are based on universal moral orientations toward coexistence with others, including love, compassion, generosity, tolerance, and solidarity. According to Kim, these social values encourage members of society to act in solidarity with and provide support for the vulnerable. While they promote cooperation and coexistence, they explicitly oppose violence, murder, exclusion, discrimination, and oppression.

In contemporary Korea, certain social values in the first sense continue to be upheld, as some values remain widely recognized and approved by the majority of Koreans. However, while values such as solidarity, compassion, and human rights are universal moral social values in the second sense, they do not hold the status of social values in the first sense, as they are not yet widely accepted by most members of Korean society.

As a result, some groups advocating for these values strive to elevate them to the status of social values in the first sense by enacting laws, which serve as formal mechanisms of social approval. For instance, in Chap. 4, Soo-Ah Kim highlights how human rights organizations in Korea are working to pass a law prohibiting LGBTQI+ discrimination. Similarly, in Chap. 9, Minah Kim examines how members of the Itaewon Disaster Movement advocated for the enactment of the "10.29 Itaewon Disaster Special Law." On the other hand, some chapters in this volume illustrate how certain values claim the status of social values in the first sense and are appropriated to marginalize minority groups—often without a legitimate process of social agreement but simply in the name of the majority. In this process, social values in the second sense, which are universal and moral, are disregarded and suppressed by the majority.

For instance, in Chap. 3, Yohan Yoo demonstrates how Korean residents in Daehyeon-dong, Daegu, held a whole-pig barbecue party in front of a mosque construction site. They justified their actions by arguing that cooking and sharing pork is part of Korean culture, implying that Muslim migrants, who do not consume pork, are unfit to be part of their community. In this sense, coexistence with minority groups was rejected in the name of the majority's culture. Similarly, in Chap. 5, Song Chong Lee examines how major societal institutions—mainstream religions, media, the government, and academia—contribute to the exclusion of new religious movements in Korea, without relying on any agreed-upon social value. These institutions impose their own values as if they were socially approved, thereby treating them as social values in the first sense.

In a different vein, this volume also explores the possibility of shaping social values rooted in moral orientations. These values are universal in nature, as they extend to all human beings—or even to all beings—according to Kim (2024, 298–303). They are also considered universal because they align with what most societies throughout history have pursued, or, at the very least, aspired to. Despite the cultural differences, all societies, in some way, recognize and appreciate these values. As Terry Eagleton states, "There are no British values. No nation has a monopoly on justice and humanity, fairness and compassion" (Eagleton 2009, 151).

Kim highlights that while these universal and moral social values are often devalued, excluded, and suppressed by economic logic and survival-driven values, they resurge with intensity during moments of upheaval, such as unexpectedly erupting popular uprisings (Kim 2024, 245). However, it is also notable that those who uphold universal social values persistently resist—and at times overcome—the dominance of economic and political logic, despite the general prevalence of survival-oriented values.

While universal social values are often repressed, they continue to be sought after in everyday life by certain individuals and institutions, many of whom are guided by religious values and identity. Rather than reemerging through sudden upheavals, universal moral social values—such as "justice and humanity, fairness, and compassion"—have been actively upheld and realized in Korea. For instance, Jung, in Chap. 6, highlights a religious tradition that takes the lead in shaping moral social values to protect and support minority groups. Similarly, in Chap. 9, Kim demonstrates how religious individuals have developed various ways to empathize with and support the bereaved families of Itaewon Disaster victims, even as the social majority refuses to officially mourn or commemorate them.

Moreover, the concept of social value is inseparably intertwined with that of identity. While identity can be understood in many ways, I rely here on Manuel Castells's clear and persuasive definition: "the process of construction of meaning on the basis of a cultural attribute, or related set of cultural attributes, that is/are given priority over other sources of meaning" (Castells 2010, 6). When a society shapes a social value—that is, when a virtue is desired and prioritized—it must establish criteria based on cultural foundations, and in this process, identity plays a crucial role. As a mechanism for constructing meaning and prioritizing certain cultural attributes over others, identity is shaped by social values—those qualities that a society desires and appreciates. In turn, identity reflexively serves as a criterion for recognizing and legitimizing what is pursued as an object of desire, thereby transforming it into a social value.

Castells also emphasizes that the social construction of identity occurs "in a context marked by power relationships," proposing three forms and origins of identity construction (Castells 2010, 7). The first, "legitimizing identity," is introduced by the dominant institutions to extend or justify their authority. The second, "resistance identity," emerges as a means of constructing "trenches of resistance" based on principles opposed to those of dominant institutions (8). In Chap. 5, Lee illustrates a case of legitimizing identity, showing how key social institutions in Korea use the doctrines of mainstream religions as a standard for distinguishing authentic religions from so-called heresies. He also presents an example of resistance identity, demonstrating how new religious movements—often stigmatized as heretical by mainstream religions and other major institutions—construct a foundation for resistance through doctrines that diverge from those of dominant groups.

On the other hand, Castells describes a third form of identity construction, in which social actors build a "project identity" that redefines their position and transforms social structures (8). Liora Sarfati, in Chap. 7, demonstrates this form of identity building by examining contemporary Korean shamans who, based on their new identity as cosmopolitans, redefine their sphere of practice from specific regions in Korea to a global stage. Similarly, in Chap. 9, Kim argues that performing rituals rooted in Buddhism within a social movement helped participants establish their identity as active agents of that movement.

It is important to note that value and identity are not fixed but changeable depending on social circumstances. While, as Eagleton argues, social values in the second sense are often universally pursued and shared, they can be acknowledged and realized in entirely different ways. For instance, nationalism in Korea once embodied universal moral social values, as Young Chae Seo aptly asserts. During Korea's liberation from Japanese colonization and the Cold War era, nationalism functioned as an ethical framework for human liberation—one of the core aspirations of post-colonial nations that gained independence after World War II (Seo 2022, 462). In this historical context, nationalism corresponded to social values in the second sense because it pursued the universal ethics of human liberation. At the same time, it also functioned as a social value in the first sense, as it was widely recognized and approved by most Koreans.

However, as times have changed, nationalism has lost its relevance and appeal as a universal social value in Korea. Although Korea has long been considered a homogeneous country, the twenty-first century has brought a significant increase in migrant populations. In a homogeneous society, nationalism—as both a value and an identity—naturally served as a prioritized source of meaning. However, in contemporary multicultural Korea, nationalism has increasingly taken on the character of far-right exclusionism, functioning as an ideology that hinders support for universal human solidarity (Seo 2022, 462). Seo argues that it is difficult to advocate for the imperative of universal human liberation under the banner of nationalism, which inherently operates as a force that distinguishes insiders from outsiders, centering on the nation at its core (Seo 2022, 463). In short, nationalism, which once served as a vehicle for achieving universal moral social values, is now appropriated as a tool for marginalizing minority groups. Chapter 3 illustrates this shift by showing how ethnic Korean residents overemphasize pork consumption as an essential part of Korean traditional culture to exclude migrant minorities. This example demonstrates how nationalism no longer functions as a universal social value in contemporary Korea.

I would like to highlight another concern regarding nationalism, particularly in relation to the characteristics of Korean studies that this volume aims to illuminate by citing Seo once more. Seo argues that *gukhak*—which can be literally translated as "nation studies" and typically refers to Korean studies conducted in Korea by Korean scholars—can hardly be neutral, as its primary objective is to establish national self-knowledge. He explains, "On the basis of that self-knowledge, identity and self-esteem that a nation cherishes are entrenched" (Seo 2022, 463).

The Contemporary Korean Studies Project, in which the authors of this volume have participated, seeks to develop a neutral and objective approach to Korean studies rather than producing self-knowledge rooted in national identity. As they examine issues of value and identity in Korea, they approach these topics with fairness and impartiality. Their goal is to develop balanced and appropriate guidelines without favoring Korea's perspective or granting it special status.

With this in mind, the following chapters thoroughly and equitably explore various dimensions of value and identity in contemporary Korea: Chap. 2 examines BTS's Korean value and identity in the American market; Chaps. 3 and 4 discuss the religious value and identity of Muslim migrants and members of new religious movements, respectively; Chap. 5 explores universal human values pursued by human rights organizations in support of LGBTQI+ identities; Chap. 6 investigates how religious individuals and institutions work to realize universal human values; Chap. 7 analyzes the cosmopolitan identity of contemporary shamans; Chap. 8 explores the spiritual value and identity sought by "religious nones"; Chap. 9 examines the new social identity that participants develop through engagement in a social movement; and Chap. 10 focuses on the subcultural and sub-ethnic value and identity of "Itaewoner" artists.

3 Korean Cases Demonstrating Various Forms of Value and Identity in a Changing World

The authors of the following nine chapters examine how value and identity shape social behaviors and individuals' lives in a rapidly changing world. Part I, which includes Chaps. 2, 3, 4, 5, and 6, focuses on the processes of rejection and acceptance of various groups that are "otherized" based on their value systems and identities in contemporary Korea.

In Chap. 2, Grace Kao examines one of the most prominent examples of contemporary Korean cultural influence—the global success of BTS, the world-famous Korean boy band—in the American music industry. She demonstrates that expressing one's identity can lead to either exclusion or acceptance by dominant groups. Kao highlights how Korean identity and values are negotiated and, at times, compromised when K-pop groups engage with global audiences. While BTS aims to maintain its Korean identity and embrace the values of *Hallyu* (the Korean wave), it explicitly shows that identity in music can sometimes be a disadvantage in the global market.

Kao emphasizes this tension: BTS and other K-pop groups strive to preserve their identity as "a Korean group first and foremost," yet they also recognize that achieving success in the American market often requires minimizing overt Korean elements. This dilemma is particularly evident in their music. BTS's most commercially successful songs in the US contain no Korean lyrics and lack direct visual or thematic references to Korea, even though the group consciously works to incorporate Korean identity into their broader artistic expression. At the same time, BTS continues to produce songs rich in Korean cultural references, reinforcing the role of K-pop groups as cultural ambassadors.

Before BTS, Korean artists who gained international recognition typically did so either by conforming to conventional American perceptions of Asians or by stripping their music of overt Korean elements. However, Kao notes that BTS resists this trend. Despite knowing that openly asserting their Korean identity may hinder their chances of topping the US Billboard Hot 100, they refuse to fully abandon their cultural roots. As RM, BTS's leader, stated: "We don't want to change our identity or our genuineness to get the number one." Although this chapter does not explicitly discuss religion, it remains integral to the volume's broader theme of value and identity in contemporary Korea. Kao's analysis demonstrates that identity struggles—often linked to religious issues—can emerge in global markets even without direct religious connections.

The tension between expressing and suppressing identity, which BTS navigates, is also evident in public spheres and workplaces in Korea. For instance, as Yohan Yoo illustrates in Chap. 3, many Muslim migrants in Korea seek to express their religious identity, even though doing so often hinders their social and professional acceptance. Similarly, as Soo-Ah Kim examines in Chap. 4, Korean conservative Protestants and broader society frequently pressure LGBTQI+ individuals to conceal their sexual identities. Many Koreans who engage with news articles on LGBTQI+ issues, whether through comments or upvotes, express the view that sexual minorities should remain invisible, tolerating them only as long as they do not openly assert their identities.

Yoo examines how non-religious ethnic Koreans resist coexisting with migrants who openly express their religious identity. He argues that many Muslim migrants, despite their legal status and economic contributions, are "otherized" through the appropriation and adaptation of Muslim religious rhetoric by native ethnic Korean community members. These migrants often find social acceptance when they refrain from visibly expressing their religious identity. However, those who openly display their religious beliefs and practices are frequently excluded from Korean social spaces, which are largely dominated by ethnic Koreans.

Yoo points out that invoking impurity is a common strategy for social exclusion, typically by labeling others as impure. In such cases, impure "others" are rejected, and coexistence with them is denied. However, he identifies a notable inversion of this strategy in Daehyeon-dong, Daegu, where native Korean residents opposed the construction of a mosque in their neighborhood. By cooking whole pigs and displaying pig heads near the construction site, the residents emphasized their own impurity to Muslim migrants as a way to signal the impossibility of coexistence. This chapter examines the rhetoric of impurity as a tool to justify hatred and discrimination against otherized migrants. Yoo extends this analysis and articulates the broader mechanisms of social exclusion by comparing the Korean case with those from many different cultures of varying historical periods.

In the concluding part of the chapter, Yoo relates the exclusion of others based on religious identity to a matter of social values. According to him, rejecting coexistence with a group that is part of society by suppressing or ignoring its religious identity not only disregards cultural diversity but also betrays universal social values. He also points out that the claim—frequently made by many Koreans—that these values are not respected in some Islamic countries does not justify denying Muslims in Korea the right to enjoy the values upheld in society. Contemporary Korea aspires to justice, humanity, fairness, compassion, and equality, and thus should uphold these principles for all members of society.

While Chap. 3 examines how a non-religious community rejects religious minorities, Chap. 4 shifts the focus to religious groups that discriminate against non-religious minorities. Kim investigates the social exclusion of sexual minorities in contemporary Korea, particularly through the influence of conservative Protestant values. She argues that conservative Protestants have positioned homosexuality as their primary adversary, opposing gender equality based on a rigid binary understanding of sexuality. According to Kim, these groups wield a significant influence over public opinion, even preventing sexuality education books from being made available in school libraries by filing civil complaints under the guise of democratic participation.

Kim contends that this legalistic approach disguises systemic discrimination against LGBTQI+ individuals. She further examines how non-religious Koreans tacitly endorse the conservative Protestant stance. For instance, major conservative newspapers rarely cover LGBTQI+ events, effectively marginalizing them from public discourse. Moreover, mainstream media often portray debates over gender equality as conflicts between two opposing groups—Protestants and sexual minorities—rather than as human rights issues. As a result, LGBTQI+ claims for rights are frequently dismissed as mere controversies rather than legitimate social concerns. Kim ultimately argues that the human rights of sexual minorities are systematically overlooked under the guise of democratic neutrality.

In Chap. 5, Song Chong Lee shifts the discussion to another marginalized group: members of new religious movements (NRMs). While Lee acknowledges that objections can be raised against any social, legal, or moral wrongdoings of NRMS, he critically evaluates the unfair practice of labeling NRMs as *idan* (heresy or cult) or *saibi* (pseudo-religion). He examines how four key societal institutions—mainstream religions, the media, the government, and academia— contribute to the exclusion of NRMs in Korea.

According to Lee, these four "stakeholders" have not recognized NRMs as entitled members of society. As a result, the general perception of NRMs contradicts the democratic and civic culture that many Koreans believe they embody; instead, it is marked by suspicion, hostility, hatred, and intolerance. Lee argues that these negative views have been shaped by the rhetoric of anti-cult activists, who are predominantly associated with conservative Protestant church communities. Dominant societal institutions judge NRMs as corrupted versions of established religions and as socially unacceptable "others," assessing their legitimacy based on how different their doctrines and practices are from those of mainstream religious traditions.

Drawing on rational choice theory, Lee proposes an objective framework for the moral evaluation of religion as a market player that provides religious services and commodities. In this framework, NRMs and established religions function equally as suppliers, whereas participants and the public serve as potential buyers. Here, the issue is not whether the founder of an NRM identifies as the incarnation of an omnipotent God or whether the leader claims sacred status as a messenger of God. Instead, Lee suggests four criteria by which the public can evaluate and critique religions, including NRMs: legality, transparency, fair competition, and social responsibility. While acknowledging alternative approaches to addressing social problems, Lee also opens the possibility that broader social values—discussed in the second section of this chapter and exemplified in Chap. 5 by "the rule of law, civil liberties, human rights, pluralism, and more"—can be fairly applied to NRMs.

The authors of Chaps. 2, 3, 4, and 5 focus on cases in which major groups fail to recognize minor identities based on value systems. While most of the value systems examined in these chapters are primarily rooted in religious beliefs and practices—either their own or those of marginalized minorities—some, such as market demand, have also emerged as powerful forces. However, in Chap. 6, Hyunjoo Jung presents an example demonstrating that religious activities grounded in religious identity can, in fact, facilitate the acceptance and inclusion of foreign migrants in Korea.

Jung examines the emergence of multicultural spaces in metropolitan Seoul. While most multicultural spaces are scattered across small or medium-sized industrial areas, often separated from ethnic Korean residential zones, those in major cities—including Seoul—are established in central urban areas, integrating into existing infrastructure. These spaces lack clear boundaries and are thus not exclusionary. The most prominent example of a multicultural space in Seoul is Little Manila, located in the Daehangno area around the Hyehwa-dong Cathedral, where Filipino migrants gather for a weekend marketplace and social activities. Notably, according to Jung, Filipinos are not the "ruler" of the space but rather "co-user" alongside Koreans and migrants from other countries, as they temporarily occupy a section of a public space in Seoul. Under Korea's government-driven top-down immigration policies, a non-governmental religious institution, the Catholic Church, has played a crucial role in shaping the multicultural space in Daehangno. This area, one of the most vibrant and popular cultural hubs for young Koreans, has become a unique example of religiously facilitated multiculturalism. Jung vividly illustrates how the religious community has fostered a multicultural space where diverse ethnicities and cultures coexist, without any single group dominating or exclusively claiming it.

Jung argues that the Hyehwa-dong Filipino community, also known as Little Manila, could not have emerged in the heart of metropolitan Seoul without the support of the Catholic Church, despite the influence of various other factors. For instance, since 2001, the Filipino Ministry Center under the Archdiocese of Seoul has rented a four-story building near the Hyehwa-dong Cathedral to the Filipino Catholic Community free of charge. The cathedral also offered a Tagalog-language Mass for the Hyehwa-dong Filipino Catholic Community, which later became the Seoul Filipino Catholic Community and now has over 2000 members.

Above all, Raphael Clinic, originally established as a free medical service for migrant workers by volunteer Catholic professors from Seoul National University College of Medicine, treats over 300 foreign nationals weekly, with Filipinos accounting for approximately 30 percent of its patients. Jung illustrates how the Catholic commitment to human rights, labor rights, and the welfare of marginalized groups—extending beyond religious and ethnic boundaries—has contributed to the formation of a multicultural space where diverse races and cultures coexist without being dominated by any single group.

She demonstrates that religions can inspire members of the dominant group to coexist with and support minorities, providing a moral framework for inclusive coexistence. This case is an important example of how religion can realize and sustain universal and moral social values, without resorting to a sudden, violent, and intense return to social values triggered by "accidental moments that burst out unexpectedly" (Kim 2024, 245).

The four chapters in Part II, titled "New Flows of Value and Identity in Contemporary Korea," adeptly and meticulously explore the evolving issues of value and identity in twenty-first-century Korea, a society undergoing rapid transformation within a radically changing world.

In Chap. 7, Liora Sarfati examines the evolving identity of Korean shamans (*mudang*) as cosmopolitans—an identity shift that began in the late twentieth century and accelerated with the rise of internet communication in the twenty-first century. Traditionally, Korean shamanism (*musok*) has been regionally defined, deeply rooted in local traditions, with shamans regarded as "unique local practitioners." However, Sarfati identifies a newly emerging identity among a group of these practitioners—one characterized by cosmopolitan cultural engagement and geographic mobility. She explores the hypermodern environment of the global market by analyzing shamanic rituals conducted outside Korea or performed for non-Korean clients and spirits. Sarfati argues that these shamans have redefined their self-awareness, which was once confined to their regional contexts, by reinterpreting their religious experiences in ways that align with "a globalizing, technology-dependent, media-saturated society." As globalization facilitates encounters with non-Korean others, vernacular practitioners increasingly feel the need to expand their regional scope of beliefs and rituals.

Sarfati further argues that this new, flexible interpretation of the shamanic tradition is possible precisely because of its vernacular nature, even as it expands the scope of shamanic beliefs and rituals beyond conventional regional boundaries. Since vernacular traditions are not institutionalized or fixed by documented texts but are instead transmitted orally, shamans can reinterpret their practices to fit diverse life contexts, adapting their rituals to an evolving global landscape.

At the same time, Sarfati highlights that these cosmopolitan shamans continue to perceive their identity as deeply rooted in Korean traditional spirituality, which often serves as a source of spiritual authority—despite their departure from older forms of belief and practice. For example, a German shaman who neither speaks Korean nor performs traditional Korean shamanic songs and chants emphasizes her spiritual genealogy, tracing her initiation to one of Korea's most highly respected shamans, Geum-hwa Kim. Conversely, a Korean American shaman practicing in the United States in English underscores her fluency in Korean and her deep knowledge of traditional chants, songs, and scripts. Through these cases, Sarfati reveals the complex transformation of traditional religious identity, illustrating how practitioners of vernacular Korean shamanism become cosmopolitan while still emphasizing their Korean roots to maintain spiritual authority.

In Chap. 8, Hae-Young Seong observes a sharp increase in the number of young Koreans who identify as religiously non-affiliated, or "religious nones." Seong notes that contemporary Korea is witnessing both a high proportion and rapid growth of religious nones, alongside a rising indifference among younger generations toward organized religion. However, Seong also underscores a countertrend—the growing popularity of *templestay* programs and meditation practices.

Although *templestay* programs, organized and offered by Buddhist temples, encourage participants to engage in Buddhist practices such as prostration and meditation, a growing number of non-Buddhists and even non-religious individuals voluntarily take part in them. Similarly, while meditation has traditionally been a distinctly Buddhist practice, it is now widely adopted in secular contexts, including healthcare, education, and psychological counseling. This broader trend reflects a significant shift in Korea's religious landscape, where adherence to established religions is declining; however, more people are engaging in practices traditionally associated with specific religions without intending to formally join them. Seong demonstrates that in twenty-first-century Korea, religious identity is shifting from institutional affiliation to a focus on ideas and activities that fulfill individual spiritual needs.

Chapter 8 illustrates how Buddhist meditation serves a religious function for individual Koreans, even when practiced in a non-religious context. Similarly, in Chap. 9, Minah Kim examines the nuanced application of Buddhist rituals in contemporary Korea, focusing on *samboilbae* (walking three steps and bowing down to the ground) and *ochetuji* (full-body prostration involving two elbows, two knees, and the forehead). These rituals were adopted by the civic organization "10.29 Itaewon Disaster Movement." The movement emerged in response to the tragic crowd crush in Itaewon, Seoul, where 159 people—mostly in their 20s and 30s, celebrating Halloween—lost their lives. In the aftermath of the disaster, bereaved family members and concerned citizens organized the movement to demand accountability from the government, an official apology for the negligence in safety management, and the implementation of measures to prevent similar incidents. To establish a legal framework for these demands, they advocated for the enactment of the "10.29 Itaewon Disaster Special Law." Throughout this process, *samboilbae* and *ochetuji* were actively performed by movement members as expressions of demonstrating sincerity and urgency in their calls for justice and reform.

According to Kim, these Buddhist rituals were performed regardless of participants' religious affiliation, with their overt religious meanings—such as lowering oneself, paying respects to the Buddha, and taking refuge in the Buddha—stripped away. Rather than emphasizing Buddhism as a specific religious tradition, Kim argues that these rituals allowed participants to engage with spirituality in a broader sense, prompting reflection on the meaning of death and the value of life. Moreover, she notes that these rituals helped participants cultivate physical empathy with the victims and bereaved families while also fostering emotional bonds among themselves. Through this shared practice, participants established their identity as active agents within the social movement.

While Kim, in Chap. 9, acknowledges that the participants of the movement mourned the Itaewon Disaster and urged the public to do the same, Merose Hwang, in Chap. 10, analyzes the disaster's implications and consequences from a different perspective. Hwang emphasizes that many members of the general public, at least officially, refused to grieve for it.

Hwang examines two distinct approaches to remembering and commemorating disasters in twenty-first-century Korea. The first disaster discussed is the Sewol Ferry Disaster, which occurred on the morning of April 16, 2014, when the ferry MV *Sewol* sank while en route from Incheon to Jeju Island. Of the 476 passengers on board, 304 lost their lives, including 250 students from Danwon High School in Ansan. In response, bereaved family members established a memorial space to preserve the collective memory of the victims. Hwang argues that this memorial space mirrors a traditional shamanic ritual space (*gutdang*). She further suggests that the bereaved families' commemorative practices function as *piacular* rites, serving a ritual purpose of atonement or expiation. Additionally, these memorial practices are believed to establish a spiritual connection with the ghosts of deceased children and siblings, reinforcing their presence in memory.

Hwang then examines the Itaewon Disaster, previously discussed in Chap. 9. She argues that, compared to the Sewol Ferry Disaster, the Itaewon tragedy was assigned a different level of significance, resulting in distinct social memories of the two events. Unlike the Sewol Ferry Disaster, Hwang notes, no dedicated memorial space was established for the Itaewon victims due to government opposition and the lack of public consensus. As mentioned earlier, many Koreans refrained from officially mourning the victims, attributing responsibility to those who lost their lives while celebrating Halloween.

In response to this societal reluctance, young artists active in the Itaewon area created an alternative form of memorial ritual that diverges entirely from traditional shamanic practices. Instead of relying on conventional mourning rituals, they process their trauma through both ordinary, everyday activities and extraordinary celebrations. A collective of "Itaewoner" artists has dedicated itself to mourning the tragedy by documenting and exhibiting mundane activities such as eating, chatting, dancing, and playing—practices they propose as a subcultural form of remembrance. Hwang argues that this commemorative approach emerges from these artists' "in-between" or "fringe" identity. While they may be ethnically Korean, they do not fully identify as culturally Korean or entirely foreign, instead positioning themselves as a subcultural, sub-ethnic group. In this context, young individuals with new identities are reshaping how disasters are commemorated in contemporary Korea.

The chapters in this volume are not merely independent research projects contributed by scholars who happened to convene due to a shared Korean heritage or interest in Korean culture. Rather, the authors have engaged in a collaborative intellectual process—critically examining each other's work, raising questions, and seeking answers together. This collective effort unfolded through six colloquiums organized by the Value and Identity Team of the Seoul National University Contemporary Korean Studies Project and a dedicated session at the 1st International Conference for Contemporary Korean Studies, held at Seoul National University on August 23–24, 2024.

I believe the nine chapters that follow will illustrate how value and identity shape new ways of life in contemporary Korea, dynamically interacting with those of other members of the global community. Beyond mere observations, these chapters will reflexively explore how these emerging ways of life, in turn, reshape and redefine value and identity. Ultimately, I hope this volume will contribute to reimagining the general characteristics of value and identity while establishing new explanatory frameworks for their study.

References

Castells, Manual. 2010 [1997]. *The Power of Identity*. Malden, MA: Wiley-Blackwell.

Eagleton, Terry. 2009. *Reason, Faith, and Revolution: Reflections of the God Debate*. New Haven, CT: Yale University Press.

Eliade, Mircea. 1982 [1978]. *Ordeal by Labyrinth: Conversations with Claude-Henri Rocquet*. Translated by Derek Coltman. Chicago, IL: University of Chicago Press.

Graeber, David. 2001. *Toward an Anthropological Theory of Value: The False Coin of Our Own Dreams.* New York: Palgrave.

Kim, Hong-Jung. 2024. *Seobaibeollist modeoniti (Survivalist Modernity).* Seoul: Ieum. (In Korean).

Seo, Young Chae. 2022. *Ujeong-ui jeongwon (Garden of Friendship).* Paju: Munhakdongne. (In Korean).

Smith, Jonathan Z. 1982. *Imagining Religion: From Babylon to Jonestown.* Chicago, IL: University of Chicago Press.

Yoo, Yohan. 2024. *Korean Religious Texts in Iconic and Performative Rituals.* Sheffield, UK: Equinox.

PART I

Excluding or Embracing Others Based on Identity and Value

CHAPTER 2

How K-Pop's Pursuit of the US Billboard Hot 100 Charts Shifts Its Value and Identity

Grace Kao

1 Introduction

K-Pop, or Korean Popular Music, usually refers to the single-sex boy or girl group that performs in synchronized and heavily choreographed dances while singing various genres of pop songs. In South Korea, the trainee system usually requires that pre-teens or young teenagers audition to be a trainee at an entertainment company such as HYBE (the home of BTS and SEVENTEEN), SM (home of Super Junior, EXO, NCT127, Girls Generation, SHINee, etc.), or JYP (Stray Kids, TWICE, The Wonder Girls). These trainees work for many years (although the actual range can be from a few months to 10 years) before some have the opportunity to debut as part of a group formed by the entertainment company. These are usually single-gender groups with four to nine members, and traditionally they include a leader (often the oldest or most mature member), center (main face of the group), visual (the most handsome or beautiful member of the group), lead singers, dancers, and rappers.

G. Kao (✉)
Department of Sociology, Yale University, New Haven, CT, USA
e-mail: g.kao@yale.edu

© The Author(s), under exclusive license to Springer Nature Singapore Pte Ltd. 2025

Y. Yoo, S. C. Lee (eds.), *Reimagining Korea*, Palgrave Series in Contemporary Korean Studies,
https://doi.org/10.1007/978-981-96-6990-5_2

As evidence of its popularity worldwide, K-Pop songs have made appearances on music charts outside of South Korea and East Asia. Because the US has the largest music market in the world (IFPI 2024) in terms of revenue and due to American hegemony in terms of popular culture (Scripps 2024), K-Pop has been in pursuit of the US Billboard Hot 100 Chart since the inception of idol groups. In a survey of individuals from 17 countries, Pew Research Center found that 71% of those outside of the US believe American entertainment is the best or above average (Scripps 2024). Moreover, K-Pop artists may also seek validation from Western measures of success. Since the first appearance of a K-Pop single in 2009 when The Wonder Girls hit #76 with "Nobody" and the second appearance of a K-Pop song with Psy's "Gangnam Style" (2012), K-Pop artists and their entertainment companies view this goal as not just aspirational, but attainable.

This chapter examines the history of K-Pop singles on the US Billboard Hot 100 Chart. I argue that by pursuing the US charts, K-Pop songs and music videos have to grapple with the loss of Korean content and identity as well as shifting values of Hallyu (or Korean Wave). I do so by first briefly summarizing the history of this chart. Next, I delineate every K-Pop song that has appeared on the US charts, along with the dominance of BTS from the late 2010s to the present. Finally, I discuss how the pursuit of the success in the Western market by entertainment companies may shift the most successful K-Pop songs away from Korea (exemplified by "Butter" or "Dynamite" by BTS, which are entirely in English). However, K-Pop artists such as BTS may rebel against purely market-driven decision-making about the content of their songs.

2 Description of the History of the US Billboard Hot 100

The *Billboard Advertiser* was first published on November 1, 1894 as a trade publication for the bill-posting industry, and proclaimed that it was "developed to the interests of advertisers, poster printers, advertising agents and secretaries for fairs" (Anand 2005, p. 145). Even then, it included columns that focused on "stage gossips," which reported on the private lives of celebrities (Anand 2005). The magazine included a mail forwarding service for traveling entertainers, which coincided with its publication of their tour dates. Because of this service, Billboard became an essential part of the entertainment industry (Anand 2005).

By 1913, Billboard created its first chart, "Popular Songs Heard in Vaudeville Theaters Last Week," which covered the most popular songs from live venues in New York, Chicago, and San Francisco (Anand 2005). However, this chart did not last long, and the first chart that is closest to the modern charts we are familiar with is the "Jukebox Record Buying Guide" (later called the "Most Played in Juke Boxes" chart) by April 1938. In July 1940, there was a chart for "Best Selling Retail Records" and by July 1940, they introduced the "Disks with Most Radio Plugs," later known as "Most Played by Jockeys" in 1945 (Anand 2005).

By 1949, RCA invented the 45 rpm (revolutions per minute) records, popularly known as the "45." These records held a few minutes of music per side, which was perfect for a single. They were inexpensive, and later jukeboxes were designed to play one single at a time. In his 1961 book, *The Adolescent Society: The Social Life of the Teenager and Its Impact on Education*, sociologist James Coleman talked about the development of the teen culture post-WWII. Here, he clearly discussed the development of an independent teen culture where feminine and masculine roles are practiced and cars and popular music become vital parts of the adolescent subculture (Coleman 1961). Mitchell Hall (2014) also argues that economic security after WWII offered middle-class adolescents the respite from transitioning immediately to adult responsibilities. Hence, a youth culture could develop for the Baby Boomer generation. Hall (2014) argues that this generation also sought out more diverse musical styles, which made it possible for rock and roll and rhythm and blues to thrive.

Almost immediately following the advent of the 45, Omaha, Nebraska radio station owner Todd Storz came up with the Top 40 Radio format in 1951. Some jukeboxes had 40 slots. This format relied on record sales from record stores. He decided that his station would play these songs most frequently, hence developing the Top-40 radio format (Radio Hall of Fame 2024; Hall 2014). His station (KOWH) listener share went from under 5% to over 45% after the transition, hence leading others to follow (Hall 2014).

Simultaneously, in 1952, radio DJ Dick Clark took over local TV show *Bandstand* in 1952–1956. It was later rebranded as *American Bandstand* in 1957, when it became syndicated on ABC. This show ran from 1957 to 1989. In its early days, Dick Clark also had a system of Top 10 singles.

Moreover, Dick Clark established the link between teenage consumers and the ranking of top singles.

The Billboard Hot 100 Chart officially began on August 4, 1958. This chart essentially combined three of Billboard's charts (including the aforementioned "Most Played by Jockeys" chart). The first number one song was "Poor Little Fool" by Ricky Nelson, which clocks in at 2:43 minutes with a 1-6-4-5 progression in C Major. Interestingly, while many music journalists lamented the shrinking length of today's K-Pop songs, traditional rock and roll songs were about the same length. Compare "Poor Little Fool's" song duration of 2:43 minutes to NewJeans' 2023 song "Super Shy," which is 2:34 minutes in length.

Since then, *Billboard* magazine has introduced hundreds of different charts, some lasting longer than others. Moreover, the names of some genres are credited to *Billboard* magazine staffers. In 1942, records made by African Americans were listed on the "Harlem Hit Parade" chart, which was later called "Race Records" by February 1945. Eventually, an employee suggested "Rhythm and Blues," and the name was adopted in June 1949. Currently, the name remains as "Hot R&B Songs."

3 Today's US Billboard Hot 100 Chart

Despite the plethora of chart rankings, the US Billboard Hot 100 remains the gold standard of singles charts. The list of 100 singles is published weekly, and tracks physical and digital sales, radio play, and online streaming. Since July 2015, the chart has begun its data count for sales and streaming from Friday to Thursday, while the radio play is counted from the following Monday to Sunday. Then, the list is published on Tuesdays. In an article published in *Billboard* magazine, Trust states: "Today, airplay is still among the chart's data mix, with downloads largely continuing the legacy of sales, and streaming—now the chart's most dominant metric, on average—essentially a modern-era, more personalized digital jukebox" (Trust 2022). While the precise formula that Billboard uses is proprietary, Wallace (2023) suggests that "radio airplay impressions are divided by 8,000, sales numbers are divided by 10" (Wallace 2023). For streams, professionals guess that "paid streams get divided by 1250, free streams by 3,750, and programmed streams by 5,000" (Wallace 2023). While the measure for pure sales is weighed heavily, it probably accounts for only 1–3% of the points used to calculate their position in the Hot 100.

4 History of K-Pop on the US Billboard Hot 100 Before BTS's Appearance

The first K-Pop song that appeared on the US Billboard Hot 100 was The Wonder Girls' "Nobody" in 2009. The Wonder Girls is from JYP Entertainment, and its CEO (songwriter, producer, and performer Park Jin-young, popularly known as JYP) wrote this song. This is a Motown-inspired song, both in its sounds and visuals, with an indelible hook. They recorded both Korean and English versions of the song, and the English version of the song appeared on the October 31, 2009 chart at #76 for 1 week. As a result of their success, The Wonder Girls opened for The Jonas Brothers on their tour that year. One might expect that this feat would have set the stage for other K-Pop songs to follow. Moreover, the appearance on the chart may have added pressure for other groups to release songs with only English lyrics (Wikipedia, 2024).

However, no other song would appear on the chart until Psy's "Gangnam Style," which charted on September 22, 2012, and reached a peak of #2 on this chart. It stayed on the charts for 31 weeks, a record for a K-Pop song that would be only surpassed by BTS's "Dynamite" (which appeared on the charts for 32 weeks).

Psy's "Gangnam Style" was not in English. For most in the Western World, this was seen as a comedic novelty song with memorable horse-like dance moves. In a 2012 CNN article, Justin Bellini compares it to "Macarena" by Los Del Rio, another campy song that became popular despite having decidedly unhip musicians in the music video. Psy's caricature of himself is also atypical of pop stars and especially K-Pop idols. Bellini further writes:

> It was cute for a while. We had some fun. And a few Americans even learned to locate South Korea on a map. (I think it's near Pittsburgh.)
>
> But now it's time for all of us to come together and stop the madness. Thus, let it be known that I hereby declare October 12, 2012, as the day "Gangnam Style" died.
>
> Sorry, folks. We're done. It's officially no longer a thing. Psy seems like a really good dude, and I hate to have done this to his song, but this morning I slowly walked "Gangnam Style" out into the backyard, thanked it for the good times and shot it. (Bellini 2012)

Of course, Bellini was wrong. The song stayed on the charts for six more months after the article was written and has maintained its status in the history of K-Pop. As of December 2024, the video has enjoyed 5.3 billion views, much more than any other K-Pop music video (unless you count Pinkfong's "Baby Shark," which has 15.4 billion views). Psy clearly set the stage for other K-Pop acts, although Psy was decidedly not an image of a handsome Asian male. Instead, he served as a comedic counterpart to the typical handsome Western male pop star.

Table 2.1 lists all K-Pop songs that appeared on the US Billboard Hot 100 Chart from 2009 to 2016, just before BTS's appearance on the chart (Wikipedia 2024). There is a total of six songs, with most enjoying just a brief appearance on the chart. The notable exceptions are Psy's "Gangnam Style" and "Gentlemen," the latter reaching #2 and staying on the chart for 15 weeks. "Gentlemen" is also interesting because the imagery shows exactly the opposite of the idealized appearance and behavior of K-Pop idols. In the video, Psy is shown to be anything but a gentleman—he pulls chairs from under women as they sit down, delays an elevator as another person is rushing to use the restroom, etc. One could argue that he plays into the image of Asian American men as being seen as less attractive and unlikely romantic interests (Kao et al. 2019; Kao and Shinkoda 2021). During the pre-BTS era, four of the six songs are by Psy, and all his

Table 2.1 K-Pop songs on US Billboard Hot 100 Chart: 2009–2016 (prior to BTS)

Number	*Date*	*Artist*	*Song title*	*Highest position*	*# of weeks*
1	October 31, 2009	Wonder Girls	"Nobody"	76	1
2	September 22, 2012	Psy	"Gangnam Style"	2	31
3	April 27, 2013	Psy	"Gentleman"	5	15
4	June 28, 2014	Psy feat. Snoop Dogg	"Hangover"	26	1
5	December 19, 2015	Psy feat. CL	"Daddy"	97	1
6	October 22, 2016	CL	"Lifted"	94	1

Source: Wikipedia, https://en.wikipedia.org/wiki/List_of_K-pop_songs_on_the_Billboard_charts and author's own calculations

songs follow the caricature that is consistent with Western images of Asian men as geeky and undesirable.

As Psy's single "Daddy" featured CL (leader of 2NE1), this likely helped elevate CL's own single "Lifted," which reached #94 on the US Billboard Hot 100 Chart on October 22, 2016. Like many songs from YG, this song is co-written by Teddy Park. This song is completely in English and heavily refers to beer (40 oz refers to the size of a malt liquor bottle and is a euphemism for it) as well as getting "lifted" or high. These are not typical themes for a K-Pop song and reveal no Korean content (unless you count CL herself).

During the era prior to BTS, the few K-Pop songs that made it to the US charts were consistent with American images of Asian men (as in the case of Psy). For The Wonder Girls and CL, they had to produce a product absent any Korean content. In other words, for a K-Pop song to be successful in the US, the identity of K-Pop songs that were in Korean was still interpreted within the traditional confines of Asian Americans. The other option for K-Pop artists was to erase any trace of Korean-ness and act as if they were simply American, hence obliterating any of the cultural content of K-Pop. All of these songs failed to disrupt the expectations of American audiences for Asian cultural products. BTS would change these expectations in the coming years.

5 Entrance of BTS to the US Charts in 2017

It is impossible to talk about the history of K-Pop on the US Billboard Hot 100 Chart without mentioning BTS. BTS (Bangtan Sonyeondan, literally Bulletproof Boy Scouts or 방탄소년단) is a seven-member group that originally comes from Big Hit Entertainment. The members are leader RM (Kim Namjoon), Jin (Kim Seokjin), Suga (Min Yoongi), J-Hope (Jung Hoseok), Jimin (Park Jimin), V (Kim Taehyung), and Jungkook (Jeon Jungkook). Unlike the typical K-Pop group today, all members are native Koreans and have not spent any time abroad. Moreover, none of them are from Seoul—this is an important part of their origin story since they were seen as a group of boys from secondary cities (such as Gwangju, Daegu, and Busan) and produced by a small and previously unsuccessful company. They were the underdog K-Pop group. In fact, their story matches that of South Korea, who were previously overshadowed by its larger East Asian counterparts, China and Japan.

Their founder and manager, Bang Si-hyuk, formed the group, and they debuted in June 2013. By 2019, BTS accounted for 97% of the Big Hit's revenue, although by 2020, BTS accounted for 85% of Big Hit's revenue as they acquired other companies (allkpop 2022a). Due to the group's popularity, Bang was able to spin Big Hit into the conglomerate HYBE in March 2021. HYBE is now the largest K-Pop company, with a market cap of over US $5 billion as of September 2024 (Tencer 2024). Previously, SM Entertainment, JYP Entertainment, and YG Entertainment were historically hailed as the "Big Three" in K-Pop. Moreover, Bang bought Scooter Braun's Ithaca Holdings, previously the management company of Justin Bieber, Ariana Grande, and others. Scooter Braun is now the CEO of HYBE North America. Bang's vision of K-Pop expands far beyond Korea, and he has often said in interviews that he imagines a global pop music rather than something that is only local to Korea.

BTS actually began its Twitter account two years before debuting—this may not seem surprising today, but at the time it was unheard of (Herman 2023). In Korea, there are many weekly TV shows that feature K-Pop musical acts. On network SBS's *The Show* in May 2015, BTS won its first award on one of these shows for "I Need U." By November 2015, BTS began making their appearance on the Billboard 200 charts (for record albums). In October 2016, BTS first topped the Billboard Social 50 Chart. While the chart became inactive by 2020, BTS spent 210 weeks at number 1 on the Billboard Social 50 Chart. Eventually, they became the first K-Pop group to debut at #1 on the Billboard 200 charts with *Love Yourself: Tear* (June 2018) (Herman 2023).

As of 2021, the *Guinness Book of World Records* notes that BTS holds 23 world records, but of course, their popularity has continued to soar since then. In terms of album sales, they are one of the best-selling artists in the past 30 years, just behind Eminem and Taylor Swift (AllKPop 2022b).

Table 2.2 presents the list of K-Pop songs on the US Billboard Hot 100 Chart from 2017 to October 2019, just prior to the lockdown due to the COVID-19 pandemic. This also marks the period of BTS prior to reaching their record-breaking Number 1 singles. Even Blackpink pales in comparison to the dominance of BTS. Note that I have numbered the songs sequentially, starting from the first K-Pop song on the chart, The Wonder Girls' "Nobody." This column provides a total tally of the K-Pop songs that appear on this chart.

BTS achieved their first appearance on the US Billboard Hot 100 on the October 7, 2017, Chart with the song "DNA," which peaked at #67

Table 2.2 K-Pop songs on US Billboard Hot 100 Chart: 2017–June 2024 (BTS arrives)

Number	*Date*	*Artist*	*Song title*	*Highest position*	*# of weeks*
7	October 7, 2017	BTS	"DNA"	67	4
8	December 16, 2017	BTS feat. Desiigner	"MIC Drop" (Steve Aoki remix)	28	10
9	June 2, 2018	BTS	"Fake Love"	10	6
10	June 30, 2018	Blackpink	"Ddu-Du Ddu-Du"	55	1
11	September 8, 2018	BTS feat. Nicki Minaj	"Idol"	11	3
12	November 3, 2018	Dua Lipa & Blackpink	"Kiss and Make Up"	93	1
13	November 10, 2018	Steve Aoki feat. BTS	"Waste It on Me"	89	1
14	January 12, 2019	Pinkfong	"Baby Shark"	32	20
15	April 20, 2019	Blackpink	"Kill This Love"	41	4
16	April 27, 2019	BTS feat. Halsey	"Boy with Luv"	8	8
17	April 27, 2019	BTS	"Make It Right"	76	2
18	October 12, 2019	J-Hope feat. Becky G	"Chicken Noodle Soup"	81	1

Source: Wikipedia, https://en.wikipedia.org/wiki/List_of_K-pop_songs_on_the_Billboard_charts and authors' own calculations

and stayed on the charts for four weeks. They looked nothing like Psy. Even in "DNA," they are presented as handsome young men, typical of teenage idols with whom Western audiences have been familiar since the beginning of the US Billboard Hot 100 Chart. In fact, Ricky Nelson, whose 1955 song was the first #1 song on this sound, personified the teenage idol at the time. Still, the members of BTS danced in sync and sported brightly colored hair—this would be the first exposure of a K-Pop boy band to most Americans. Like Psy, however, most of the lyrics in BTS's "DNA" are in Korean, and fans would have to learn the lyrics either by memorizing a sequence of syllables (which many did) or by learning Korean. The boon to Korean language studies worldwide certainly owes some debt to BTS. In fact, according to the Colleen Baer in the Modern Language Association (MLA), from the period from 2016 to 2021, foreign-language enrollment decreased by 16.6%, but in contrast, Korean grew by 38.3% (Baer 2023).

Before Psy's "Gangnam Style," very few non-English songs ever made it to the chart. According to Billboard, as of October 2023, only 36 non-English songs have ever appeared on the US Billboard Hot 100 Chart. Most of these singles are in Spanish. If we only consider non-Western languages, all but one ("Sukiyaki" by Kyu Sakamoto, which reached #1 in 1963) are in Korean. K-pop has clearly put Asia on the American pop music landscape.

In the same year as "DNA," their next song, "Mic Drop," peaked at #28 and spent 10 weeks on the US Billboard Hot 100. This song enjoyed a remix from Asian American DJ and producer Steve Aoki (interestingly, son of the entrepreneurs behind the restaurant chain Benihana). By June 2018, they enjoyed their first Top 10 single, "Fake Love," which spent 6 weeks on the chart. That same month, Blackpink enjoyed their first appearance on the US Billboard Hot 100 Chart with "Ddu-Du Ddu-Du," but it only reached number 55 and stayed on the chart for just a single week. While I have included "Baby Shark," a popular children's song in this table, it is not K-Pop in the traditional sense. Still, I include it given that it likely promotes the Hallyu.

When evaluating the list of songs on Table 2.2, with the exception of "Baby Shark," all of the songs include at least some Korean lyrics. To any viewer of these music videos, it is clear that these songs are from K-Pop groups hailing from Korea and singing Korean lyrics. In the case of "Chicken Noodle Soup," J-Hope (BTS) and Becky G (Mexican American singer)'s cover of a classic hip-hop song by DJ Webstar and rapper Young B from 2006, the song is in English, Korean, and Spanish and features a multi-ethnic group of dancers. The video was shot in Los Angeles.

In general, it is rare for listeners to hear non-English language songs on American radio. Given that radio airplay still accounts for a non-trivial share of the score used to determine a song's chart position, K-Pop fans rightly feel that K-Pop songs are disadvantaged. In 2017, BTS ARMY (the name of BTS's fandom) in the US organized themselves to call their local DJs to play BTS songs. The network they created was BTSx50 States (Chang 2017). Moreover, some fans sent American DJs flowers and other gift baskets to thank them for interviewing BTS. For example, on October 4, 2017, a DJ for 103.7 KISS FM in Chattanooga tweeted a photo of a bouquet of flowers and a card that thanked them for playing BTS (@KissChattanooga 2017).

5.1 Korean Language as an Expression of Identity

In terms of K-Pop songs and music videos, its producers must present products that are appealing to a wide range of audience members. To some extent, it may be tempting for them to simply increase the English language content of their song lyrics. Is it important for K-Pop songs to be in the Korean language to properly express its Korean identity? Do members of K-Pop groups have to be Korean or from the Korean diaspora? Since the first K-Pop idol group, H.O.T., there have been Korean American members. Later, Super Junior introduced a Chinese member, but all of these groups were still dominated by Korean members born and raised in South Korea. To what extent does the pursuit of success on the American charts require the erasure of Korean-ness?

6 BTS and the COVID-19 Pandemic

From December 2019 to January 2020, a new illness that caused pneumonia-like symptoms was discovered in China. By January 23, 2020, the city of Wuhan, China, was placed on complete lockdown due to the new virus termed 2019 Novel Coronavirus (later COVID-19). By March 2020, many cities in the US and Korea mandated people to stay at home as much as possible (Centers for Disease Control 2024). As of December 2024, there have been approximately 777 million reported cases of COVID and 7 million deaths (World Health Organization 2024) from COVID.

While all of us spent more time at home, we were also more likely to watch YouTube. According to the Pew Research Center, 73% of Americans used YouTube in 2019. By 2021, this had increased to 81%. Among 18- to 29-year-olds (presumably the age group that is most likely to follow pop music), 95% said they used YouTube (Pew Research Center 2024a). For those ages 13–17, in 2024, 93% reported using YouTube (Pew Research Center 2024b).

By March 2020, most public gatherings were shut down, and this, of course, included live music concerts, including K-Pop performances (Lee and Kao 2023). K-Pop companies were especially quick to innovate. SM Group SuperM held its *Beyond Live* online concert in April 2020, while TVXQ and Super Junior both held their online concerts in May 2020. BTS held a teaser event called *Bang Bang Con* on YouTube in May 2020 and broadcast many of its earlier concerts for free. They then announced that they would have an online concert called *Bang Bang Con: The Live* in June 2020. This concert earned about $20 million from 756,000 viewers who paid a range of prices, averaging about $45 each. A few months later, in October 2020, they held another online concert titled *Map of the Soul ON:E*, which took place over one weekend. These shows garnered 993,000 viewers from 191 countries and earned over US $40 million. By June 2021, BTS held two more online concerts, which sold 1.33 million tickets and earned $71 million in sales revenue. In total, these three sets of concerts generated more money than the 31 stadium performances they held in 2019 ($113.6 million) (Lee and Kao 2023). In fact, during a year where there were no in-person concerts, Big Hit Entertainment (the parent company of BTS before HYBE was formed) reported $716.7 million in revenue for 2020 compared to $507.9 million in revenue in 2019.

Table 2.3 lists all of the K-Pop songs that appeared on the US Billboard Hot 100 Chart from February 1, 2020, to February 15, 2025. Again, the songs are numbered consecutively starting from Table 2.1 so that we can see a total tally of the songs. Overall, there have been 97 songs since The Wonder Girls' "Nobody" in 2009. Note that 58 of the 97 songs on the list are by BTS or its members. We can also see that most songs appear on the chart for just a week before disappearing. If we were to total the number of weeks that these singles stayed on the chart, BTS's dominance would be even more dramatic.

Table 2.3 K-Pop songs on US Billboard Hot 100 Chart post–COVID-19: February 2020 to February 2025

Count since 2009	*Date*	*Artist*	*Song title*	*Highest position*	*# of weeks*
19	February 1, 2020	BTS	"Black Swan"	57	1
20	March 7, 2020	BTS	"On"	4	2
21	March 7, 2020	BTS (Jungkook solo)	"My Time"	84	1
22	March 7, 2020	BTS (Jimin solo)	"Filter"	87	1
23	June 6, 2020	Suga (Agust D)	"Daechwita"	76	1

(*continued*)

Table 2.3 (continued)

Count since 2009	*Date*	*Artist*	*Song title*	*Highest position*	*# of weeks*
24	June 13, 2020	Lady Gaga and Blackpink	"Sour Candy"	33	2
25	**June 27, 2020**	**Jawsh 685, Jason Derulo, and BTS**	**"Savage Love" (Laxed—Siren Beat)"**	**1**	**14**
26	July 11, 2020	Blackpink	"How You Like That"	33	2
27	**September 5, 2020**	**BTS**	**"Dynamite"**	**1**	**32**
28	September 12, 2020	Blackpink and Selena Gomez	"Ice Cream"	13	8
29	October 17, 2020	Blackpink	"Lovesick Girls"	59	1
30	**December 5, 2020**	**BTS**	**"Life Goes On"**	**1**	**3**
31	December 5, 2020	BTS	"Blue & Grey"	13	1
32	December 5, 2020	BTS	"Stay"	22	1
33	December 5, 2020	BTS	"Fly to My Room"	69	1
34	December 5, 2020	BTS	"Telepathy"	70	1
35	December 5, 2020	BTS	"Dis-ease"	72	1
36	March 27, 2021	Rosé	"On the Ground"	70	1
37	April 17, 2021	BTS	"Film Out"	81	1
38	**June 5, 2021**	**BTS**	**"Butter"**	**1**	**20**
39	**July 24, 2021**	**BTS**	**"Permission to Dance"**	**1**	7
40	September 25, 2021	Lisa	"Lalisa"	84	1
41	**October 9, 2021**	**Coldplay & BTS**	**"My Universe"**	**1**	**17**
42	October 16, 2021	Twice	"The Feels"	83	1

(*continued*)

Table 2.3 (continued)

Count since 2009	*Date*	*Artist*	*Song title*	*Highest position*	*# of weeks*
43	November 6, 2021	Lisa	"Money"	90	2
44	December 25, 2021	Juice Wrld & Suga	"Girl of My Dreams"	29	1
45	January 8, 2022	V	"Christmas Tree"	79	1
46	February 26, 2022	Jungkook	"Stay Alive"	95	1
47	May 14, 2022	Psy feat. Suga	"That That"	80	1
48	June 25, 2022	BTS	"Yet to Come"	13	2
49	June 25, 2022	BTS	"Run BTS"	73	1
50	July 9, 2022	Charlie Puth feat. Jungkook	"Left and Right"	22	17
51	July 16, 2022	J-Hope	"More"	82	1
52	July 30, 2022	J-Hope	"Arson"	96	1
53	August 20, 2022	Benny Blanco, BTS & Snoop Dogg	"Bad Decisions"	10	5
54	September 3, 2022	Blackpink	"Pink Venom"	22	6
55	October 1, 2022	Blackpink	"Shut Down"	25	3
56	November 12, 2022	Jin	"The Astronaut"	51	1
57	December 17, 2022	RM with Youjeen	"Wild Flower"	83	1
58	January 28, 2023	NewJeans	"Ditto"	85	5
59	January 28, 2023	Taeyang feat. Jimin	"Vibe"	76	1
60	February 4, 2023	Twice	"Moonlight Sunrise"	84	1
61	March 18, 2023	J-Hope with J. Cole	"On the Street"	60	1

(*continued*)

Table 2.3 (continued)

Count since 2009	*Date*	*Artist*	*Song title*	*Highest position*	*# of weeks*
62	April 1, 2023	Jimin	"Set Me Free Pt. 2"	30	1
63	April 1, 2023	Fifty Fifty	"Cupid"	17	25
64	**April 8, 2023**	**Jimin**	**"Like Crazy"**	**1**	**5**
65	May 6, 2023	Agust D	"Haegeum"	58	1
66	June 3, 2023	Kodak Black & NLE Choppa feat. Jimin, Jvke, Muni Long	"Angel Pt. 1"	65	2
67	June 24, 2023	BTS	"Take Two"	48	1
68	July 22, 2023	NewJeans	"Super Shy"	48	8
69	**July 29, 2023**	**Jungkook feat. Latto**	**"Seven"**	**1**	**15**
70	August 5, 2023	NewJeans	"ETA"	81	1
71	August 5, 2023	NewJeans	"Cool with You"	93	1
72	August 26, 2023	V	"Love Me Again"	96	1
73	September 23, 2023	V	"Slow Dancing"	51	1
74	October 14, 2023	Jungkook & Jack Harlow	"3D"	5	9
75	November 4, 2023	The Kid Laroi, Jungkook & Central Cee	"Too Much"	44	6
76	November 18, 2023	Jungkook	"Standing Next to You"	5	19
77	November 25, 2023	Stray Kids	"Lalalala"	90	1
78	December 30, 2023	The Weeknd, Jennie, Lily-Rose Depp	"One of the Girls"	51	15
79	March 9, 2024	Le Sserafim	"Easy"	99	1
80	March 30, 2024	V	"Fri(end)s"	65	1

(*continued*)

Table 2.3 (continued)

Count since 2009	*Date*	*Artist*	*Song title*	*Highest position*	*# of weeks*
81	April 20, 2024	Illit	"Magnetic"	91	1
82	May 25, 2024	Stray Kids feat. Charlie Puth	"Lose My Breath"	90	1
83	June 22, 2024	Jungkook	"Never Let Go"	97	1
84	July 13, 2024	Lisa	"Rockstar"	70	1
85	July 13, 2024	Jimin feat. Loco	"Smeraldo Garden Marching Band"	88	1
86	August 3, 2024	Jimin	"Who"	14	1
87	August 3, 2024	Stray Kids	"Chk Chk Boom"	49	1
88	August 31, 2024	Lisa feat. Rosalía	"New Woman"	97	1
89	September 14, 2024	Le Sserafim	"Crazy"	76	2
90	September 21, 2024	Megan Thee Stallion & RM	"Neva Play"	36	2
91	October 26, 2024	Jennie	"Mantra"	98	2
92	November 2, 2024	Rosé & Bruno Mars	"Apt."	3	16
93	November 30, 2024	Jin	"Running Wild"	53	1
94	December 13, 2024	V & Park Hyo-shin	"Winter Ahead"	99	1
95	December 21, 2024	Rosé	"Toxic Until the End"	90	1
96	December 21, 2024	V & Bing Crosby	"White Christmas" (remix)	93	1
97	February 15, 2025	Jennie & Dominic Fike	"Love Hangover"	96	1

Number 1 songs are in bold
Note that 58 of 97 songs are by BTS or its members
Source: Wikipedia, https://en.wikipedia.org/wiki/List_of_K-pop_songs_on_the_Billboard_charts and author's own calculations

6.1 K-Pop and BTS's First Number Ones

The beginning of 2020 marked the start of the COVID-19 pandemic. As mentioned previously, not only were music fans spending more time at home, concerts, including the BTS tour that would have supported *Map of the Soul:7*, were canceled. This album was released in February 2020 and included 20 tracks. The album reached music charts all over the world, from Argentina to Denmark, Estonia to Mexico, and reached #1 on the US Billboard 200 (US chart for album sales). Like almost all K-Pop albums, an EP *Map of the Soul: Persona* was released one year earlier, and previewed some of the songs which would appear on *Map of the Soul: 7*. BTS already enjoyed the success of "Boy with Luv," which reached #8 in April 2019.

The new album included "Make It Right" (reaching #76), "Black Swan" (#57), and "On" (#4) as well as the solo songs "My Time" (Jungkook's solo, #84) and "Filter" (Jimin's solo, #87). These songs are primarily in Korean, and with the exception of "Boy with Luv," received little radio play. In fact, even for "On," their highest charting single from the album, Vox writer Aja Romano noted in March 2020, "BTS just landed an unprecedented spot on the Hot 100—with virtually no radio play" (Romano 2020). In the same article, Romano quotes BTS's RM (Kim Namjoon) in their goal to hit #1 on the US Billboard Hot 100. In a 2019 Entertainment Weekly article by Leah Greenblatt, she also mentions that "mainstream radio airplay—a huge component of Hot 100 domination—still eludes them stateside" (Greenblatt 2019).

Even then, BTS noted the struggle between reaching their goals and abandoning their identities. In the same article, RM says:

> You know, Latin pop has its own Grammys in America, and it's quite different. I don't want to compare, but I think it's even harder as an Asian group. A Hot 100 and a Grammy nomination, these are our goals. But they're just goals—we don't want to change our identity or our genuineness to get the number one. Like if sing suddenly in full English, and change all these other things, then that's not BTS. (RM as quoted in Greenblatt 2019)

In fact, RM expressed this sentiment many times in various interviews. He often emphasized that they were a Korean group first and foremost. Interesting, RM discusses their identity as well as their values as being "genuineness."

Technically, BTS hit #1 on June 27, 2020, through a remix of a song by Jawsh 685 and Jason Derulo titled "Savage Love." They actually added Korean rap lyrics to the song. However, after the success of their online concerts, they released the single "Dynamite" on August 21, 2020. This would be their first original #1 single on the Billboard Hot 100 Chart, debuting at #1 on the September 5, 2020, US Billboard Hot 100 Charts. It became the first song to enjoy 100 million views on YouTube within 24 hours. However, directly contradicting what leader RM said in previous interviews, this song was completely in English.

In fact, it was primarily written by two English songwriters, David Stewart and Jessica Agombar. Unlike almost all of BTS's other songs, the members were not listed as songwriters on this single. The music video is a dreamy amalgam of an imaginary Los Angeles of the 1980s, complete with pastel colors reminiscent of "Ocean Pacific" shirts and the famous Randy's Donuts. However, Jungkook first appears in a bedroom draped in a 1970s color scheme of browns and greens, but the room also includes a poster of the film *Terminator* (released in 1984). It also featured a large Disco sign that felt out of place in this landscape, given that Disco disappeared from the US in 1979 after Disco Demolition Night in Comiskey Park in Chicago, IL, on July 12, 1979 (Sclafani 2009). The record store in the music video also sold CDs, which were not available until 1983. They sport disco-inspired outfits from Gucci. However, at the end of the video, they are wearing pastel-colored (from the 1980s) outfits clearly inspired by American boy bands from the 1990s (see Boyz II Men's music video for "Water Runs Dry" from 1994). They referred to these outfits and scene as "Teletubbies" (which began airing in 1997). Despite its jarring imagery, it is a very catchy song, and as of December 2024, the music video has 1.9 billion views.

The visual elements are borrowed from "retro" styles of the 1970s, 1980s, and 1990s America, but there are no signs of Korea or Korean-ness except that the BTS members are Korean. There are no Korean lyrics in the song, nor does the music video include any obvious or hidden signs of Korea. There are no Korean movie posters in the bedroom Jungkook sings in, nor are there albums featured by Korean artists in the record store from which RM sings his verses. Even the burger and donut shop does not sell any Korean food. In other words, BTS had to eliminate all signs of their Korean identity and abandon their aforementioned values as Korean artists to hit #1 on the US Billboard Hot 100 Chart. Still, this song is a landmark in K-Pop history in the US. It remained on the chart for 32 weeks, beating Psy's "Gangnam Style" by one week.

A few months later, in November 2020, BTS released *BE.* All the singles from this album debuted on the Billboard Hot 100 Chart, with "Life Goes On" hitting #1, and the other songs ranging from #13 to #72. Given that BTS had three number-one songs on the US Billboard Hot 100 in three months, they became the fastest group to do so since the Bee Gees. Not only that, "Life Goes On" became the first song primarily sung in Korean to reach number one. Moreover, all of the other songs are primarily in Korean. However, only "Life Goes On" lasted more than 1 week on the chart. The music video was shot primarily in outdoor locations in Seoul, and it was clear that they were in Korea. The indoor scenes showed them at home in their pajamas—also presumably in Seoul. Moreover, the music video was directed by maknae (youngest member of a group) Jungkook. As of December 2024, the music video has had 556 million views on YouTube.

BTS's next #1 singles were "Butter," "Permission to Dance," and "My Universe." "Butter" reached #1 on the US Billboard Hot 100 Chart dated June 5, 2021, and stayed on the charts for 20 weeks. This was a 1980s-inspired synth-pop number that was completely in English and not written by any of its members. The sets were primarily indoor sets, with no signs of Korea in its visuals. As of December 2024, this song has 1 billion views on YouTube.

"Permission to Dance" appeared on the chart dated July 24, 2024, and was primarily written by Ed Sheeran and included various English and Canadian songwriters. Again, this song was not co-written with any of the BTS members. The introduction of the music video showed a cast of characters that were multi-ethnic, and the setting looked like suburban America. It begins with a waitress holding a stack of pancakes topped with butter, presumably referring to their last single. The scenes with the members in Western-inspired outfits (with denim and fringes) were shot in a newly constructed laundromat. These shots were interspersed with scenes clearly shot in middle America. As of December 2024, this music video has about 660 million views.

Finally, in "My Universe," a song written by Chris Martin of Coldplay, BTS and Coldplay appear in a science fiction universe set in outer space, complete with aliens. The storyline is that in this universe, there are three bands, DJ Lafrique's Supernova 7, Coldplay, and BTS, and they are collaborating on a song via a "holoband" device despite being many miles apart. Here, BTS abandons any choreography but sings primarily in Korean (with the exception of the chorus). Interestingly, the fictional band also has no standalone part in the song. While BTS is not recognizable as a K-Pop idol group, they do primarily sing in Korean. This song was on the US Billboard Hot 100 charts for a total of 17 weeks, and as of December 2024, the video has had 330 million views.

Given that BTS began as a hip-hop/rap group (see their first music videos "No More Dream" and "We Are Bulletproof, Pt. II"), their number one songs are a far departure from their roots. Their old songs had almost no English, with the exception of the titles and a few hooks that repeat the title. Even their big hits in Korea, such as "Run," "I Need U," "Fire," "DOPE," "DNA," "Fake Love," and "Spring Day," sound very different. BTS wrote their own lyrics and imbued them with meaning. They admitted that "Dynamite," "Butter," and "Permission to Dance" were just light songs with no meaning (and no Korean words or visuals). The latter three were written by Western songwriters.

Many other K-Pop songs were also on the charts during the period from February 2020 to December 2024. Besides BTS and its members, most of the songs are from Blackpink or its members (Lisa, Jennie, and Rosé). Stray Kids, Fifty Fifty, NewJeans, TWICE, LeSerafim, Illit, and even Psy (in a collaboration with Suga of BTS) made appearances on the charts. However, outside of BTS or their members' songs and with the exceptions of Fifty Fifty's "Cupid" (#17 and a total of 25 weeks on the charts), "One of the Girls" by The Weeknd, Jennie, and Lily-Rose Depp, Rosé (#51 with 15 weeks on the charts), Blackpink and Selena Gomez's "Ice Cream" (#13 with 8 weeks on the charts) and Rosé and Bruno Mars's "Apt." (#8 with 6 weeks on the charts), NewJeans's "Ditto" (#85 with 5 weeks on the charts), and NewJeans's "Super Shy" (#48 with 8 weeks on the charts), most non-BTS (and even some BTS) K-Pop songs that appear on the charts stay for no longer than one or two weeks. Still, many of these songs have some Korean content, although a few are also only in English ("One of the Girls," "Cupid," "Money," "Rock Star," and "Mantra"), besides many of BTS's top-charting songs. In fact, of the 97 K-Pop songs that have ever appeared on the US Billboard Hot 100 Charts, 58 are from BTS or its members (RM, Jin, Suga or Agust D, J-Hope, Jimin, V, and Jungkook). Only Jungkook and Jimin have had #1 songs as solo artists, and only BTS and its members have had #1 songs.

US radio is not ready for non-English songs, but that has not prevented K-Pop fans from making up for it in terms of streaming and sales. As with all of the most popular K-Pop artists, BTS's position on the charts is due, in part, to fans buying multiple copies of their records. According to Wallace (2023), in Spring 2021, when "Butter" hit Number 1 while Olivia Rodrigo's "Good 4 U" hit #2, the ratio of sales to streaming is notable. For the charted dated June 5, 2021, "Butter" debuted at #1 with 248,800 pure sales and 32.2 streams, while "Good 4 U" had 19,000 sales with 62.3 million streams. In other words, "Butter" owes about 68% of its ranking points to sales, while the record sales of "Good 4 U" only accounted for 7% of its ranking points (Wallace 2023). However, Wallace does not mention the importance of YouTube streams, where K-Pop fans are stellar in their use in promoting their favorite groups.

According to the IFPI's Global Albums Sales Charts, including sales from all physical formats and album downloads, nine of the top 10 albums sold were K-Pop albums. Looking at the Top 20 albums, 19 were by K-Pop artists. The only exception was Taylor Swift's 1989 (Taylor's Version), at #6. The top 10 albums sold were Seventeen's *FML* (6.4 million units sold), Stray Kids's *5-STAR* (5.3 million), and NCT DREAM's *ISTJ* (4.6 million sold), down to #10 (V's *Layover* with 2.2 million sold) (IFPI 2024).

Why is this the case? In part, K-Pop groups release multiple versions of the same album. They often provide different photocards and other memorabilia. If fans want to collect a variety of merchandise, they have to buy multiple copies of the same album. Moreover, fans believe that they must support their artists. According to an article in the *Korea JoongAng Daily*, pre-order sales from GS25's mobile app suggested that foreign buyers bought 47 albums each (Kim 2024). For example, Seventeen's FML has 19 versions of the same album (Photobook, 3 versions; Carat Class, 13 versions; Weverse, 1 version; Deluxe, 1 version, and KIT, 1 version) (allkpop 2023). NMIXX's *A Midsummer NMIXX's Dream* includes one random polaroid card and one random photocard. According to an article, there are more than 150 photocards per member, which means that with six members, there are more than 900 possible photocards to collect (Koreaboo 2023).

What does this all mean? Given the number of views on YouTube, album sales, and other streaming data, K-Pop groups, and especially BTS, are doing exceptionally well. Without clear data and information on the formulas used to calculate positionality of songs on the Billboard charts, it is reasonable to suspect that radio plays are the primary culprit behind why K-Pop groups do not appear on the US charts more often. However, this has not stopped K-Pop groups from pursuing the US Billboard Hot 100 Charts. It is now commonplace for music videos to be released on Thursdays at midnight US Eastern time in order to accommodate the timing of when Billboard Hot 100 Charts begin tracking for the following week.

7 Value and Identity

Given that the power of the Hallyu is that it transmits Korean cultural products across its borders, is it still part of the Hallyu if the product has no Korean content? What counts as Korean content? Certainly, most of us would agree that having Korean language, Korean members, Korean locations, Korean objects, Korean references, and Korean songwriters would qualify. In Youjeong Oh's book, she also argues that "Korean television dramas and pop music not only project an international image of Korean consumer goods and services but brand Korean cities by cultivating and displaying their images and meanings therein" (Oh 2018). She states that this is what attracts Korean tourists to Korea. Until recently, BTS served as brand ambassadors not only for large companies like Hyundai and Samsung, but also in tourism campaigns for Seoul. However, if music videos are increasingly shot in Los Angeles or New York, how does K-Pop continue to promote Korean content and places? In contrast to BTS's "Dynamite," which appears in a fictional Los Angeles of the 1980s, compare their song "Paldogangsan" (or Satoori Rap), which is literally about the provinces of Korea, or RM's song "Seoul."

In the case of K-Pop, is it enough that there are Koreans involved? There is no doubt that BTS members are Korean. But Lisa of Blackpink is Thai. If her solo work, as evidenced by "Rock Star," is not produced by a Korean entertainment company, nor is it in Korean, does that still count as K-Pop? The video also shows scenes of Bangkok, and none of the songwriters are Korean. Still, she was trained by YG Entertainment in Korea, and she was part of the most popular K-Pop girl group of all time, and I think this is enough to claim her songs as K-Pop. However, it would be reasonable to disagree.

Companies like HYBE are pushing the boundaries of K-Pop. Bang Si-hyuk has claimed that he does not believe K-Pop is a genre and instead argues, "K-Pop has to drop the K and become 'just pop' if it wants to become the true mainstream genre of the world" (Yoon 2024). Yoon also argues that Lee Soo-man (founder of SM Entertainment) predicted in 2011 that Hallyu 3.0:

> or the third phase of the Korean Wave, or Korean content export – follows the first phase in which Korean content is simply exported to foreign markets, and the second where overseas companies or celebrities collaborate with Korean content, finally ending at a point where Korean companies export the 'culture technology' of Korea by establishing joint ventures with overseas companies in a true realization of localization. (Yoon 2024)

New groups such as KATSEYE (a HYBE and Geffen Records collaboration) or Dear Alice (an SM and Moon&Back Media venture) further question the boundaries of K-Pop. KATSEYE includes one Korean member and one multiracial Chinese member, but their songs are not in Korean, and the members are not trained there.

Dear Alice is a British group whose debut was the subject of a six-part documentary, titled *Made in Korea: The K-Pop Experience*. There are no Korean or East Asian members. They were trained for 100 days by SM in Korea—compare this to the many years that K-Pop idols work as trainees before their debut. Along with the title of the show, they once performed live at the British Embassy in Korea. They are clearly being marketed as a novelty act. From my views of their videos, their dance choreographies pale in comparison to any current K-Pop boy groups. Would anyone view them as a legitimate K-Pop group? It is doubtful. Still, they represent the export of the Hallyu and perhaps work to highlight the high level of skills necessary to be in a K-Pop idol group.

With the exception of the large entertainment companies such as HYBE, SM, JYP, and YG, others are promoting more traditional K-Pop idol groups, whose members are primarily Korean ethnics and whose songs are sung mostly in Korean. Their identities as K-Pop artists from Korea are fully intact.

For the most successful groups, such as BTS, hitting #1 and staying there seems to require Americanization—although this Americanization can be conceived by non-Americans.

8 Conclusion

What does this suggest for the future of K-Pop? As it becomes globalized, one strategy is to localize it so that it is accepted by other non-Korean markets (a process sometimes referred to as glocalization). For songs to appear on the US Billboard Hot 100 Charts, especially via radio play, K-Pop songs are compelled to be performed solely in English. Not only that, when examining songs like "Dynamite," "Butter," or "Permission to

Dance," BTS's number one songs on the US Billboard Hot 100 Chart, they seem to eliminate all traces of Korean-ness in its lyrics and visuals in the music video. These songs appeared despite BTS's leader RM stating that they are a Korean band and that, through their United Nations appearances, young people must "Speak Yourself" and his earlier claims for maintaining their identity and their genuineness.

BTS clearly battles against these pressures. Their most successful songs were ordered by HYBE and had no participation by the members in terms of its composition or production. There were no Korean lyrics. However, for all of the other BTS songs and in most of the members' solo work (with the exception of Jungkook's 2024 singles), their songs were composed with the input of the members and contain primarily Korean lyrics and often about Korean subjects. For RM, K-Pop is Korean because it requires its idols to reach perfection. He states in a 2023 interview:

> Korea is a country that has been invaded, exploited and divided in two. It was a country that had nothing 70 years ago. Nowadays, the entire world is looking at Korea. How do think it was possible? It's because people are working [expletive] hard to improve themselves. (RM, in Korea JoongAng Daily, 2023)

Currently, K-Pop has expanded such that there are groups that fit many definitions of what the "K" means in K-Pop idol groups. For most, it requires that one has participated in the trainee system and heavily choreographed dance numbers. The other elements may include Korean members, Korean producers, Korean lyrics, Korean cultural content, or Korean visuals. Some might insist that it should be made in Korea. What happens when one or all of these elements are absent? Would that group or song without these characteristics still be considered K-Pop?

Ideally, the Hallyu should work to expose other countries to Korea, and by doing so, increase the cultural impact and soft power of South Korea. By extension, when the Hallyu reaches the West, it can promote the acceptance of East Asia and also East Asian Americans or other East Asians in the diaspora. However, if the characteristic of the Hallyu simply emulates those of the West, what are the values and identities that are transmitted from Korea to other countries? For the Korean or Asian diaspora, many of us hope that some element of Korean-ness is maintained in K-Pop. It is clear that while market-driven forces are driving K-Pop songs toward a generic Westernization, many fans actually enjoy the Korean content found in K-Pop.

References

@KissChanttanooga. 2017, October 4. @BTS_twt YOU HAVE THE BEST FANS EVER! No Fanbase Has EVER Sent Me Flowers I'm Crying. Twitter. https://x.com/KissChattanooga/status/915585442568957952. Accessed 11 December 2024.

Allkpop. 2022a, February 11. A Business Analyst Gives His Insight to the Statement That "HYBE is an agency that only has BTS and nothing else." Allkpop. https://www.allkpop.com/article/2022/02/a-business-analyst-gives-his-insight-to-the-statement-that-hybe-is-an-agency-that-only-has-bts-and-nothing-else. Accessed 12 December 2024.

Allkpop. 2022b, August 2. BTS Climbs Up to #3 in Global Artists Who Sold the Most Albums Over the Past 30 years. Allkop. https://www.allkpop.com/article/2022/08/bts-climbs-up-to-3-in-global-artists-who-sold-the-most-albums-over-the-past-30-years. Accessed 12 December 2024.

Allkpop. 2023, May 18. How Many Versions of One Album Are K-Pop Idol Groups Selling These Days? Allkpop. https://www.allkpop.com/article/2023/05/how-many-versions-of-one-album-are-k-pop-idol-groups-selling-these-days. Accessed 17 December 2023.

Anand, N. 2005. Charting the Music Business: Billboard Magazine and the Development of the Commercial Music Field. In *The Business of Culture: Strategic Perspectives on Entertainment and Media*, ed. J. Lampel, J. Shamsie, and T. K. Lant. Oxford: Taylor & Francis Group.

Baer, C. 2023. New MLA Report Highlights the Need for Investment in Language Study. Modern Language Association. https://news.mla.hcommons.org/2023/11/15/new-mla-report-highlights-the-need-for-investment-in-language-study/. Accessed 21 December 2024.

Bellini, J. 2012, October 15. Apparently This Matters: R.I.P., 'Gangnam Style' CNN. https://www.cnn.com/2012/10/12/tech/web/apparently-this-matters-gangnam-style/index.html. Accessed 10 December 2024.

Center for Disease Control Museum. 2024. COVID-19 Timeline. https://www.cdc.gov/museum/timeline/covid19.html. Accessed 15 December 2024.

Chang, D. 2017, December 22. Catching Fire: Grassroots Campaign That Sold BTS to Mainstream America. Yonhap News Agency. https://en.yna.co.kr/view/AEN20171222003200315. Accessed 9 December 2024.

Coleman, J. S. 1961. *The Adolescent Society: The Social Life of the Teenager and Its Impact on Education*. New York: Free Press of Glencoe.

Greenblatt, L. 2019, March 28. The Greatest Showmen: An Exclusive Look Inside the World of BTS. Entertainment Weekly. https://ew.com/music/2019/03/28/bts-exclusive-cover-story/. Accessed 16 December 2024.

Hall, M. K. 2014. *The Emergence of Rock and Roll: Music and the Rise of American Youth Culture. Critical Moments in American History*. New York: Routledge.

Herman, T. 2023, June 13. How BTS Took Over the World: A Timeline of the Group's Biggest Career Moments. Billboard. https://www.billboard.com/lists/bts-timeline-biggest-career-moments/july-2011/. Accessed 11 December 2024.

IFPI. 2024. Global Music Report: 2024. State of the Industry. https://ifpi-website-cms.s3.eu-west-2.amazonaws.com/IFPI_GMR_2024_State_of_the_Industry_db92a1c9c1.pdf. Accessed 21 December 2024.

Kao, G., and P. Shinkoda 2021, April 12. Media Bears Responsibility for Reinforcing Asian American Stereotypes. Variety. https://variety.com/2021/film/news/media-asian-american-stereotypes-1234949658/. Accessed 9 December 2024.

Kao, G., K. Joyner, and K. Stamper Balistreri. 2019. *The Company We Keep: Interracial Friendships and Romantic Relationships from Adolescence to Adulthood*. New York: Russell Sage Foundation.

Kim, J. 2024, September 24. Foreign K-Pop Fans Flock to Convenience Stores to Buy Albums in Bulk. *Korea JoongAng Daily*. https://koreajoongangdaily.joins.com/news/2024-09-24/business/industry/Foreign-Kpop-fans-flock-to-convenience-stores-to-buy-albums-in-bulk/2139799. Accessed 17 December 2024.

Koreaboo. 2023, November 28. NMIXX Is the Latest K-Pop Group to Draw Controversy for Extremely High Photocard Numbers. Koreaboo. https://www.koreaboo.com/news/kpop-nmixx-latest-group-draw-controversy-extremely-high-photocard-numbers/. Accessed 17 December 2024.

Lee, W., and G. Kao. 2023. 'I Need U': Audience Participation in BTS's Online Concerts During COVID-19. *Journal of Popular Music Studies* 35 (1): 46–66. https://doi.org/10.1525/jpms.2023.35.1.46.

Oh, Y. 2018. *Pop City: Korean Popular Culture and the Selling of Place*. Ithaca, NY: Cornell University Press.

Pew Research Center. 2024a. Americans' Social Media Use. Pew Research Center. https://www.pewresearch.org/internet/2024/01/31/americans-social-media-use/. Accessed 15 December 2024.

Pew Research Center. 2024b. Teens and Social Media Fact Sheet. Pew Research Center. https://www.pewresearch.org/internet/fact-sheet/teens-and-social-media-fact-sheet/. Accessed 15 December 2024.

Radio Hall of Fame. 2024. https://www.radiohalloffame.com/todd-storz.

Romano, A. 2020, March 2. BTS Just Landed an Unprecedented Spot on the Hot 100 – With Virtually No Radio Play. Vox. https://www.vox.com/2020/3/2/21158499/bts-on-hot100-chart-position-record. Accessed 16 December 2024.

Sclafani, T. 2009, July 10. When 'Disco Sucks!' Echoed Around the World. Today.com. https://www.today.com/popculture/when-disco-sucks-echoed-around-world-1C9410502. Accessed 16 December 2024.

Scripps News, July 24. 2024. The Pervasiveness of U.S. Pop Culture. *Scripps News*. https://www.scrippsnews.com/us-news/the-pervasiveness-of-u-s-pop-culture. Accessed 21 December 2024.

Tencer, D. 2024, September 10. Who Owns K-Pop Giant HYBE? Music Business Worldwide. https://www.musicbusinessworldwide.com/who-owns-k-pop-giant-hybe123/. Accessed 21 December 2024.

Trust, G. 2022, August 4. 64 Fun Facts from the Billboard Hot 100's First 64 Years: From Ricky Nelson to Lizzo & More. Billboard. https://www.billboard.com/music/chart-beat/hot-100-64-years-fun-facts-ricky-nelson-lizzo-1235122282/. Accessed 9 December 2024.

Wallace, K. 2023, June 22. The Billboard Hot 100 Deconstructed. *Firebird Magazine*. https://firebirdmagazine.com/birds-eye-view/thebillboardhot100deconstructed. Accessed 11 December 2024.

Wikipedia. 2024. List of K-pop songs on the Billboard charts. https://en.wikipedia.org/wiki/List_of_Kpop_songs_on_the_Billboard_charts. Accessed 10 October 2024.

World Health Organization. 2024. WHO COVID-19 Dashboard. https://data.who.int/dashboards/covid19/cases?n=o. Accessed 15 December 2024.

Yoon, S. 2024, February 17. Dropping the K: Can K-pop Ever Be Just Pop? *Korea JoongAng Daily*. https://koreajoongangdaily.joins.com/news/2024-02-17/entertainment/kpop/Dropping-the-K-Can-Kpop-ever-be-just-pop-/1982607. Accessed 17 December.

CHAPTER 3

Rejection of Coexistence Through Impurity: Opposition to Mosque Construction in Contemporary Korean Multicultural Society

Yohan Yoo

1 Otherizing Muslim Migrants in the Multicultural Society of Contemporary Korea

Although the Republic of Korea was considered a racially homogenous nation until several decades ago, it has rapidly evolved into a multicultural society in the twenty-first century. As of 2024, over 2.5 million migrants

The photos in this chapter were taken in Daegu by Chi-Yeong Choi, a graduate student in the Department of Religious Studies at Seoul National University, to whom I am grateful for their use.

Y. Yoo (✉)
Department of Religious Studies, Seoul National University, Seoul, Korea (Republic of)
e-mail: yohanyoo@snu.ac.kr

© The Author(s), under exclusive license to Springer Nature Singapore Pte Ltd. 2025

Y. Yoo, S. C. Lee (eds.), *Reimagining Korea*, Palgrave Series in Contemporary Korean Studies,
https://doi.org/10.1007/978-981-96-6990-5_3

reside in Korea, accounting for approximately five percent of the population. Many of these migrants play essential roles in various sectors, particularly in physical labor that Koreans often avoid. Despite their legal status and significant contributions, Muslim migrants in Korea face challenges in being accepted as integral members of Korean society and are frequently otherized. Notably, local Koreans tend to be more tolerant of Muslim migrants' presence within residential neighborhoods as long as these migrants do not overtly express their religious identity. However, those who openly practice or display their religious identity are more likely to be perceived as impure beings incapable of coexisting within the Korean insider realm and are subsequently marginalized.

There are several reasons that may contribute to this hostile attitude toward Muslims in Korea, including practical inconveniences arising from cultural differences and the negative influence of media coverage on conflicts involving Muslim migrants and native residents in Western countries. However, the focus of this chapter is not to uncover these reasons. Instead, I seek to examine the religious discourses and expressions that often underpin the exclusion of these otherized migrants from the realm of native ethnic Koreans.

By examining this situation in Korea, I aim to highlight two notable characteristics that contribute to a general and theoretical formulation. First, it is important to recognize that conflicts between native Korean residents and Muslim migrants did not arise merely from the presence of the latter, but rather from their attempts to build a mosque—an act that formally signaled their religious identity. As will be demonstrated, residents in Daehyeon-dong, Daegu, oppose Muslims under the pretext of religious concerns. Similarly, in many so-called modernized and developed countries, migrants are labeled as inferior or impure not on the basis of race or nationality but because of their religion. Terry Eagleton aptly identifies this phenomenon as a prevailing trend in contemporary Western countries.

> A supercivilized brand of cultural supremacism, one which would no doubt find itself offended by common-or-garden racism, is now much in fashion, not least among the literary intelligentsia. Since branding others as inferior because of their race is no longer acceptable, relegating them to the outer darkness because of their religion may serve instead. (Eagleton 2009, 95)

As Eagleton insightfully observes, while cultured modern people hesitate to discriminate against migrants based on their race or nationality, they feel relatively unrestrained in stigmatizing them for their religion. In the strong opposition of Daehyeon-dong residents to the construction of a mosque, we see evidence of a heightened sensitivity to the display of religious and cultural identity compared to differences in race or nationality.

Second, the rhetoric of purity and impurity is strategically employed to exclude Muslim migrants in Korea. I have previously explored the concept of purity in relation to how specific cultures divide and structure realms within their cosmological worldviews (Yoo 2005, 2013; Yoo and Watts 2021). In this framework, purity refers to the necessary conditions or qualities attributed to each realm within a cosmological understanding, while impurity signifies a state that fails to meet these requisite conditions. As noted, "Purity and impurity ideas come about when people distinguish the realms of various beings in the world and accord different conditions to each realm" (Yoo and Watts 2021, 11). Social exclusion based on the dichotomous division between the pure and the impure is typically achieved by labeling others as impure. By doing so, impure others are marginalized from the social sphere, and coexistence with them is largely discouraged.

This chapter investigates how the rhetoric of impurity is utilized to justify hatred and discrimination against otherized migrants in contemporary Korea. Interestingly, residents of Daehyeon-dong do not argue, "You are impure to us," but rather, "We are impure to you." This response reflects a distinctly different application of the purity concept compared to the common approach, if not an unprecedented one. Residents opposing the construction of the mosque do not argue that Muslim others are impure to "us," but rather that "we" are impure to them. This is exemplified by their emphasis on practices such as displaying and consuming pork, which is a staple in the daily lives of most Koreans but is considered unclean or impure and avoided by Muslims. As will be demonstrated, when residents were unable to prevent the legally sanctioned construction of the mosque, they escalated their actions by displaying a pig's head—eventually increasing the number to three—and sometimes substituting them with plastic replicas in front of the main gates of houses surrounding the construction site. Additionally, unidentified white liquid waste was spread in front of the site, which Muslims suspected was done by some residents. The residential community also organized pork parties in close proximity to the site.

These residents have persistently argued that Muslim others do not belong among them because "we" and "they" adhere to fundamentally different concepts and practices of purity. Before analyzing this exclusionary strategy through the lens of purity and impurity concepts, the next section will provide a brief account of the events that have unfolded around the mosque construction site in Daehyeon-dong, Daegu.

2 Conflicts Between Korean Residents and Muslims in the Residential Area, Daehyeon-dong, Daegu

2.1 The Sequence of Events

Daehyeon-dong is a neighborhood in Buk-gu, a district in Daegu, one of South Korea's six *Gwangyeoksi* (Metropolitan cities), with a population of approximately 2.37 million. The ongoing conflict between Korean residents and Muslim migrants is centered near the Western Gate of Gyeongbuk National University, the largest university in both Daegu and Gyeongsangbuk-do Province. This area is an established residential neighborhood where native citizens have lived for many years.[1]

Starting about twenty years ago, Muslim international graduate students from various countries—including Pakistan, Bangladesh, Indonesia, and Nigeria—began settling in this area. Currently, the neighborhood is home to approximately eighty international Muslim students, along with some of their family members.

In November 2014, five Muslims purchased a 264 square meter traditional Korean-style house and began using it as a *musalla* (prayer hall). This location later became the site where construction of a mosque was initiated, although the construction has been halted. The Muslim community planned to build a mosque with a dome roof capable of

[1] There is one mosque and six prayer halls in Daegu. However, conflicts between Korean residents and Muslim migrants are rare in other areas, primarily because these facilities are located in industrial complexes rather than residential neighborhoods. In contrast, the prayer hall in Daehyeon-dong has become a focal point of tension due to its location in a residential area. Unlike most laborers who come to Korea without their families, many international graduate students in Daehyeon-dong reside there with their family members, making their religious activities more noticeable to local residents (Kim 2021c). For reference, according to the Korean Muslim Federation's website (https://www.koreaislam.org), there are twenty mosques in Korea. Additionally, it is estimated that there were about 180 prayer halls as of 2019 (Nam 2019).

accommodating up to 200 people at one time (Jeong 2022).[2] In September 2020, the local government approved the construction of a three-story mosque to be used as a religious assembly hall. Meanwhile, in May 2020, the Muslim community purchased another 132-square-meter house to serve as a temporary prayer hall during the construction (Kim 2021a, 2021b).

Although the construction began in December 2020, it was halted after the steel structures were erected due to strong objections from local residents. These residents opposed the project and submitted a petition with 350 signatures to the Buk-gu district office, prompting the office to suspend construction on February 16, 2021. On the same day, they also filed an online petition on the national petition board of the Office of the President, titled "We are opposing the Islam mosque within the highly residential area of Daegu." In response, the district office immediately issued an order to cease the construction (Kim 2021a).

The Muslim community in the area appealed to the court, arguing that the order to discontinue the mosque's construction was unlawful. The district office defended its decision, citing concerns over the infringement of property rights and the emotional disturbance of residents, while acknowledging the possibility that the measure might infringe upon religious freedom. However, on December 1, 2021, the Daegu lower court ruled that the office should not halt solely based on collective complaints. The court further emphasized that the district office "should have notified the Muslim community about the halt well beforehand and provided them an opportunity to submit their own opinions about the office's decision" (Kim and Yi 2022). Subsequent rulings reinforced the decision. The second trial court in April 2022 and finally the Supreme Court in September 2022 ruled against the residents, upholding the lower court's decision (Yang 2022).

However, even the Supreme Court ruling failed to resolve the issue, as Korean residents remained steadfast in their opposition to the mosque

[2] Although the official name of the building under construction is "Darul-Emaan Gyungpook Islam Center," it is referred to as a mosque, rather than a prayer hall, on the "Local Muslim News" board of the Korea Muslim Federation's website (https://www.koreaislam.org/en/local-muslim-news/?pageid=2&uid=4414&mod=document). A mosque typically includes specific architectural features, such as a *minbar*—a pulpit where an imam, the prayer leader, stands to deliver sermons—and a *mihrab*, a niche in the wall that indicates the direction of the Kaaba, the sacred shrine at the center of the Great Mosque in Mecca. In contrast, a prayer hall generally lacks these features.

being built in their neighborhood (Kim and Yi 2022). Members of the Muslim community attempted to resume construction on August 8, 2022, but their efforts were unsuccessful due to the residents' vigorous resistance. Some residents lay down in front of trucks carrying materials, others blocked laborers from entering the site, and some resorted to using offensive and abusive language toward Muslims and laborers. A second attempt to resume construction two days later was again thwarted by the residents' stiff opposition (Yang 2022).

Construction only resumed with police assistance, but residents continued their efforts to disrupt the work. On August 30, 2022, two residents were arrested for persisting in their efforts to obstruct construction despite police warnings (Sim 2022). Over the following year, the Muslim community managed to complete approximately 80 percent of the mosque, but the construction was halted again on December 14, 2023, by order of the Buk-gu office. The office also reported the construction company to the police for failing to comply with directives issued by the construction supervisor, specifically regarding the installation of additional stud bolts on the steel girder supporting the second floor, which the company had neglected to implement (Ryu 2023).

In March 2024, a new conflict arose between Muslim clients, who filed a civil suit against the construction company to recover payments they had made, and the company, which demanded additional costs to cover delays caused by construction disruptions (Hwang 2024). As of July 2024, residents continued to strongly oppose and disrupt the construction. On July 5, two residents were fined for parking their cars to block the access road to the site. Later that month, on July 25, approximately twenty residents staged protests in front of the Daegu Bukbu Police Station and the Daegu District Court (Yun 2024).

2.2 *Strategic Use of Pork to Prevent the Construction*

During the conflict, residents strategically appropriated pork as a symbolic tool to express their indignation and to hinder the mosque's construction. The first pig head appeared near the construction site in October 2022, placed by Daehyeon-dong residents in front of the gate of a house as a form of protest (Song 2022). The number of pig heads increased to two by November 9, 2022, and to three on December 26 of the same year (Cha 2022; Kim and Yi 2022). Shortly thereafter, several pig feet were displayed alongside the heads (Kim 2023). As of July 2024, pig heads continued to be displayed near the site. When the heads began to decay and emit a foul odor, they were stored in a refrigerator placed outside a resident's main gate. In addition to real pig heads, a pig head replica was also displayed.

Another incident, perceived by Muslims in the area as an attack involving pork, occurred on March 8, 2023. Two individuals spread a white liquid waste on the street in front of the construction site while concealing their actions under the cover of an umbrella. Muslims believed the substance to be pig fat, which caused significant distress within the community (Choi 2023). Although the National Forensic Service later identified the liquid as vegetable oil (Hwang 2023), the incident successfully provoked Muslims due to its initial perception as pig fat.

Another effective tactic used to agitate Muslims was organizing parties where pork was prominently featured. The pork-themed gatherings were held near the construction site shortly after the first pig head was displayed. "The Emergency Planning Committee to Stop the Construction of the Mosque," comprised primarily of Daehyeon-dong residents, hosted a *tongdwaeji* (whole pig) barbeque party on December 15, 2022, which they referred to as the "Daehyeon-dong year-end party" (Han 2022b). This event was believed to have escalated tensions with the Muslim migrant community in the area (Song 2022). Shortly thereafter, on February 2, 2023, residents prepared and ate 100 servings of boiled pork while drinking distilled spirits at tables set up in the alley directly in front of the construction site (Kim 2023).

It is true that the displayed pig heads were the type commonly sold in Korean traditional markets for dishes like pork meat soup and boiled pork slices. Members of the committee refuted criticism that their pork disrespected Islamic culture, arguing, "It is Korean culture to cook and share pork dishes. Since when has any explanation been required for residents having a party?" (Kim 2023). Residents also defended their actions, claiming they were legal and that placing pig heads on private property was within their rights (Han 2022a). However, some admitted that the act was a form of protest. The owner of the house where pig heads were displayed in front of the main gate refused the demand to remove them, stating, "I cannot, because this is the last protest I can make" (Cha 2022).

In summary, the display of pig heads was a deliberate strategy by residents to antagonize Muslim migrants while technically avoiding legal repercussions, especially after physical obstruction became unfeasible due to the court ruling and police enforcement. The form of protest was not only symbolic but also direct and tangible, as evidenced by its high level of effectiveness. I will elaborate further on this effectiveness in Sect. 4.

Muslims in the area expressed deep discomfort and distress over the presence of what they considered impure and forbidden food, according to the Quran. They requested that the Korean residents remove the pig heads, explaining the emotional suffering caused by their display. However, the residents refused to comply. The Muslim community regarded the act as highly provocative and warned that it had the potential to escalate into hate crimes. One Muslim doctoral student emphasized, "Placing pig heads in front of another person's house [because one's main gate in a narrow alley is just in front of another's house] or drinking alcohol in front of a religious facility is not real Korean culture but Islamophobia" (Kim 2023) (Figs. 3.1 and 3.2).

3 Opposing Opinions in News Article Comments and Social Networks: Refusing to Coexist with Muslim Others Manifesting Their Religious Identity

Regarding the construction of the mosque in Daehyeon-dong, Daegu, some Koreans have expressed support for the Muslim community. For example, students from Gyeongbuk National University and members of the civic group Daeguchamyeoyeondae (People's Solidarity for Participatory Democracy in Daegu) have taken the position that the mosque should be built without interference. On February 18, 2021, two days after the district office ordered the construction to halt, the civic group issued a statement asserting that the decision should be reversed, arguing that it violated freedom of religion, universal human rights, cultural diversity, and administrative fairness (Kim 2021a).

On December 15, 2022, a student and a graduate of Gyeongbuk National University confronted residents as they attempted to post a handwritten sign supporting the Muslim community on the wall of the university's Western Gate (Han 2022b). Online, posters and commenters on news articles related to this conflict have argued that it is shameful for freedom of religion and universal human rights to be blatantly violated in contemporary Korea. They emphasize that upholding the universal values of modern democratic society is of paramount importance.

Fig. 3.1 Pig heads in a refrigerator. (© Chi-Yeong Choi)

However, it is evident that supporters of the mosque are significantly outnumbered by its critics. Among the general public, the majority aligns with the local residents of Daehyeon-dong, Daegu, who oppose the mosque's construction. An extreme example of this disparity is a message posted on the "Forum" bulletin board of the Office of the President on September 3, 2021, titled "Opposition to the Daegu Islam Mosque." The

Fig. 3.2 A replica pig head and a placard opposing the construction. (© Chi-Yeong Choi)

post garnered 519 upvotes and only seven downvotes, illustrating the overwhelming support for the opposition.[3]

Above all, as we have seen, the residents living near the site are the most vocal in their opposition to the construction. Some express concerns that real estate prices will decline if the neighborhood becomes associated with a growing Muslim residential area. Others cite discomfort with living alongside Muslims due to perceived lifestyle differences, including noise, food smell, and waste management. One resident complained, "Muslims

[3] This post is preserved on the website of the Presidential Archive, managed by the Ministry of Interior and Safety in Korea, at http://webarchives.pa.go.kr/19th/www.president.go.kr/forums/341889. I refer to this ratio as "an extreme example" because it does not necessarily represent the general opinion of Koreans. It should also be noted that the interviews with residents of Daehyeon-dong, quoted in news articles and referenced in this section, may be overstated. Nevertheless, both the ratio and the interviews highlight a growing tendency to avoid and oppose Muslims in Korea.

do not properly sort waste, creating a lot of trash. They hang around in groups until two or three a.m., making noise" (Oh and Seong 2021). Another resident shared with a journalist, "Dozens of Muslims frequently come and go every day. I feel especially distressed during the festival [Ramadan] because of the peculiar odor coming from their cooking and eating together very late every night" (Kim 2021a, 2021b).

Residents have openly expressed their complaints through placards and pickets displayed in the alley. While some placards simply state that residents strongly oppose the construction, others provide specific reasons for their opposition. From the beginning, residents have asserted messages, such as "The mosque will smash our right to live and right to pursue happiness." Some placards go further, "The mosque will kill us" (Oh and Seong 2021). These messages suggest that they cannot live with Muslims who openly demonstrating their religious identity and that residents believe they cannot coexist with Muslims who openly demonstrate their religious identity, nor can they achieve happiness while living alongside them. One picket reveals a deep entrenched prejudice against Muslims, reading, "Although not all Muslims are terrorists, all terrorists are Muslims" (Yi 2021; Kim and Yi 2022). Such statements reflect a perception that they cannot live in the same neighborhood alongside Muslims because they could pose a threat. Some placards, which were later removed by the district office for containing discriminatory content, employed even stronger language of hatred, the details of which I am unwilling to include here (Jeong 2022).

Criticisms found on the internet regarding the mosque controversy can generally be divided into two categories. The first type focuses on the perceived characteristics of Islam itself. Many critics argue that Islam is an exclusive religion, claiming that it does not attempt to engage with other cultures while expecting accommodations from them. Some commenters specifically criticize that Muslims in Korea for building mosques in residential areas, contrasting this with the lack of allowance for temples or churches in many Islamic countries. One comment sarcastically remarks, "If a Korean opens a pork rib restaurant in the center of an Islamic country, he or she will be beheaded." Another states, "Islamic male-centered culture is unfair to women and makes Korean women feel uneasy."

The conclusion of many negative comments is that Muslims should not act disrespectfully in Korea and should instead return to their own countries, effectively proclaiming the impossibility of coexisting with them. Examples of such comments posted on an online news website include:

Fig. 3.3 A placard and picket in the alley leading to the construction site. (© Chi-Yeong Choi)

"Islam is a religion that never concede to the cultures of other countries." "We respected their culture, but they do not show appreciation." "They are haughty, expecting to receive more and more even though they have been respected enough." "They came to study in Korean knowing there were no mosques near the university. How dare they demand a mosque now?" These comments reflect the perception that Muslims exhibit cliquey and intransient attitudes, leading critics to argue that they should leave Korea (Fig. 3.3).[4]

The second type of critic focuses on the perceived inconveniences of living in the same area as Muslims. These critics express concerns about

[4] Most of the comments cited are from a news video about the struggle over the Daegu mosque, posted on the YouTube channel of KBS news, dated May 1, 2023. https://youtu.be/IuwSsRK45g4?si=W9eUYEPh3R_W8wUF. The comment regarding the male-centeredness of Islam is from a news video on the YouTube channel of BBS news, dated April 1, 2022. https://www.youtube.com/watch?v=kP-egalKAlU.

disruptions to their daily lives, such as food smells and noise, echoing complaints raised by residents of Daehyeon-dong. Some specifically grumble about the *adhan* (the call to prayer), which those living near a mosque should hear five times a day. Others highlight differences in culinary traditions, arguing that it is uncomfortable for pork-loving Koreans to live alongside Muslims who avoid pork. One commenter even stated, "If Islam culture is approved in Korea, we may not able to eat pork in our own country." The conclusion drawn from these complaints is often the same: Muslims should return to their own countries, reinforcing the argument that coexistence with Muslims is impossible.

Another expression of the perceived impossibility of coexistence with Muslims is the refusal to accept them as official members of Korean society. Some critics voice fears that Muslims will gradually take over Korea if they are allowed to integrate into society. They argue that Muslims will become the majority in areas where their demands are accommodated and will continue to expand their presence in Korea without showing respect for Korean culture.[5]

As demonstrated, many Koreans are reluctant to live in the same neighborhood as Muslims who openly express their religious identity and engage in public religious practices. They often perceive that Muslims, by asserting their religious identity, are refusing to respect Korean *ethos* and *pathos* and will ultimately become unmanageable. It is clear that Islamic practices conducted within their immediate vicinity evoke significant discomfort.

This uneasiness, however, is not confined to Muslims alone. A broader tendency exists in contemporary Korean society to disregard the religious orientations of others and favor the absence of religion. This sentiment is encapsulated in the widely accepted advice: "Never talk about religion." Not only in contemporary Korea, but also in many other cultures and historical periods, people have felt more comfortable living among others who do not openly reveal their religious identity. In such contexts, otherizing a group of people often involves dismissing their religion as

[5] I referred to comments posted on several online debate boards discussing newspaper articles about the conflict over the Daegu mosque. These include: https://theqoo.net/index.php?mid=square&document_srl=2676754928, posted on December 27, 2022; https://www.instiz.net/pt/7295189?frompc=1, posted on December 28, 2022; and https://gall.dcinside.com/board/view/?id=dcbest&no=201014, posted on January 20, 2024.

insignificant or even non-existent. For instance, when stronger nations encounter weaker ones that they wish to influence or rule, they often belittle the latter's religion. Western visitors in the late nineteenth century commonly claimed that Korea lacked religion altogether (Bang 2023, 120–147). While it may have been challenging for these visitors to clearly observe religious activities in the major cities where they primarily stayed, it is also evident that they were unwilling to recognize the practices and beliefs of premodern Koreans—whom they regarded as marginalized others—as legitimate religions.

Similarly, in the eighteenth and nineteenth centuries, European colonizers in India and Africa sought to diminish the power and scope of the religions practiced by the colonized. These efforts involved marginalizing the colonized people by "representing religious practices and ideas as otherworldly and apolitical" and "truncating their political meanings and social functions" (Peterson and Walhof 2002, 2). By redefining these religions as detached from political and social issues, colonial rulers confined them to the realm of the otherworldly, furthering their efforts to exert control.

Likewise, many contemporary Koreans feel uncomfortable around migrant others who openly express their religious identity. Consequently, the religious orientations of others in Korea are often dismissed or deemed insignificant. In some cases, the religion of migrant others—especially Islam, which is among the most unfamiliar to contemporary Koreans of the major world religions—is expected to remain concealed. For instance, Korean in-laws often expect Muslim migrant women who marry into Korean families to avoid revealing their religious identity. In Daehyeon-dong, Korean residents have similarly refused to coexist with Muslim neighbors who wish to build a mosque and engage in public religious practices. This rejection stands in stark contrast to the tolerance they previously exhibited toward these Muslims before they openly expressed their religious identity.

4 Excluding Muslim Others by Using Pork Impurity

Most Koreans who hold negative opinions of Islam—whether based on criticism of the religion itself or discomfort with living alongside Muslims—are unwilling to coexist with those who openly express their religious and cultural identity. This rejection is articulated in various ways, from opposing the construction of a mosque in the neighborhood to making hostile remarks, such as suggesting that Muslims should return to their own countries. Moreover, as discussed in Sect. 2.2, the strategy of employing the concept of pork impurity serves as another means of expressing the rejection of coexistence. This tactic highlights a deliberate effort to use cultural and religious differences as a basis for exclusion, reinforcing the perceived impossibility of living alongside Muslim others.

Jews and Muslims have long regarded pork as impure food, based on teachings from the Hebrew Bible and the Quran. The Hebrew Bible presents more comprehensive and complex dietary laws (Leviticus 11, 17: 10–14; Deuteronomy 14), while the Quran imposes simpler rules. However, the Quran explicitly forbids eating pork, along with carrion and blood, in several verses:

> He has only forbidden you to eat carrion, blood, swine, and what is slaughtered in the name of any other than Allah. (Quran 2:173)

> Forbidden to you are carrion, blood, and swine; what is slaughtered in the name of any other than Allah; what is killed by strangling, beating, a fall, or by being gored to death; what is partly eaten by a predator unless you slaughter it; and what is sacrificed on altars. You are also forbidden to draw lots for decisions. (Quran 5:3)[6]

Another verse in the Quran states that swine is forbidden because it is "impure" (Quran 6: 145). Because pork is repeatedly prohibited and explicitly labeled as impure in the Quran, Muslims firmly believe that they must abstain from eating pork, much like Jews adhere to the dietary laws outlined in the Hebrew Bible.

Jews and Muslims typically avoid breeding or slaughtering pigs and abstain from eating pork. Some also prohibit pork within their living spaces, refusing to share their living environment with pork eaters. In their daily lives, activities and individuals associated with eating pork are often regarded as impure. Purity ideas and practices serve as tools for affirming a group's identity by distinguishing its members from those who do not

[6] For the English translation of the verses in the Quran, I referred to Quran.com (https://quran.com).

share these beliefs and practices. In this sense, those who consume pork may be viewed as impure by Jews or Muslims who abstain from pork.

However, as previously mentioned, the residents of Daehyeon-dong have a different perspective. They do not argue, "You are impure to us," but instead claim, "We are impure to you, and so you should leave." This represents a distinctly different application of the purity concept compared to the conventional approach—if not an unprecedented one.

In many cultures and historical periods, foreigners were often regarded as a source of pollution, particularly during times of conflict. Defining others as impure was a common way to express hatred toward them, signaling that coexistence was impossible. The concept of impurity frequently carried implications of hostility and the necessity for removal. For ritually or morally impure activities, objects, animals, and people, the Hebrew Bible uses terms strongly associated with disdain, such as "abominable" (abomination) (KJV) or "detestable" (NIV, NASB), and prescribes their removal. In such contexts, concepts of purity and associated rituals have often been employed to exclude others.

In ancient Jewish culture, "the paired terms 'pure' and 'impure' were employed in various ways not only to describe but also inscribe socio-cultural boundaries between Jews and Gentile others" (Hayes 2002, 2; 223). During the postexilic period, Israelite religious leaders viewed gentiles as genealogically distinct, claiming that the holy seed of Israel had been defiled through intermarriage with gentiles. This perspective further reinforced socio-cultural boundaries (Hayes 2002, 26; see Ezra 9:1–10:15). Similarly, in Egypt, after the Assyrian invasion in 667 BCE, purification rituals were required for all temples attacked by the Assyrians (Blackman 1998, 16). In Greece, following the Persian withdrawal in 479 BCE, Greeks extinguished "the fire in the country, since it had been polluted by the barbarians, and fetched pure fire from the common hearth at Delphi" (Parker 2001 [1983], 23).

In Korean traditions, defining others as impure has similarly been used to declare the impossibility of coexistence. Those who cannot coexist with "us" should be banished from our realm, or separate realms must be established for each group. For example, in Jeju *bonpuri* (myths), when a god or goddess calls another deity "impure" or describes their coexistence as "full of impurity," they are proclaiming the impossibility of living together (Yoo and Watts 2021, 86–87).

In Korean history, by the time Christianity was introduced in the eighteenth century, traditional and newly imported religions had long recognized similarities and coexisted, though they often emphasized their own superiority. However, Christianity, as a new religion, was excluded and persecuted because it was deemed impossible to coexist with. In Joseon governmental records of the criminal investigation and trial of Catholics in 1801, Catholicism is described as dirty, and conversion to Catholicism is portrayed as pollution (*Chuangeupgukan* 2014, 25, 171, 414). The language in these records clearly conveyed impurity and expressed hatred.

The separation of others using purity concepts related to food is not unprecedented in history. In many ancient cultures, food has played a crucial role in purity notions and regulations, serving to distinguish "us" from "others" (Yoo and Watts 2021, 45–46). For instance, in the eighth century BCE, three of the four Egyptian princes who came to pay homage to the Nubian conqueror Piye were denied royal audience because they ate fish, which was considered an abomination (Lichtheim 1980, 66–83). Only the one prince who "was clean and did not eat fish" was permitted to enter the palace (Lichtheim 1980, 80).

In a slightly different context, Jews during the Second Temple period were prohibited from eating with gentiles. According to Paul, even Peter, one of the leaders of the early church, refrained from eating with gentiles for fear of judgment from fellow Jews (Galatians 2: 12). In the Book of Acts, Peter received a vision in which God commanded him to kill and eat "impure or unclean" animals before he was invited by Cornelius, a centurion of Roman army (Acts 10: 9–16). Both Peter and the Romans he visited understood "how unlawful it is for a man who is a Jew to associate with a foreigner or to visit him" (Acts 10: 28). For Jews, non-Jews and impure food were inseparably linked.

In the examples of Ancient Egypt, Greece, and Israel, nations occupying dominant realms often used the rhetoric of purity to compare their own purity with the impurity of gentile or barbarian others, excluding them from their realms. This was a common strategy for inscribing boundaries between "us" and "others." However, in some cases, a smaller and weaker group may emphasize its own impurity relative to a dominant group as a strategy to preserve its distinct identity. For instance, in the Book of Genesis, Joseph, the prime minister of Egypt, advised his family from Palestine to say to Pharaoh, "Your servants have been keepers of livestock from our youth even until now, both we and our fathers." This ensured that they would be allowed to live in the land of Goshen, separate from the Egyptians, "for every shepherd is loathsome to the Egyptians"

(Genesis 46: 34). By intentionally highlighting their perceived impurity, Joseph and his family intentionally ensured they would be avoided by the Egyptians and allowed to maintain their separateness. Importantly, Joseph's family did not share or accept the Egyptian concepts and practices of impurity but appropriated them as a strategy to distinguish themselves. This illustrates how a minor migrant group can emphasize its own impurity in the eyes of a dominant majority to preserve its identity.

Yet another example of appropriating impurity can be observed in the actions of the residents of Daehyeon-dong, Daegu, who strongly opposed the construction of a mosque in their neighborhood by cooking a whole pig or displaying a pig's head near the construction site. The residents sought to exclude Muslims by emphasizing their everyday practice of eating pork, framing it as an impure activity in conflict with Muslim beliefs. In this case, the majority group highlighted its own impurity to the minority in order to underscore the perceived impossibility of coexistence.

It is evident that the Korean majority group does not subscribe to the Muslim concepts and rules regarding pork impurity. Instead, members of the majority appropriated these notions as a strategic tool for separation. They utilized the impurity concepts belonging to others—concepts they themselves do not share—in a way reminiscent of the minor migrants in Genesis. However, the key difference lies in intent: whereas the migrants in Genesis used impurity to maintain their identity and achieve separation, the majority in Daehyeon-dong deployed these notions to insult and oppress the minority group.

Just as in the case of Daehyeon-dong, pork is a favored food in some cultures while being considered unclean and to be avoided in others. Due to this stark difference, pork has historically been weaponized by dominant groups to target weaker or minority groups, aiming to make them feel religiously defiled. For example, during the Seleucid and Roman periods, persecutors of Jews used pork to offend Jewish sensibilities. The Seleucid king, for instance, "had built an idol altar upon God's altar, he killed swine upon it, and so offered a sacrifice neither according to the law, nor the Jewish religious worship in that country" (Josephus 1999, 404). In modern societies, beyond Daehyeon-dong, similar uses of purity concepts related to pork can be observed as tools for insulting minority groups. For instance, on December 6, 2015, a pig's head was thrown at a mosque in Philadelphia, USA, from a pickup truck that drove by the building twice that night. The police identified this act as a hate crime, and the mayor at the time remarked, "Someone tried to desecrate the mosque"

(Izadi 2015). Similarly, pigs have been used to provoke social tensions between majority and minority groups. In 2012, when a pig's head was discovered outside a mosque in Kuala Lumpur, Malaysia, tensions escalated between the majority Muslims and the minority Christians. Although the perpetrator remained unknown, the act was widely believed to be an attempt to "flame tensions among Muslims and non-Muslims" (BBC 2012).

As we have observed, purity ideas and practices function to differentiate "us" from "others" in various ways. They play a significant role in establishing group identity and maintaining social order. However, they can also be weaponized to reject coexistence with others and justify hatred. These concepts can be used not only to assert our own purity to others but also to persuade others of our impurity by emphasizing what they consider impure as a means of insult and provocation.

Scholars have only recently begun to examine how purity ideas and practices operate in diverse ways such as these. In *Purity and Danger*, Mary Douglas, arguably the most influential scholar on this topic in the twentieth century, explored impurity and pollution "as analogies for expressing a general view of the social order" (Douglas 2002 [1966], 4). She emphasized the role of purity ideas and rituals in maintaining social order and creating "one single, symbolically consistent universe" (Douglas 2002 [1966], 85). However, in the preface to the 2002 edition of *Purity and Danger*, Douglas herself acknowledged that ideas of purity can function in more multi-layered and complex ways.

> The examples of taboo that I gave to illustrate the themes in *Purity and Danger* are mainly conservative in effect. They protect an abstract constitution from being subverted. If I had anticipated the political implications of taboo, I could have mentioned radical taboos … If I were to write the book again, I would know what to look out for to balance the original account. (Douglas 2002, xix–xx)

In the case of Daehyeon-dong, we observe a situation where protection and subversion operate in the reverse order of what Douglas illustrated in *Purity and Danger*. When the residents were unable to stop the construction of the mosque, which had been permitted by the local government, they used pork to demonstrate that the area where the mosque was being built was impure to Muslims. They relied on the purity ideas and taboos of the "otherized" Muslims—concepts originally designed to protect

Muslim society from subversion, as Douglas noted—but instead weaponized these concepts to subvert them.

The residents did not emphasize impurity or pollution to avoid within their own realm; rather, they appropriated the purity concepts of Muslims, which they do not share, to emphasize that "we" are impure to the "otherized" Muslims. This strategic inversion shifted the usual dynamic of impurity, from "you are impure to us" to "we are impure to you." By doing so, they aimed to preserve their own realm and disrupt the religious cosmos of the Muslim community, which they do not believe in, thereby asserting the impossibility of coexistence.

5 Conclusion: Strategic Inversions of Impurity

In the introduction, I suggested that we should focus on two key aspects observed in the conflicts between the Korean residents of Daehyeon-dong, Daegu, and the Muslims attempting to build a mosque there. First, the native residents feel significantly more uncomfortable when Muslims explicitly express their religious identity than when they do not. As discussed in Sect. 3, both criticisms on Islam itself and complaints about the discomfort of living alongside Muslims in the same area ultimately converge in a rejection of coexistence. Second, an important strategy for excluding Muslims involves leveraging religious ideas and rhetoric related to impurity. Considering that the notion of pork impurity was invoked only after the mosque's construction began, it is clear that the strategy emphasizing impurity is employed in Daehyeon-dong when Muslims' religious identity becomes more visibly pronounced.

Muslim international graduate students' attempt to establish a sacred space within their residential area has been disrupted by the Korean residents' declaration: "Because we are impure to you, you should avoid us," symbolized by the display of pig heads and ongoing pork parties. By appropriating Muslim concepts and practices of pork impurity—beliefs they neither share nor accept—the residents effectively provoked the Muslim community, causing significant distress after physical attempts to stop the mosque's construction were thwarted by court orders and police enforcement.

While the majority groups typically attack minority groups by emphasizing the impurity of the latter within their own realm, the residents in this case inverted this dynamic. They targeted Muslim others by demonstrating that their own way of life is impure to Muslims. As discussed in

Sect. 4, the majority's self-identification with impurity is uncommon, though not entirely unprecedented, and remains an underexplored topic in academic discourse. By arguing not that "you are impure to us" but rather that "we are impure to you," the residents adopted a strategic inversion to assert the impossibility of coexistence.

It is increasingly evident that contemporary Korea is a multicultural society. As Terry Eagleton aptly observes, "so-called multiculturalism" in modern and Westernized countries has emerged from "great tides of global migration" driven by economic liberalism (Eagleton 2009, 150). Most Muslims in Korea play vital roles in many fields, from academic research to physical labor. They have come to this country not only out of necessity for themselves but also to contribute to Korean society. They are an integral part of this multicultural fabric.

A healthy multicultural society does not solely emphasize diversity; it also upholds universal human values such as justice, humanity, fairness, compassion, and equality (Eagleton 2009, 151, 154). This is not to suggest that residents must endure all inconveniences or unconditionally accept new religious facilities in established residential neighborhoods. It is natural to express concerns about inconvenience; however, these concerns must not be articulated through rhetoric of exclusion or a rejection of coexistence, especially in multicultural contemporary Korea.

If we, as Koreans, reject coexistence with a group that is part of this society by suppressing or ignoring its religious identity, we are not only disregarding cultural diversity but also betraying these universal human values. The argument that these values are not respected in some Islamic countries does not justify denying Muslims in Korea the right to enjoy the values upheld in this country. We live in contemporary Korea, a society that aspires to justice, humanity, fairness, compassion, and equality. The ongoing debates surrounding the mosque will serve as a touchstone for determining whether Korea will evolve into a more dynamic, creative, and, above all, healthier multicultural society.

References

Bang, Wonil. 2023. *Gaesingyo Seongyosa-wa Hanguk Jonggyo-ui Mannam* (Protestant Missionaries' Encounters with Korean Religions). Seoul: Somyeong Chulpan. [In Korean]

BBC. 2012. Pig's Head Outside Malaysia Mosque Causes Outrage. An Article on *BBC New Asia* with No Byline. 2 February. https://www.bbc.com/news/world-asia-16854036.

Blackman, Aylward M. 1998. *Gods, Priests, and Men: Studies in the Religion of Pharaonic Egypt*. New York: Kegan Paul International.

Cha, Eunji. 2022. Daegu Islamsawon Galdeung Jisok: Dwaejimeori Dugaero Neureo (Ongoing Conflict Over the Mosque in Daegu: Increasing Number of Pig Heads to Two). *Hangukgyeokje*. 9 November. https://www.hankyung.com/society/article/2022110986377 [In Korean]

Choi, Jeong-yoon. 2023. Suspected Animal Fat Sprayed in front of Mosque Construction Site in Daegu. *The Korea Herald*, 9 March. https://news.koreaherald.com/view.php?ud=20230309000661&md=20230312003133_BL

Chuangeupgukan 73-75: Sunjo 1 (Records of Criminal Investigation and Trial in 1801). 2014 [1801]. Annotated and Translated from Classical Chinese to Korean by Sangsik Yi. Jeonju: Heureumchulpansa.

Douglas, Mary. 2002 [1966]. *Purity and Danger: An Analysis of Concepts of Pollution and Taboo*. 2nd ed. New York: Routledge Classics.

Eagleton, Terry. 2009. *Reason, Faith, and Revolution: Reflections on the God Debate*. New Haven: Yale University Press.

Han, Jiyeon. 2022a. Daegu Islamsawon Geonchuk Hyeonjang ap Dwaejimeori-ga (A Pig's Head Placed in Front of the Mosque Construction Site in Daegu). *Daegusinmun*. 31 October. https://www.idaegu.co.kr/news/articleView.html?idxno=399359 [In Korean]

Han, Seunggon. 2022b. Daegu Islamsawon ap Tongdwaeji Babikyu Eoddeoke Saenggakasimnigga (What Do You Think of a Whole Barbequed Pig in Front of the Mosque [Construction Site] in Daegu). *Asiagyeongje*. 18 December. https://view.asiae.co.kr/article/2022121613505704056 [In Korean]

Hayes, Christine E. 2002. *Gentle Impurity and Jewish Identities: Intermarriage and Conversion from the Bible to the Talmud*. Oxford: Oxford University Press.

Hwang, Subin. 2023. Gukgwansu 'Daegu Islamsawon ap Huinsaek Aekche Singmulseong Gireum-euro Chujeongdwae (National Forensic Service Identifies the White Liquid in Front of the Mosque in Daegu as Vegetable Oil). *Yeonhapnews*. 8 March. https://n.news.naver.com/mnews/article/001/0013820506. [In Korean]

Hwang, Subin. 2024. Daegu Islamsawon Geonchukju, Sigongeopche Sangdae Gongsabi Banhwan Sosong (Mosque Builders in Daegu File a Lawsuit Against Construction Company for Refund of Construction Costs). *Yeonhapnews*. 8 March. https://www.yna.co.kr/view/AKR20240307152600053?input=1195m [In Korean]

Izadi, Elahe. 2015. 'Ignorant Act': Severed Pig's Head Thrown at Philadelphia Mosque Door. The Washington Post. 9 December. https://www.washingtonpost.com/news/acts-of-faith/wp/2015/12/08/severed-pigs-head-thrownat-philadelphia-mosque-door/

Jeong, Hanbyeol. 2022. Daegu Islamsawon Geonchuk Jumin Bandae … Muslim Chabyeol Nollan (Residents Oppose Construction of Islam Mosque in Daegu:

Debate over Whether It Constitutes Discrimination). *Hanguknewstoday*. 28 August. http://www.koreanewstoday.co.kr/news/articleView.html?idxno=68161. [In Korean]

Josephus, Flavius. 1999 (c. 75, c. 94). *The New Complete Works of Josephus*. Translated by William Whiston. Grand Rapids, MI: Kregel Publications.

Kim, Ilu. 2021a. Daegu Jutaegga Islamsawon, Jumin Bandae-e Geollib Jungdan (Construction of Mosque in Daegu Residential Area Halted Due to Residents' Objection). *Hangyeore*. 19 February. https://www.hani.co.kr/arti/area/yeongnam/983682.html [In Korean]

Kim, Jeonghye. 2021b. Gyeongbukdae Jumindeul Islamsawon Geollib-e 'Jutaegga Jonggyosiseol-e Bandae (Residents Near Gyeongbuk University Oppose Construction of Mosque in Residential Area). *Hankookilbo*. 14 February. https://www.hankookilbo.com/News/Read/A2021021415540003215?did=NA. [In Korean]

Kim, Taehun. 2021c. Muslim yuhaksaeng-ui nunmul (Tears of Muslim Foreign Students). *Kyeonghyangsinmun*. 4 September. https://m.khan.co.kr/national/national-general/article/202109041302001?utm_source=urlCopy&utm_medium=social&utm_campaign=sharing [In Korean]

Kim, Jeongseok. 2023. Dwaejimeori Jeonsi-e Suyuk Pati-ggaji: Haebeop Chajji Motaneun Daeugu Islamsawon Galdeung (From Pig Head Displays to Boiled Pork Parties: No Resolution to the Conflict Over the Mosque in Daegu). *Joonangilbo*. 2 February. https://www.joongang.co.kr/article/25137763#home [In Korean]

Kim, Yoon-ho, and Sung-eun Yi. 2022. Civic Group Files Petition to UN as Daegu Locals Continue to Oppose Construction of Mosque. *Korea JoongaAng Daily*. 26 December. https://koreajoongangdaily.joins.com//2022/12/26/national/socialAffairs/korea-muslim-daegu//20221226184644574.html

Lichtheim, Miriam. 1980. *Ancient Egyptian Literature*. Vol. 3. Berkeley: University of California Press.

Nam, Jeongmi. 2019. Oneroom Geonmulinjul alanneunde 'mosque' yeonne: Islam Sawon Muryeo 200 yeogae (It Looks Like a Studio Apartment but It's a Mosque: There Are as Many as 200 Islamic Temples). 14 December. *Chosunilbo*. https://www.chosun.com/site/data/html_dir/2019/12/13/2019121302753.html?utm_source=naver&utm_medium=original&utm_campaign=news. [In Korean]

Oh, Jinyeong, and Siho Seong. 2021. Muslim-man Jumin-igo Daegu Simin-eun Gae-inga: Jibjibmada Geollin Mosque Bandae Hyeonsumak (Are Only Muslims Residents While Daegu Citizens Are Dogs? Anti-mosque Placards Hung on Every House). *MoneyToday*. 17 September. https://news.mt.co.kr/mtview.php?no=2021091613054645784. [In Korean].

Parker, Robert. 2001 [1983]. *Miasma: Pollution and Purification in Early Greek Religion*. Oxford: Oxford University Press.

Peterson, Derek R., and Darren R. Walhof, eds. 2002. *The Invention of Religion: Rethinking Belief in Politics and History.* New Brunswick, NJ: Rutgers University Press.

Ryu, Suhyeon. 2023. Chaggong Samnyeon Daegu Islamsawon Gongsa Jungji Myeongryeong … Ibeon-en Busilsigong Doma Wiro (Oder to Halt Construction of Mosque in Daegu Three Years after It Began: This Time Due to Poor Construction). *Hankookilbo.* 20 December. https://www.hankookilbo.com/News/Read/A2023121402250004648?did=NA [In Korean]

Sim, Sangseon. 2022. Daegu Islamsawon Gongsa Banghae Chilsipdae-nyeo Deung Dumyeong Gyeongchal Josa (Police Investigates Two Individuals for Disrupting Mosque Construction in Daegu, Including a Woman in Her Seventies). *Gyeongbukmaeil.* 26 September. http://www.kbmaeil.com/news/articleView.html?idxno=939594 [In Korean]

Song, Jung-hyun. 2022. Residents of Daegu Protest Mosque Construction with Pork Barbecue. *The Korea Herald.* 16 December. https://news.koreaherald.com/view.php?ud=20221216000112&md=20230204120139_BL

Yang, Gwanhui. 2022. [Simcheung] Islamsawon Geonchuk Magaseon An Doenda: Boebwon Pangyeolggaji Najjiman Yeojoenhan Yokseol-gwa Pongryeok ([In-Depth Report] Mosque Construction Should Not Be Hindered: Curses and Violence Persist Despite Court's Ruling). *Daegu MBC.* 17 August. https://dgmbc.com/article/TCJ3OxWIJrylb [In Korean]

Yi, Myeongik. 2021. Islam hyeomo hyeonsumak, muslim ai-neun ingneunda (Muslim Children Read Islamophobic Placards). *Sisain.* 7 September. https://www.sisain.co.kr/news/articleView.html?idxno=45478 [In Korean]

Yoo, Yohan. 2005. *A Theory of Purity from the Perspective of Comparative Religion.* Ph.D. Dissertation, Syracuse University.

Yoo, Yohan. 2013. Sin-deul Sai-ui Yeongyeok Gubyeol, Sin-gwa Ingan-ui Yeongyeok Gubyeol: Jeju Tochak Juonggyo-ui Jeonggyeol Gaenyeom-e Gwanhan Yeongu (Separation between the Realms of Gods and Separation of the Divine Realm from the Human Realm: A Study of Purity Idea in the Indigenous Religion of the Jeju Island). *Religion and Culture* 25 (2013): 27–65. [In Korean].

Yoo, Yohan, and James W. Watts. 2021. *Cosmologies of Pure Realms and the Rhetoric of Pollution.* Abingdon, UK: Routledge.

Yun, Sujin. 2024. Daegu islamsawon bandae jumindeul 'Oegugin muslimman bohohana' … gyeongchal·beobwon gyutan (Residents Opposing Islam Mosque in Daegu Denounce Police and Court, Asking 'Do You Only Project Foreign Muslims?'). *Maeilsinmun,* 24 July. https://www.imaeil.com/page/view/2024072512590670865 [in Korean]

CHAPTER 4

Anti-LGBTQIA+ Discourse and Hate Speech in Korean Protestant Organizations: Focusing on Sexuality Education Discourse in Schools

Soo-Ah Kim

1 Introduction

This chapter addresses the issue of banning sexuality education books th.at is currently taking place in South Korea. Conservative Protestant groups oppose gender equality education in schools and the banning of sexuality education books from school libraries. This is one of the many regressive phenomena that emerged in the 2010s as Korean Protestantism has made homosexuality its greatest enemy (Johannemann 2020). In October 2024, a unified worship service was conducted by Korean conservative Protestant organizations, namely, the United Christian Churches of Korea (Hangukgyohoe Chongyeonhap) and the Council

S.-A. Kim (✉)
Department of Communication/Interdisciplinary Program in Gender Studies, Seoul National University, Seoul, Republic of Korea
e-mail: sooah@snu.ac.kr

© The Author(s), under exclusive license to Springer Nature Singapore Pte Ltd. 2025

Y. Yoo, S. C. Lee (eds.), *Reimagining Korea*, Palgrave Series in Contemporary Korean Studies,
https://doi.org/10.1007/978-981-96-6990-5_4

of Presbyterian Churches in Korea (Daehanyesugyo jangnohoe chonghoe). A booklet containing 100 prayer requests distributed before the event (1027 Korean Churches 2 Million Unity Worship and Big Prayer Event Organizing Committee (10.27 Hangukgyohoe 2baengman yeonhabyebae Jojigwiwonhoe) 2024) reveals the thematic focus of the event. Sections 15–30 are dedicated to "Prayer Requests Regarding the Anti-Discrimination Act and Gender Revolution," while sections 31–45 address "Prayers on Gender Conflict, Non-Maritalism, and Low Birthrates." The first 15 prayers focus on the sacraments of the conference, underscoring the conference's primary mission, which it identifies as the most significant Protestant mission in Korea. This mission, as outlined in the prayer, is to resist discourse related to homosexuality and feminism. The title of the prayer, "Healthy Families and a Holy Nation," serves as a symbolic declaration, suggesting that the primary adversaries of Korean Protestantism today are the existence of LGBTQIA+ individuals and feminist ideas.

In other countries, the debate over LGBTQIA+ rights is often at odds with religion. Those who wish to maintain certain religious beliefs claim that discrimination against LGBTQIA+ people is a matter of religious freedom. Furthermore, they seek to actively intervene in the political process for LGBTQIA+ rights through means such as civil society organizations. The situation is not different in South Korea. Protestant conservative groups, such as Korean Churches' Anti-Homosexuality Coalition (Hangukgyohoe bandongseongae gyodanyeonhap) and Anti-Homosexuality Christian Solidarity (Bandongseongae gidoksiminyeondae), exert political influence in various forms and construct anti-LGBTQIA+ discourse. Moreover, Korea still does not have an explicit law prohibiting LGBTQIA+ discrimination. In the absence of a Comprehensive Anti-Discrimination law, few laws and institutions explicitly list sexual orientation as grounds for discrimination. For example, sexual orientation is not included among the grounds for discrimination and degradation regulated by the Korea Communications Standards Commission (hereinafter KCSC). In this situation, various human rights organizations formed the Anti-Discrimination Law Enactment Coalition (hereinafter ADLEC) in 2011 and have been working to amend the Comprehensive Anti-Discrimination Law; however, the law has not yet been enacted.

The slow progress in enacting this law is largely due to political pressure from Protestant conservatives at various levels. Korean Protestantism is generally conservative and right-wing, with an anti-communist ideology and anti-homosexuality sentiment. Within Korean Protestantism, the ecumenical Kijang Presbyterian, which is a minority, has a progressive perspective in terms of *Minjung* theology, and some churches, such as the Hyangrin Church, are active in supporting the rights of sexual minorities (Han 2020). The Protestant right-wing in South Korea, which began to increase its political visibility in the 1990s, became an important pillar of the national security discourse, centered on "the doctrine of anti-communism" (Heo 2021, 87). In other words, it was the left that was set up as the main antagonist in the identity formation and political behavior of Christian conservatives, and this antagonism was justified in the context of national security. However, around the 2010s, when the influence of the de facto security discourse began to decline, Protestant conservative groups developed a discourse of LGBTQIA+ organizations as a dangerous force to the state, which they condemned in the context of national security (Chen 2023, 519). Korean Protestantism has experienced a decline in the number of believers and public criticism, and its moral superiority is being questioned. North Korea, which was created as an internal enemy to overcome this, has become a reality that is not an existential threat due to South Korea's appeasement policy and the acceleration of North Korea's internal collapse. On the other hand, the legalization of same-sex marriage in the West was perceived as a defeat for Christianity, and homosexuals were re-created as external enemies as challengers to the core doctrines of Protestantism (Lee 2021, 1927–1927). In other words, the scope of those who should not be recognized to defend the state was broadened from the left wing to LGBTQIA+ people.[1]

Conservative Protestant groups share similar values with various conservative forces in society, such as defending the family, advocating for traditional gender roles, opposing abortion, resisting LGBTQIA+ rights, and other related issues, and they seek to form an identity as patriots who defend the country. *The Men's Solidarity* (*Namseong Yeondae*), which began to gain influence in the online space in the 2010s, has also presented the value of defending healthy families and the homeland. To defend the unity of family and nation, conservative civic organizations characterize homosexuality as undermining the stability of the family and consider any argument or discourse that seeks to recognize it as a social

[1] *Anti-Homosexuality Christian Solidarity* was formed in 2015, and *the National Alliance Against Gay Marriage* was formed in 2017. Currently, among the Protestant denominations in South Korea, some churches affiliated with the National Council of Churches in Korea (Hyangrin Church, for example) support the Anti-Discrimination law, but the voices of other churches are almost identical in their opposition to homophobia and the Anti-Discrimination law.

evil. They argue that opposition to comprehensive anti-discrimination laws should be viewed as a "right to express conscientious hatred," meaning that discriminatory or hate speech is constitutionally protected freedom of expression and that people have the freedom to abhor behavior that is contrary to public morality or good customs (Ji 2021, 197). Even in countries where same-sex marriage has been legalized, Protestants often claim that their freedom of expression is being restricted by LGBTQIA+ people, citing religious freedom (Gelber 2023). In South Korea, conservative Protestant groups have been active in pressuring the National Assembly, forming civil society organizations, and organizing events, all while arguing that religious freedom should take precedence over the obligation not to engage in hate speech.

The latest case of conservative efforts to shut down the discussion of homosexuality in the legal and institutional realm, including attempts to enact Anti-Discrimination laws and Civil Partnership Act legislation, is in the area of education. Two issues have become battlegrounds for Christianity versus feminism and the queer movement: the Students' Human Rights Ordinance and sexuality education. The Students' Human Rights Ordinance was opposed by conservative Protestant groups because it recognizes sexual orientation, and some citizens criticized the ordinance for supporting the infringement of teachers' rights. In 2024, the Chungnam Provincial Assembly and the Seoul Metropolitan Council decided to repeal the ordinance, leading to a confrontation in which the Seoul Metropolitan Office of Education took legal action in response.

Complaints about the content of the curriculum have also continued, and references to gender equality in the curriculum have also been the subject of debate. It has been argued that the curriculum violates the Constitution by conceptualizing gender equality as advocating homosexuality (Lee and Yu 2023). When the curriculum was revised in 2022, the Ministry of Education did not actively respond to the complaints of these conservative organizations, resulting in the removal of the phrase "sexual minorities and gender equality" during the revision process, making it difficult to discuss LGBTQIA+ issues in school sexuality education (Oh 2022). Conservative Protestant groups have complained about sexual education books in school libraries since 2023. In the name of civil society organizations, there is a growing trend of protesting against comprehensive sexuality education (hereinafter CSE) and especially against gender equality books, which leads to libraries and schools removing them or restricting access to them in such a way that they only exist as check-out symbols and cannot be checked out anymore.

The purpose of this chapter is to examine the discourse strategies used by conservative Protestant groups to remove sexuality education books from schools and to highlight the problems with the current complaint system that justify this setback. This article shows how conservative Protestant parent groups have used the discursive strategy of denigrating sexuality education books and critically analyzes the fact that this has allowed homophobic groups to use the system to their advantage. To do so, this article used "What's the Problem Represented to Be? (WPR)" methodology, a policy analysis methodology that is a critical discourse analysis (Bacchi 2009, 2012). The questions this methodology raises are as follows: what is the problem represented, what are its assumptions and presuppositions, in what contexts do these representations emerge, what is silenced in these representations, what are the discursive effects of these representations, and how and where are these representations produced and disseminated? Bacchi's work is primarily used for policy analysis, but it can also be used to challenge assumptions and reveal what they represent, as seen in the case of the analysis of media coverage (Silfver and Nordström 2023). This method of analysis is a critical discourse analysis methodology that can analyze "historical genealogies and social repercussions" (Pringle 2019, 2). This methodology is used to analyze the ways in which "problems are constituted, elicit particular forms of subjectivity, and influence how we see ourselves and others" (Bacchi 2012, 22). Using this analytical framework, I examine what a conservative Protestant parent organization's challenge to a sexuality education book represents as a problem, explore the historical context of school sexuality education in which this challenge occurred, and analyze the discursive effects of these challenges and the mechanisms through which they are produced within the institution of complaint. Finally, I demonstrate how this case is signified in society through media coverage.

2 2023–2024 Sexuality Education and Gender Equality Book Removal from Libraries

The complaints about sexuality education books and the subsequent book destruction are as follows. The book removal movement began in earnest in May 2023, when a letter was sent to all libraries under the Chungcheongnam-do Office of Education from organizations such as the *Kkum-kium Institute for Growth* (hereinafter, *Kkum-kium*). The letter provided a list of books on gender equality and sexuality education, claiming that they violated the 2022 revised curriculum and should be removed from the libraries. In May 2023, around the same time, *the Parents' Alliance for the Next Generation* produced and distributed a promotional material titled "Keeping My Child Alive in the Library," which emphasized the need to protect children from homosexuality.

Conservative Protestant organizations, including the *National Network for the Normalization of Education*, which has been advocating for the removal of "gender" and "LGBTQIA+" from textbooks in the 2022 revised curriculum, have actively intervened in public hearings on curriculum revision, ultimately resulting in the removal of the terms "gender" and "sexual minority" from the curriculum (Kim 2022). This allowed the argument that the subsequent inclusion of related topics in the curriculum was "illegal."

Civic groups from conservative Protestant backgrounds that identified themselves as parents' organizations formed around October 2022. They framed their discourse under the pretext of an academic process, for example, issuing a statement stating, "Immediately stop the recent attempt to revise the 2022 curriculum to brainwash the next generation with the ideology of the sexual revolution and legalize anti-discrimination laws and same-sex marriage," and co-hosting a seminar on "the Unconstitutionality and Dangers of the 2022 Revised Curriculum (draft) (November 2, 2022) with the *Alliance Against Evil Anti-Discrimination Laws for True Equality (Health Society)*. According to the seminar presentations and discussion papers released at the time, South Korea's curriculum introduced topics such as sexual self-determination, recognition of sexual minorities, contraception, and abortion to adolescents, asserting that this contributed to the phenomenon of "early sexualization."

The concepts of sexual self-determination and contraceptive education that these seminars highlight are those of CSE. This puts them at odds with feminist education organizations that advocate for CSE, and raises issues related to LGBTQIA+ discrimination. Lee (2024) analyzed that the 2022 curriculum includes all areas except core concepts 7 and 8 in UNESCO's guidelines for CSE, but since core concept 7 is sexuality and sexual behavior and core concept 8 is sexual and reproductive health, it can be said that the curriculum is, in fact, one that removes contraceptive education and sexual minorities-related discussions as claimed by Protestant groups.

The library initially did not respond to complaints that the sexuality education and gender equality books violated the 2022 curriculum but later stated that it was compelled to take action after receiving a continuous stream of complaints. While the library continued to receive complaints, other public institutions, such as the Office of Education and the City Council, also responded to the complaints and took the lead in the process of removing the books. The controversy began in July 2023, when a Seoul Metropolitan Council member demanded that all libraries in the city report the purchase of 17 books on sexuality education from private publishers. This sparked a backlash from librarians, as only sexuality education books were checked for purchase. In November, the Gyeonggi Provincial Office of Education sent a letter to elementary schools in the province, saying, "The provincial council and the National Assembly have pointed out that some sex education books have a negative impact, such as being sensationalist and promoting homosexuality, on teenagers." It has instructed libraries to "take action against books containing inappropriate and controversial content related to sexuality education." This forced libraries to restrict access to books requested by conservative civil society organizations (Mong 2024, 5). The conservative Protestant groups requested the Korea Publication Ethics Commission (hereinafter KPEC) to review a total of 68 books as harmful and inappropriate for young people, but the committee ruled that 67 books were not harmful, and one book designated as harmful was withdrawn a month later. However, regardless of the outcome of these deliberations, as of June 2024, 2528 books (517 titles) related to gender equality and sexuality education in Gyeonggi-do alone have been removed or restricted due to ongoing complaints (Mong 2024, 6).

3 Context of South Korea's Institutionalization of Sexuality Education and CSE

A common argument against sexuality education and gender equality books is that they are considered obscene because of their detailed descriptions of sex or their inclusion of LGBTQIA+ individuals. Traditionally, conservative discourse on sex has tended to make public references to sex as taboo. When sexuality education is framed in the context of science, conveying scientific knowledge about pregnancy and childbirth is the only information that is not pornographic (Lee 2021, 305–306).

This context of "healthy sexuality" has a discursive effect in the context of the current state of gender equality education or sexuality education in Korea. Sexuality education in South Korea is mandatory under the Sexual Violence Prevention and Victims Protection Act, which has the effect of placing sexuality education in the context of sexual violence (Kim 2015, 59). In addition, school sexuality education is typically conducted either by the school's health teacher directly or by inviting outside instructors. However, especially when inviting outside instructors, the system is more vulnerable to complaints. If one receives a complaint, the organization is unlikely to re-invite him or her, and if one is a freelance instructor, his or her reputation will suffer. Just because one is a school teacher doesn't mean he or she is safe. If one receives a complaint about the content of sexuality education, one will be penalized in various administrative processes. In such a situation, the content of gender equality and sexuality education can only be done cautiously in anticipation of complaint (Jeong et al. 2023).

In this social climate, teachers view sexuality education and gender equality education as dangerous. In fact, transgender issues are difficult to address because they do not occupy an important place in the curriculum, and their content is prone to protest. Therefore, gender equality education or sexuality education in schools is often limited to criticizing the sexism of existing gender norms and breaking down gender stereotypes. Um and Shin (2019) criticized the limitations of school gender equality education and sexuality education, which claim the values of feminism but have the effect of reproducing gender norms and narrowing gender equality awareness to the level of individual ethics. Nam and Lee (2022) also noted that school sexuality education must be combined with citizenship education to develop an understanding of sexual citizenship.

The problem is that in an environment where sexuality education itself is becoming difficult, even criticizing gender stereotypes is becoming a challenge. As a result, sexuality education in schools has become an increasingly shunned topic, making it difficult for students to acquire knowledge about sexuality and gender equality through public education. This has led to a situation where students are turning to books to develop their sexual awareness and sensitivity to gender equality. The growth of the sexuality education book market was intended to respond to the needs of women and LGBTQIA+ youth. These topics, discussed in the context of CSE, were tailored to the needs of female youth who, in the wake of #MeToo, were asking for a different understanding of gender equality.

These books have been called into question in the recent controversy over the removal of sexuality education books from libraries. The sexuality and gender equality education books that conservative parent groups are calling for review are typically those that promote sexual subjectivity, which is a woman's understanding of her body, sexual desire, and how to respect her queer peers.

Of course, these topics were not only addressed in sexuality education books. Around the 2010s, civic organizations were implementing CSE in a Korean context, and discussions on sexual agency and self-determination based on an understanding of the body, gender identity, and sexual orientation were conducted by civic organizations such as the *AHA Sexuality Culture Center*. However, in 2015, the National Standards for Sexuality Education, released by the Ministry of Education, revised the content of sexuality education and gender equality education, which had been reorganized into CSE. It deleted content about LGBTQIA+ people, portrayed women and men in essentialist ways, and stated that sexual violence can be prevented by not going to dangerous places. The content of the proposed curriculum was shaped by the conservative views of conservative civic and health organizations. It is said that the curriculum was composed through consultation with conservative Protestant organizations (Kim 2016, 12). However, as the backlash against the proposed curriculum grew and civil society voices were organized into public opinion, the sexuality education standard was effectively scrapped.

In a world where "proper sexuality education" is becoming increasingly unattainable and where students have multiple routes to gender equality knowledge outside of schooling, it is perhaps a natural progression for conservative Protestant organizations to revisit sexuality education books as a key issue. Following the 2020 complaints about the *Nadaum* program,[2] the 2023 complaint to remove sexuality education books from libraries is a repeated attempt by conservative Protestant parent organizations to enforce what they claim to be "proper sexuality education."

[2] The *Nadaum* Children's Books Program, organized by the Ministry of Gender Equality and Family, recommends gender equality education books for children and young adults. The program began in 2019 but was suspended in 2020 due to opposition from conservative political parties and Protestant groups. The distribution program stalled after Conservative Protestant groups claimed that the children's sexuality education books explicitly depicted sex, leading to early sexualization.

4 Defending "healthy sexuality" and the Family

Conservative parenting organizations' definition of healthy and proper sexuality is limited to procreation. Protestant organizations and researchers have explained that the most important aspect of the discussion of sexuality is moderation or taboo. These taboos are important because, first, sexuality is meant to be practiced solely within marriage; therefore, it is argued that sexual desire before marriage is not a desire that needs to be quenched, but rather one that needs to be subdued or sublimated, which can take the form of religious discipline (Go 2021, 420–425).

In the discourse on sexuality education based on the theory of youth protection, it is important to emphasize scientific knowledge of physical development and the risks of sexual practice. It is based on the idea that sexual practice should be postponed until one is ready for marriage and that sexual urges should be controlled. However, sexual urges themselves are not addressed in sexual education. Conservative parent groups argue that teaching contraception encourages adolescents to become sexually active and that discussing homosexuality promotes homosexuality (*Kkumkium* et al. 2023).

How can language that promotes homosexuality be considered transphobic? Ruin (2015, 321–322) suggested that heterosexual, non-transgender individuals who participate in a queer parade might be deeply affected by the experience, feeling troubled, shaken, and changed afterward. He pointed out that the claim made by conservative Christian groups that attending a queer festival makes you queer, might hold some truth in certain cases. Learning about homosexuality can be an opportunity to learn something about one's identity that one did not know before or to become more open-minded about homosexuality. The problem is not knowing about LGBTQIA+ people but not being able to respect them. In this sense, a conservative parent organization's refusal to mention homosexuality per se is both a declaration of ignorance and a statement of disrespect.

Denying queer existence often defends the traditional heteronormative family concept. The concept of reproductive temporality focuses on the life path of having children, raising children, and growing old. In contrast, queer lives aren't tied to reproduction and are seen as non-linear and unpredictable, which some might view as "promiscuous" temporality (Halberstam 2005, 6). Queer existence itself reveals heterosexual families' instability and contradictions. As long as only the heterosexual family is assumed to be the family in order to "preserve the family," queer people are bound to be represented as a crisis and problem for the family.

Sex is meant to defend the family and the nation, so the concept of obscenity is also redefined through this. Recently, TVING's[3] OTT platform-exclusive drama *Love in the Big City* (2024) has been the subject of protests and statements by various parents' organizations, as it has been called a "pornographic drama that glorifies homosexuality." Korean content regulation rules require nudity to be included in order to be judged as obscene, so this drama is not obscene in this regard. However, these groups claimed that the material was obscene because it depicted homosexuality that deviated from the dichotomous family structure of healthy sexuality and abnormal sexuality.

If the mere mention of homosexuality is obscene, then CSE will end up breaking down the family and undermining the state because it not only recognizes the existence of LGBTQIA+ people but also emphasizes respect for them. Feminism's discussion of sexual agency also jeopardizes the family. The conservative perspective does not treat sexuality as a right and therefore rejects a gender equality perspective that seeks to address the discrimination within the sexual sphere. In a feminist context, practicing sexual autonomy while respecting the rights of others is the central argument of sexuality education books, and this is the message of CSE (Berglas et al. 2014). The reason why sexuality is such a central issue in feminist education efforts is that it is not only a matter of reproduction but also a site of cultural and social power and discursive struggle. Among the rights to the body, the right to self-determination over reproduction is particularly important. Conservative groups argue that sexuality education threatens the family structure by asserting the right to terminate a pregnancy. In this context, sexuality education books are reproduced as a problem.

In order to reproduce sexuality education books as a serious social problem, conservative organizations utilize the discursive tool of "law and institutions." Until 2022, Korean official curriculum has included contraception, pregnancy interruption, and knowledge of sexuality in the health curriculum in line with CSE guidelines (Kim 2021, 8–9), and even if it does not mention LGBTQIA+ people in the realm of sexuality education, it acknowledges issues of discrimination against them in the context of

[3] TVING is a Korean OTT platform that offers entertainment programs, dramas, and movies aired by Korean broadcasters and also produces its own exclusive programs.

human rights (Moon 2012, 432). The 2022 curriculum revision has made it easier to challenge sexuality education books. Since this revision, past human rights and sexuality education content may now be considered "outlawed." This has provided a discursive resource for the removal of sexuality education books in a more formalized manner, allowing for the institutionalization of the process.

5 Abusive and Discriminatory Tactics of Parent Groups Who Abuse the System

5.1 *Complaints and the Veneer of Democracy*

Although organizations that complain about sexuality education have explicitly identified themselves as anti-homosexual organizations in the past (i.e., *Anti-Homosexuality Christian Solidarity*, hereinafter AHCS), they are now using a strategy that positions them as "parents/citizens" concerned about their children's education (i.e., *the Parents' Alliance for the Next Generation*). As parents are concerned about their children's education, they position themselves as key stakeholders and seek a greater voice alongside teachers and students, the three main actors in education. They use the complaint system as a mechanism to do so.

In Korean society, the complaint system functions as an administrative mechanism that prioritizes responding to and enforcing public demands, with institutions seeing it as their duty to address potential complaints. Although malicious complaints have recently been discussed (Lee et al. 2024), responding to complaints is recognized as an important responsibility, especially for those in public office. Civil service administration, defined as "an administration that the people want and an administration that responds to the needs of the people" (Ra et al. 2006, 243), emphasizes the democratic net function of performing a watchdog function over the public sector (Sun and Kim 2023). However, in recent years, fatigue and weakened work capacity of public officials due to repeated complaints have been identified as problems. In the private sector, responding to complaints is increasingly emphasized as a service, which often requires excessive emotional labor from service workers who respond to consumers as a priority, even if there are problems with the content of the complaint, and leads to extreme emotional exhaustion of employees (Wang et al. 2021, 278).

The definition of malicious complaints is not always clear in the legal system. Yun (2022, 116–117) categorizes malicious complaints as those that do not follow normal procedures or demand the fulfillment of illegal content, including pointlessly repeated complaints and violent complaints. According to him, malicious complaints are categorized into procedural problems, i.e., when the complainant is at fault for the process, such as repetition or violence, and when the content is illegal (Yun 2022, 117).

In this context, it is difficult to classify complaints about the removal of sexual orientation education books from libraries as malicious. Of course, we can talk about the problem of repetitive complaints, but until now, what qualifies as a repetitive complaint is often premised on the existence of a small number of problematic individuals, such as when a small number of complainants file a large number of complaints in a short period (three people filed 5142 complaints) (Yun 2022, 119). However, in some cases, such as the complaint regarding the removal of sexuality education books, a significant number of complaints were filed by a large group of individuals. This is often due to the mobilization of church communities in response to LGBTQIA+ controversies.

Regarding content-based unlawfulness, there is currently no Comprehensive Anti-Discrimination Act in place. As a result, there is no legal basis to deem claims such as "a sexuality education book is problematic because it mentions homosexuality" as unlawful. The current complaint structure does not allow public debate on complaint content. In the case of the sexuality education removal complaint, administrative action was taken first without public discussion. This is also due to the precarious position of librarians who experience library complaints. Librarians are professionals who must be deployed according to Article 12 of the School Library Promotion Act, but as of 2022, only 48% of schools deployed library professionals in elementary and secondary curricula, and only 12% of these professionals were full-time (Byun 2023). In an unstable environment where public librarians are hired and fired on a temporary basis, the numerous complaints filed make it challenging to introduce sexuality education books. According to a survey by the *Korean Teachers and Education Workers' Union* (2024, 4), 53.2% of school librarians have "directly experienced or witnessed pressure or orders to remove or restrict access to" gender equality and sexuality education books, and 48.2% have "directly experienced or witnessed pressure or orders to discourage the purchase of" the books. For librarians who face a high volume of library complaints, dismissing those voiced on behalf of parents can be challenging. Librarians can't do it alone, especially when schools choose to remove sexuality education books as a quick fix.

The use of the complaint system is only a pretext for democracy. As long as the complaint is from a "citizen," and as long as there is no framework in Korean society to discuss discrimination against certain ways of expressing opinions, attacks on LGBTQIA+ individuals through complaints remain permissible. This can be referred to as the "Veneer of Democracy" (Fetman 2017, 265). This concept was coined within the education process to name the ways in which certain policies or arguments are presented in an acceptable form so that political and bureaucratic systems can be maintained, but whose effects ultimately contribute to individuals affected by the policies experiencing marginalization and discrimination. The process of multiple complaints presented under the "veneer of democracy," framed as democratic action and the defense of "good mores," influence curriculum and legal changes (e.g., the Student Human Rights Ordinance), ultimately shaping laws and institutions that justify discrimination against LGBTQIA+ people. This is evident in cases such as the Queer Culture Festival, where the space where the festival was held was no longer available due to an increase in complaints against the festival, or the Seoul Metropolitan Government's decision to deny the Queer Culture Festival's application to rent a seminar room in 2024, citing concerns about the event's high number of complaints as the reason (Yang 2024). Moreover, the complaint process often involves the approval of Protestant politicians. In Seoul, Chungnam, and Gyeonggi provinces, the involvement of politicians in the debate over sexuality education and student rights ordinances was an important trigger, and the politicians took the position that they represented the people based on complaints (Jeong 2024, 33). Many processes related to LGBTQIA+ issues in Korean society effectively violate LGBTQIA+ rights through democratic processes under the guise of complaints that claim to be the "subject" of such discourse and policies.

5.2 *Refusing to Accept the Decision and Continuing to Protest*

As the removal of sexuality education books occurs in the realm of education, the strategies for using the complaint system have varied. For example, a conservative Protestant organization applied to the KPEC to designate a book as harmful to youth. If a book is designated as harmful to youth in Korea, it will naturally disappear from K-12 libraries because it is not distributed to youth. This is a more effective way to exclude sexuality education books than directly requesting libraries to remove them. In response to the complaint, KPEC reviewed 68 books in February 2024 and April 2024.

In its April 2024 review, the KPEC designated only one of its 68 books as harmful. The book was a translation of a Swedish sexuality education book, *First, Let's Do Sexuality Education*, and the reason for the decision was that the book contained detailed descriptions of erections and queer terms. In response, the Korean Publishing and Culture Association highlighted that the book has been used as an official sexuality education textbook in several countries and argued that it is not harmful. On the other hand, conservative Protestant parents' organizations protested that the KPEC had made a ruling that was problematic for LGBTQIA+ people and for the formation of healthy sexual discourse. In June 2024, after a reconsideration, it was finally decided that it was not a harmful book (Choi W. 2024a).

Parent organizations have since questioned the composition of KPEC. In addition to parent organizations that advocate for parents and education, such as *Citizens for Good Education*, *Parents for Right Education*, *Parents for the Protection of Our Children*, *Institute for Right Generation*, *Kkum-kium*, *Gyeonggi-do Parents' Organization Alliance*, *the AHCS* et al. (All of them are civic groups with Protestant backgrounds) issued a statement titled "Reprimand the members of the KPEC who abandoned their duties and immediately withdraw the selection of biased and uneducated reviewers!" on behalf of 67 civic organizations. The statement criticized the Korean National Mothers' Association as a radical feminist group and alleged that the chairman of KPEC was responsible for protecting obscene books. It further asserted that the truth remained hidden because the committee's composition, which advocates for feminism and LGBTQIA+ rights, influenced the outcome (AHCS 2024).

On the one hand, it leans on the discourse of fairness as a principle of democracy to call out "committee bias" without having filed for a review and accepted the outcome. However, the composition of the committee to ensure fairness as a democratic principle leads to many pre-determined deliberations. For example, the Korea Communications Standards Commission comprises recommendations from the ruling party, opposition party, and presidential, resulting in a 6:3 split on most political issues (Choi Y. 2024b, 3). When the above statement challenges the inclusion of a Buddhist who recommended a suitable person for deliberation but was not accepted, it can be said that it seeks to fully utilize the effect of ostensible democracy, in which the composition of the members who can hold a majority in the actual composition of the committee determines the deliberation.

The results of the discussion thus far can be summarized as follows. Conservative Protestant groups have raised the issue of sex education books, arguing that they are harmful to young people. The reason they are harmful to young people is that they contain explicit sexual content or advocate homosexuality. Accordingly, they argued that homosexuality is harmful to the nation because it makes it difficult to protect healthy families. The premise of this claim is that no gender equality courses will be offered in the 2022 curriculum. However, the removal of gender equality content from the curriculum resulted from the Ministry of Education accepting the complaints of conservative Christian parent groups. Having experienced the success of complaints, parent organizations are now using the complaint system to try to erase homosexuality from public discourse, including complaints about libraries, book reviews, and broadcasters. In the current discourse, there is almost no way to respond to these complaints, and these complaints are packaged as a practice of democracy, i.e., the veneer of democracy.

6 The Shrinking Public Sphere with Non-reporting

Kim (2021) argued that the fact that sexuality education is not a core course in the current curriculum is largely related to the social controversy raised by conservative civil society organizations. The importance attached to sexuality education has been strengthened in South Korea since "the feminist reboot" (Son 2017), as it is seen as an important discursive site for bridging feminist theory and practice. As such, controversies related to sexuality education books are more likely to be covered by liberal media, while conservative media respond with non-reporting.

Although there are not many media reports on the disposal of gender equality education books in libraries, there is a significant difference in the orientation of the media. Among national daily newspapers, *Dong-A Ilbo*, which is categorized as a conservative media, reported one story, while *JoongAng Ilbo* reported one between January 2023 and August 2024, while *Chosun Ilbo* did not report any stories. In contrast, *Kyunghyang*

Shinmun, *Hankyoreh*, and *Hankook Ilbo* reported 30, 19, and 9 stories, respectively. The *Dong-A Ilbo*'s coverage does not focus on the removal of sexuality education books as a standalone topic, but rather in relation to the Ministry of Gender Equality and Family's reduction of sexuality education programs, while the *JoongAng Ilbo* reports on the Seoul Metropolitan Council's efforts to combat pornography, effectively conflating sexuality education books with pornography without questioning the claim. On the other hand, the high number of reports in the *Kyunghyang Shinmun* reflects the significant presence of women and LGBTQIA+ individuals among its columnists, who have repeatedly raised the issue.

The phenomenon of underreporting or non-reporting is actually a difficult topic to frame in journalistic terms. There are many factors that influence the selection process of what is covered, and the fact that certain facts are not reported by the media may not in itself reflect power structures. However, in journalism ethics, the justification for not covering socially problematic events is often debated. Given the highly partisan nature of Korean media, where journalists' portrayals of events often reflect their political views, disparities in the number of reports based on political stances can create the impression that the issue is being ignored entirely (Kim and Jeong 2011). By not reporting on the controversy surrounding gender equality education, it can be said that it is normalized as not being a problem.

This clear difference is also related to the attitudes of conservative and liberal media toward LGBTQIA+ coverage in the past. Kang et al. (2019) found that conservative and liberal media significantly differ in the number of articles on LGBTQIA+-related issues. This difference is exacerbated by conservative media's preference for non-reporting. The study also found that conservative media only provide informational articles on LGBTQIA+-related events, while liberal media produce more problem-solving feature articles aimed at human rights and institutional improvement. This difference is also evident in the case of gender equality and the removal of sexuality education books, where conservative media did not report on the issue, and when they did, they only presented the position of conservative parent groups: they presented sexuality education books as pornographic and then reported that the Seoul Metropolitan Council would crack down on them, implying that the removal of sexuality education books was a normalization process.

On the other hand, progressive media outlets have been actively opposing gender equality education book banning. They have been working to create an agenda with the case, reflecting the voices of Anti-Discrimination civic organizations and feminist educators. For example, *Kyunghyang Shinmun* and *Hankyoreh* have been covering the case since July 2023. Rather than simply reporting on both sides of the issue, their reporting style emphasizes that complaints against gender equality education amount to censorship, violate libraries' intellectual freedom rights, and are driven by conservative Christian organizations disguising themselves as concerned parents. In the case of sexuality education, several feature articles have attempted to frame the controversy surrounding the removal of books in the context of LGBTQIA+ discrimination.

The phenomenon of non-reporting has the effect of reducing the number of actors in discourse and social discussion. In the discourse surrounding the removal of sexuality education books, two main mechanisms have been proposed by which the public arena becomes less open to discussion. First, by not discussing the issue, i.e., by not socially reproducing the issue itself, a discursive process is established in which the parties to the issue are reduced to two axes: Protestants and LGBTQIA+ people. This reduction is presented as a battle between different parallel epistemologies. Conservative Protestant groups are seen as expressing their freedom to hate for the sake of sexual ethics(of their own), and therefore a legitimate part of the debate, while LGBTQIA+ rights and feminist groups are seen as making identity politics or ideological claims. The juxtaposition of the issue of sexuality education books, as reproduced by Protestant organizations, and the human rights claims made by LGBTQIA+ individuals and those involved in sexuality education is seen as a conflict between different groups—an irreconcilable one. In Korean society, which lacks the discursive resources to interpret each claim and position as a matter of discrimination or human rights, the public debate is perceived as exhausting. This leads to the gradual marginalization of the LGBTQIA+ agenda. By delaying judgments on discrimination and replacing them with process/procedure-based judgments on legitimacy, this approach effectively shrinks the space for meaningful discussion. Complaint processes, protests, and public statements are all recognized as processual freedoms in a democratic process, and public authority responses to multiple complaints are legitimate administrative enforcement. As long as the "process" is allowed legally, the "content" is not a problem, despite its obvious hatred.

The case of a conservative Protestant group that included hate speech related to LGBTQIA+ people was pointed out as a problem even by the public in the case of the 2022 curriculum public hearing (Kang and Son

2023), and it can be explained that when the process of democracy is undermined, it is perceived as a problem, regardless of the judgment of the argument. Conversely, processes can always be used to violate the rights of sexual minorities. In 2024, when the Seoul Metropolitan Government refused to rent the Civic Center to the ADLEC, using the logic that the name of the event application was different from the actual name of the event, it restricted the exercise of LGBTQIA+ rights in the form of criticizing the process without mentioning the content. The decision to suspend the discrimination judgment is based on a formal process, and the majority complaint can be seen as a mechanism justified by the principle of democratic majority rule. The legitimization of process over substance is a consequence of the fact that our society has not sufficiently discussed the equality, discrimination, rights, and freedoms that democracy envisions while maintaining the appearance of democracy.

The current situation is that it has become difficult to guarantee the legitimacy of the process when it is difficult to discuss the content itself. The difficulty in ensuring the legitimacy of the "process" in the counter-discourse is due to the 2022 curriculum revision. While complaints about sexuality education books, i.e., claims that the books are not in line with the curriculum, have gained ground, schools and librarians have lost the discursive resources of the national curriculum to respond to them. The discursive resources that librarians and citizen organizations are using in response to the removal of sexuality education books are international standards. The content aligned with UNESCO's CSE guidelines, the fact that a particular book has been recognized by more than 15 countries abroad when it was designated as a historical book, and the UN Human Rights Committee's recommendation that sexuality education should include LGBTQIA+ contents are used as evidence to argue for its retention (Tari 2024). Another international standard is intellectual freedom in libraries. Criticism of censorship in libraries, which began in 1939 with the American Library Association's (ALA) Declaration of Library Rights, led to the Korean Library Association's Intellectual Freedom Guidelines for Libraries in 2024, which were prompted by the controversy over the banning of sexuality education books (Kim 2024). However, with the discursive resource of international standards providing little space for socially persuasive debate, the removal of books based on complaints is ongoing.

The WPR methodology focuses on what is seen as a problem. Conservative media do not report the removal of sex education books as a social problem, making it difficult to recognize the issue as discrimination against sexual minorities. Or they frame the issue as one where sex education books are obscene and need to be removed. In response, conservative media outlets endorse the conservative Protestant group's approach to solving the problem.

On the other hand, progressive media outlets have framed the issue as one of sexuality education books being removed because of complaints from conservative Protestant groups. Progressive media outlets have raised the issue that other considerations, such as the educational impact of the books and their contribution to the human rights of sexual minorities in our society, are not being taken into account. As a result, they call for institutional improvements to prevent public institutions from having to respond to malicious complainants such as conservative Protestant groups. However, the current issue-raising and agenda-setting by the progressive media is having no effect. Progressive media and civic organizations claimed that discrimination against sexual minorities must end through reports, forums, and protest documents, but since the libraries have complied with conservative Protestant groups' complaints, they appeared to be attempting to downplay the issue by not making any more decisions about sexuality education books. According to this perspective, these libraries' attitude can be viewed as just adopting the veneer of democracy. They are unwilling to go through any more consideration or discussion because the removal of the books was decided by a number of complaints.

7 Conclusion

The discourse of conservative Christian groups that criticize sexuality education as problematic is not the result of democratic discussion and debate but rather a repetition of circular reasoning and an act of hatred. Parent groups that have successfully obtained complaints are now using the complaint system to target libraries, book reviews, and broadcasts to remove sexual minorities from public discourse.

With the ban on references to sexuality in sexuality education, there have been reports of a growing market for private sexuality education. The "Sexuality education for son" is a sexuality education program for boys in upper elementary schools that can be quite expensive. This sexuality education, called small group sexuality education, is conducted in groups of two to six people (Song 2024). As discussions on sexuality education are disappearing from the public curriculum, it is also difficult for the voices of young people to be heard among the three main actors in the education process.

The Protestant groups' use of youth as the main discourse target reflects a sense of crisis that they are being overtaken by a generation of degenerate youth (Yoon 2024, 5). If it is not possible to edify the youth generation that has already been exposed to BL, homosexual glorification dramas, etc., and shows favorable perceptions of LGBTQIA+ people, it constitutes a strategy to build a "breakwater" to prevent the contamination of future generations. The metaphors used by anti-gay groups and organizations reflect a combination of patriarchal and Protestant doctrines of preventing contamination and preserving healthy families.

In South Korea, the debate on LGBTQIA+ issues tends to converge on the need for Comprehensive Anti-Discrimination laws. This is not just because the core activities of Protestant conservative organizations are related to opposing Anti-Discrimination legislation, but because even when opposition groups frame their discourse, they also raise the need for Anti-Discrimination laws. This is driven by the need to create a basis for content judgments, given that the strategies that naturalize homophobia have been effective in leveraging formal democratic structures that do not judge "content." Since we do not yet have a legal framework for discussing hate/discrimination in our society, we are left with the possibility of treating arguments that reproduce someone's existence as the problem itself and arguments that demand recognition of their existence, on an equal footing, and only examining the legitimacy of the opinions and the process by which they are presented. This is why the discussion of LGBTQIA+ discrimination has been stalled for decades, and why the tool for claiming rights is converging on anti-discrimination legislation. Of course, it is also clear that Comprehensive Anti-Discrimination laws are not the solution, but a starting point for a discussion. In a study of US and South Korean preservice teachers' perceptions of LGBTQIA+ people, some participants in the US remained silent when asked how they would respond to homophobia (i.e., did not express explicit homophobia), whereas participants in South Korea explicitly expressed homophobia (Shin 2019), demonstrating that social institutionalization of discrimination and hatred is only a starting point. Above all, it is imperative to discuss the substance of democracy. Approving the veneer of democracy while deferring to the discussion of discrimination enables the reproduction of social discrimination.

References

Anti-Homosexuality Christian Solidarity. 2024, August 27. Statement by Minister of Culture, Sports, and Tourism Yoo In-chon to Reprimand the KPEC Reviewers Who Abandoned Their Duties and Immediately Withdraw the Selection of Biased and Uneducated Reviewers.

Bacchi, C. 2009. *Analysing Policy*. London: Pearson Higher Education AU.

Bacchi, C. 2012. Introducing the 'What's the Problem Represented to be?' Approach. In *Engaging with Carol Bacchi: Strategic Interventions and Exchanges*, ed. A. Bletsas and C. Beasley, 21–24. Adelaide: The University of Adelaide Press.

Berglas, N., N. Constantine, and E. Ozer. 2014. A Rights-Based Approach to Sexuality Education: Conceptualization, Clarification and Challenges. *Perspectives on Sexual and Reproductive Health* 46 (2): 63–72.

Byun, J. 2023, March 10. Why Doesn't My School Library Have a Librarian? Sisain. https://www.sisain.co.kr/news/articleView.html?idxno=49724 (in Korean).

Chen, P. 2023. Queer Feminist Assemblages Against Far-Right Anti- 'Anti-Discrimination Law' in South Korea. *Journal of Lesbian Studies* 28 (3): 518–524. https://doi.org/10.1080/10894160.2023.2240551.

Choi, W. 2024a, June 26. Swedish Sexuality Education Book, 'Target of Conservative Civic Groups,' Has Been Freed from the 'harmful book' Label. Hankyoreh. https://www.hani.co.kr/arti/culture/culture_general/1146501.html (in Korean).

Choi, Y. 2024b. Failures of the Korean Broadcasting Standards System and Constitutional Reform Proposals. *Journal of Media Law, Ethics and Policy* 23 (2): 1–47. (in Korean).

Fetman, L. J. 2017. Wiping Away the "Veneer of Democracy" to Expose the School-Level Effects of Arizona's Language Policy. *Leadership and Policy in Schools* 17 (2): 264–295. https://doi.org/10.1080/15700763.2016.1278241.

Gelber, K. 2023. Free Speech, Religious Freedom and Vilification in Australia. *Australian Journal of Political Science* 59 (1): 78–92. https://doi.org/10.1080/10361146.2023.2283008.

Go, S. 2021. Christian Sex Education for Young People Against Sexuality in the Current Society. *Korea Presbyterian Journal of Theology* 53 (5): 407–431. https://doi.org/10.15757/kpjt.2021.53.5.015 (in Korean).

Halberstam, J. 2005. *In a Queer Time & Place: Transgender Bodies, Subcultural Lives*. New York: New York University Press.

Han, J. H. J. 2020. The Queer Thresholds of Heresy. *Journal of Korean Studies* 25 (2): 407–428.

Heo, A. 2021. The Christian Right and Refugee Rights: The Border Politics of Anti-communism and Anti-discrimination in South Korea. *Religion and Society* 12 (1): 86–101. https://doi.org/10.3167/arrs.2021.120107.

Jeong, E. (2024). Issues for Expanding Intellectual Freedom and Freedom of Expression: Focusing on the Censorship of Books on Gender Equality and Sexuality Education. South Korean Coalition for Anti-discrimination Legislation et al., Proceedings of the Discussion on the Response to the Restriction and Removal of Gender Equality and Sexuality Education Books. Seoul: South Korean Coalition for Anti-discrimination Legislation, pp. 33–43. 2024.8.28. (in Korean).

Jeong, E., J. Kim, and J. Koh. 2023. School Health Teachers' Gender-Sensitive Sexual Health Education Experiences in South Korea. *Sex Education* 25 (1): 81–94. https://doi.org/10.1080/14681811.2023.2272127.

Ji, Y. 2021. Discussion on Enactment of Comprehensive Anti-discrimination Law and Fake News. *The Journal of Church and Law* 7 (2): 168–224. https://doi.org/10.23116/church.2021.7.2.168. (in Korean).

Johannemann, H. 2020. Creating the Internal Enemy: Opportunities and Threats in Pro and AntiLGBT Activism Within South Korean Protestantism. *International Journal of Religion* 1 (1): 23–43.

Kang, Y., and J. Son. 2023. Analysis of Anti-homosexual Discourses on Education Policies Related to LGBT: Focusing on Hate. *Korean Journal of Sociology of Education* 33 (3): 27–73. (in Korean).

Kang, S., Y. Lee, and J. Cho. 2019. Automated Text Analysis on Media Partisanship and Sexual Minority Discourse in South Korean Society. *Information Society and Media* 20 (2): 145–174. (in Korean).

Kim, H. 2015. Searching for the Feminist 'Sexual Violence Prevention Education'. *Journal of Korean Women's Studies* 31 (2): 55–89. (in Korean).

Kim, D. 2016. Discussions with the Issue of National Level of School Sexual Education Standards. *The Korean Journal of Health Education* 2 (1): 1–23. (in Korean).

Kim, D. 2021. A Study on the Controversy Over the Selectivity of Children's Sex Education Books. *The Korean Journal of Health Education* 7 (1): 1–13. (in Korean).

Kim, B. 2022, November 22. "Abusive language to students…" Busan Curriculum Public Hearing Disrupted by Conservative Groups' Invasion. Ohmynews. https://www.ohmynews.com/NWS_Web/View/at_pg.aspx?CNTN_CD=A0002882626 (in Korean).

Kim, S. 2024. Aspects of Intellectual Freedom Restrictions in Libraries and Countermeasures. *Journal of Korean Library and Information Science Society* 55 (2): 189–217. https://doi.org/10.16981/kliss.55.2.202406.189. (in Korean).

Kim, S., and Y. Jeong. 2011. Non-reporting, Media Ethics and Ideological Conflicts in South Korea: Focus on Media Coverage Relating to Surveillance of Civilians by the National Intelligence Service and the Defense Security

Command. *Korean Journal of Communication & Information* 53:5–28. (in Korean).

Kkum-kium Institute for Growth et al. 2023, October 10. Complaint Received by the KPEC. (in Korean).

Korean Teachers and Education Workers Union. 2024. Report on the obstruction and disposal of books about gender equality and sexuality education in schools. Seoul: Korean Teachers and Education Workers Union (in Korean).

Lee, J. 2021. Searching for a Curriculum to Reconceptualize Sexuality for Youth Sex Education – Nth Room Era, New Talk of 'body' and 'sex' from a Feminist Theological Point of View. *Journal of Christian Education in Korea* 67:301–337. https://doi.org/10.17968/jcek.2021..67.009. (in Korean).

Lee, S. 2024. Exploring Gender Equality Education Teaching Methods in Practical Arts Education According to the 2022 Revised Practical Arts Curriculum. *Journal of Korean Practical Arts Education* 37 (3): 53–74. https://doi.org/10.24062/kpae.2024.37.3.53 (in Korean).

Lee, H., and C. Yu. 2023. The Danger of the Notion of Gender Equality in the 2022 Revised Curriculum: A Symbolic Policy Perspective. *Christian Education and Information Technology* 76:167–199. (in Korean).

Lee, W., T. Kim, and J. Koo. 2024. Malicious Complainant Behavior and Impact of Malicious Complaint Response System on Public Servants' Job Perceptions: Focusing on Seoul Government Employees. *The Journal of Convergence Society and Public Policy* 18 (2): 1–48. (in Korean).

Mong. 2024. Progress on the Removal of Gender Equality and Sexuality Education Books. South Korean Coalition for Anti-discrimination Legislation et al., Proceedings of the Discussion on the Response to the Restriction and Removal of Gender Equality and Sexuality Education Books. Seoul: South Korean Coalition for Anti-discrimination Legislation, pp. 2–8. 2024.8.28. (in Korean).

Moon, R. 2012. Globalisation and Citizenship Education: Diversity in South Korean Civics Textbooks. *Comparative Education* 49 (4): 424–439. https://doi.org/10.1080/03050068.2012.727677.

Nam, M., and H. Lee. 2022. An Alternative Approach to Sexuality Education in School: Focusing on Sexual Citizenship. *Journal of Korean Women's Studies* 38 (1): 37–71. https://doi.org/10.30719/JKWS.2022.03.38.1.37 (in Korean).

Oh, S. 2022, December 31. Korean Teachers Worry New Policies Will Undo Inclusive Education on Sex, Gender. Hankyoreh International. https://english.hani.co.kr/arti/english_edition/e_national/1073604.html.

Pringle, W. 2019. Problematizations in Assisted Dying Discourse: Testing the "what's the problem represented to be?" (WPR) Method for Critical Health Communication Research. *Frontiers in Communication* 4:1–11. https://doi.org/10.3389/fcomm.2019.00058.

Ra, H., M. Kim, and C. Song. 2006. Possibilities and Limitations of Reform Measures for Civil Application. *Korean Journal of Policy* 16 (3): 241–263. (in Korean).

Ruin. 2015. Rethinking Pride and the Rhetoric of Christian Fundamentalist Groups Toward LGBTQ+ People. *Silcheonmunhak* 119:317–325. (in Korean).
Shin, K. 2019. A comparative Analysis of Korean and American Prospective Teachers' Perceptions of LGBTQ Issues. *Education as Change* 23 (1): 1–22.
Silfver, E., and M. Nordström. 2023. Shifting Discourses on Giftedness in Swedish Newspaper Media – What's the Problem Represented to Be? *Scandinavian Journal of Educational Research* 68 (7): 1555–1567. https://doi.org/10.1080/00313831.2023.2259930.
Son, H. 2017. *Feminism Roboot.* Seoul: Woodpencilbooks.
Song, Y. 2024. Sex education tips for parents... Don't ask, "Are you watching porn?" out of concern about harmful content. Kyunghyang Weekly. 17. Aug. https://www.khan.co.kr/article/202408170905001 (in Korean).
Sun, W., and S. Kim. 2023. The Effect of Emotional Labor on Public Service Motivation (PSM): A Focus on the Moderating Effects of Malicious Complaints and Social Support. *Public Affairs.* 61 (4): 89–116. https://doi.org/10.24145/KJPA.61.4.4 (in Korean).
Tari. 2024. The Meaning of Gender Equality Education and Comprehensive Sexuality Education. South Korean Coalition for Anti-discrimination Legislation et al., Proceedings of the Discussion on the Response to the Restriction and Removal of Gender Equality and Sexuality Education Books. Seoul: South Korean Coalition for Anti-discrimination Legislation. pp. 13–31. 2024.8.28. (in Korean).
Um, H., and G. Shin. 2019. The Reality and Effects of Gender Equality Education in Schools: Reproduction of Gender Norms and 'Dangerous' Gender Equality Education. *Issues in Feminism* 19 (1): 51–90. https://doi.org/10.21287/iif.2019.4.19.1.51. (in Korean).
Wang, Y., T. Wang, and C. Gui. 2021. A Meta-analysis of Customer Uncivil Behaviors in Hospitality Research. *Journal of Hospitality Marketing & Management* 31 (3): 265–289. https://doi.org/10.1080/19368623.2021.1973934.
Yang, D. 2024, October 28. National Human Rights Commission of Korea "Refusal to rent out a lecture hall for a queer festival is an infringement of the right to equality" YTN. https://www.ytn.co.kr/_ln/0103_202410281815558491 (in Korean).
Yoon, D. 2024. Uncanny Model: How Korean Christian Media Portrays Sexual Minorities. Paper presented at The Korean Society for Journalism & Communication Studies; 19 Oct, Gongju, South Korea (in Korean).
Yun, Y. 2022. Status and Solutions of Malicious Complaints. *Kyung Hee Law Journal* 57 (2): 113–146. https://doi.org/10.15539/KHLJ.57.2.4. (in Korean).

CHAPTER 5

A Rational Evaluation of *Idan* and *Saibi*: A Market Approach to Religious "Troublemakers" in Korea

Song Chong Lee

1 Introduction

The recent cringe-inducing trend of prefixing "K-" to various terms to highlight or promote their significance has become increasingly prevalent in Korean academia and journalism, extending even into unexpected domains such as religion. Several news media outlets, including the national newspaper *Joongang Ilbo*, have recently published articles featuring a potential new buzzword: K-*Idan* (heresy or cult). *Idan* and *saibi* are derogatory terms used by Koreans to refer to New Religious Movements (NRMs), a concept that remains value-neutral in academic circles, particularly in the sociology of religion and religious studies, used to objectively classify and scrutinize religious deviations. The Standard Korean Dictionary by the National Institute of the Korean Language defines *Idan* as "a

S. C. Lee (✉)
Department of Religious Studies, Seoul National University,
Seoul, Korea (Republic of)
e-mail: songchonglee@snu.ac.kr

© The Author(s), under exclusive license to Springer Nature Singapore Pte Ltd. 2025

Y. Yoo, S. C. Lee (eds.), *Reimagining Korea*, Palgrave Series in Contemporary Korean Studies,
https://doi.org/10.1007/978-981-96-6990-5_5

doctrine that deviates from one's own beliefs," while *Saibi* refers to "something that appears similar on the surface but is fundamentally different in essence."[1] Unlike NRMs, whenever *idan* or *saibi* is mentioned in the media, they evoke discomfort and disparagement in the public's mind, prompting a quick defensive reaction. Korean *idans* or K-*idans* are perceived as powerful and dangerous, allegedly extending their influence even into North Korea,[2] marked by severe deception, criminality, and violence, exemplified by numerous recent incidents such as JMS (Jesus Morning Star) leader Myung Seok Jung's recent 22-year jail sentence for criminal charges and accusations against politician-turned-cult leader Gyeong Yeong Heo for political funding violations, fraud, and embezzlement.[3] While it is important for the public to be aware of the wrongful acts of NRMs, it still remains problematic to make sweeping, indiscriminate judgments against them as a unified entity as a public enemy. Every social group harbors outliers. We usually refrain from condemning the entire group, particularly in the context of mainstream religions. Why, then, should NRMs not be afforded the same consideration? Challenging unqualified generalizations is an urgent task, not primarily to defend minority religious groups due to their social vulnerability, but because the level of religious bigotry, particularly against NRMs, is a barometer reflecting the extent of religious freedom in a given society. I think that the general perception of NRMs in Korea, as drawn in this chapter from the viewpoints of four key stakeholders—mainstream religions, media outlets, the government, and academics—clearly reveals a mismatch with the democratic and civic culture that many Koreans themselves believe they embody. It is marked by suspicion, hostility, hatred, vitriol, contempt, and intolerance.

[1] National Institute of the Korean Language, Standard Korean Dictionary, accessed February 22, 2025, https://stdict.korean.go.kr/main/main.do.

[2] "*Seongpokaeng Jeongmyeongseoge Mureupkkureun Gyeongchal 20-Kidan, Bugedo Chimtu* (Eluding Justice: Myung Seok Jung's Escape from Police Pursuit, K-*Idan*, Infiltrating North Korea)," *JoongAng Daily*, accessed July 2, 2024, https://www.joongang.co.kr/article/25251894#home.

[3] "*Seongbeomjoe JMS Jeongmyeongseok Jingyeok 23nyeon Beobwon Ap sindo 200myeong Mollyeowatda* (JMS Leader Myung Seok Jung Sentenced to 23 Years for Sexual Offenses; 200 Followers Gather at Courthouse)," JoongAng Daily, accessed July 2, 2024, https://www.joongang.co.kr/article/25216953#home. Officially, JMS (Jesus Morning Star) refers to the Christian Gospel Mission (CGM). The public, however, believes that JMS refers to its founder, Myung Seok Jung.

In the following discussion, I will examine and characterize the Korean public's perception of NRMs through a general overview of the public discourse formulated by various outlets such as public statements from mainstream religions, the tone of newspaper reports and essays, the primary concerns of the government's policy efforts regarding religious intelligence and tolerance, and academic discussions. Note that the NRMs discussed in this chapter are primarily groups associated with Protestant Christianity. The attention to these groups is not due to their unique status as a religious group but because they are the primary targets of hostile public perception, which has been largely driven by Protestant churches—one of the most influential social communities in Korea. Most of the characterizations that I have drawn from the materials of this public discourse are unfortunately associated with acts of *otherizing*, such as derationalization, cultic-labeling, dehumanization, pathologization, and social criminalization. To ensure the validity of my overall evaluation or characterization of the public perception, I will first present a theoretical explanation of *otherizing* in NRM studies and then identify and discuss the pertinent markers revealed through the public discourse.

2 Theoretical Overview of *Otherizing* NRMs

The act of *otherizing* has been identified and discussed in various intellectual discourses to highlight unjust social interactions and relationships. From the inception of society, the emergence of dominant power—whether stemming from disparities in talent, resources, or physical power—has fostered privilege. This privilege allows certain groups to establish and enforce norms and public perceptions, thereby categorizing other groups and assigning them specific positions in society. Within this established hierarchy of power and status, some groups are controlled, marginalized, and subjected to *otherization*. Labeled as less competent and valuable, and perceived as threats to the established order, these marginalized groups are often excluded from equal access to both rights and resources within society. Suspicion and persecution engendered by marginalization and *otherization* have deep historical roots. The followers of ancient Egypt's Pharaoh Akhenaten in the fourteenth century BCE and Prophet Muhammad in the seventh century CE both faced persecution for their monotheistic deviation from traditional polytheism. Some groups, such as the Zoroastrians of ancient Persia during the Achaemenid rulers, the cult of Marduk in Mesopotamia under King Nabonidus, and

Confucianism during the Qin Dynasty, were oppressed by the dominant power not only to enforce a new religious understanding but also to legitimize its political regime. Similarly, the Roman Senate suppressed the Bacchanalia, early Christians endured under Nero and Diocletian, Jews and Cathars suffered during the Crusades, Pagans faced persecution in Charlemagne's Saxon Wars, Druids during the Roman conquest of Gaul, Buddhists under Pusyamitra Sunga, and various witch hunts in Western history are all examples of dramatic instances of *otherizing*.

I think that the idea of *otherizing* has been addressed in both macro and micro intellectual dimensions. The macro dimension concerns abstraction from broader human perception and organizational interactions involving power dynamics among large social groupings such as gender, race, nation, and invisible social forces. The exploration of this concept has been enriched by numerous thinkers, including Edward Said, Michel Foucault, Frantz Fanon, Judith Butler, and other notable intellectuals. The micro dimension, meanwhile, refers to the smaller milieu in which stereotyping and stigmatization target specific social groups, such as NRMs in this chapter, causing various practical problems, including discrimination, harassment, defamation, and infringement of religious freedom. For instance, NRMs in many societies have been unfairly and sometimes excessively accused of causing mental distress, psychological damage, wanton misconduct, outrageous acts, wrongful death, kidnapping, and brainwashing young adults, as well as involving minor sexual servitude. *Otherizing*, particularly against NRMs, in my personal evaluation, has been articulated with three major characteristics: derationalization/pathologization, cultic labeling, and social criminalization.

First of all, in most societies, both religiously homogenous and pluralistic, New Religious Movements and their practices are frequently derationalized and even pathologized. This perception primarily targets those who join NRMs, portraying them as emotionally fragile and mentally unstable individuals who are easily swayed, indoctrinated, and controlled. According to Wilson and Cresswell, they are seen as vulnerable targets for manipulative cult tactics, characterized by cognitive delusion, psychological dependence, and impaired judgment.[4] This negative perception extends to the legitimacy of the NRM organizations themselves. For example, their worship rituals are often portrayed as bizarre or exotic and subject to

[4]Bryan Wilson and Jamie Cresswell, *New Religious Movements, Challenge and Response* (New York: Routledge, 1999), 124.

ridicule. Their evangelism is criticized for employing aggressive, intrusive, and coercive recruitment methods, viewed as manipulative. The NRMs' worldviews are perceived as conflicting with public reason and societal norms. Their leaders are similarly depicted as delusional, egotistical, paranoid, erratic, and potentially dangerous.[5] Consequently, the conversion experienced by NRM members is often portrayed as a harmful outcome of brainwashing, necessitating deprogramming to restore normalcy and sanity. Consequently, the public, including the mainstream religions, media, and government, does not have a serious intention to engage in rational conversation with NRMs to solve problems. When some problems related to NRMs occur, they rather seek opinions and guidance from the media and anti-cultists. According to Wilson, "Even people directly affected by NRMs relied for their information overwhelmingly on the mass media."[6]

Second, NRMs are publicly *otherized* because they are viewed as cults rather than religions. The term "cult" has acquired overwhelmingly negative connotations in the general public and media, leading scholars such as Eileen Barker, James T. Richardson, James Beckford, and various sociologists to advocate for its abandonment in academic discourse.[7] According to Melton, a cult is a religious group that deviates significantly from the norms of the dominant religious culture.[8] This deviation implies more than a simple institutional or denominational differentiation; it suggests illegitimacy, unorthodoxy, and faultiness. Just as with dramatic examples such as Heaven's Gate, Branch Davidians, The Order of the Solar Temple,

[5] See Catherine Wessinger, *How the Millennium Comes Violently: From Jonestown to Heaven's Gate* (New York: Seven Bridges Press, 2000).

[6] Wilson and Cresswell, *New Religious Movements, Challenge and Response*, 124.

[7] See Eileen Barker, "Religious movements: Cult and anticult since Jonestown," *Annual Review of Sociology*12 (1986): 329–46 and *New religious movements: A practical introduction* (London: Her Majesty's Stationery Office, 1989); James T. Richardson, "Definitions of Cult: From Sociological-Technical to Popular-Negative," *Review of Religious Research* 34, no. 4 (1993): 348-56 and "A Critique of 'Brainwashing' Claims about New Religious Movements," in Cults in Context: Readings in the Study of New Religious Movements, ed. Lorne Dawson (New York: Routledge, 2018), 220–225; Paul J. Olson, "The Public Perception of 'Cults' and 'New Religious Movements,'" *Journal for the Scientific Study of Religion* 45, no. (2006); James Beckford, *Cult controversies: The societal response to the new religious movements* (London and New York: Tavistock., 1985) and "The mass media and new religious movements," in *New Religious Movements, Challenge and Response*, ed. Bryan Wilson and Jamie Cresswell (New York: Routledge, 1999), 103–19.

[8] J. Gordon Melton, "Anti-cultists in the United States: An Historical Perspective," in Wilson and Cresswell, *New Religious Movements, Challenge and Response*, 217.

Aum Shinrikyo, and the People's Temple—often referred to as Big Five NRMs—many NRMs are not just seen as new organizations with new faith and vision, but rather as groups with corrupted versions of established religious traditions. Instead of being recognized for their unique belief systems, NRMs are often perceived as misinterpreting scriptures from their related established traditions, having false prophets and messiahs, distorting fundamental tenets with unacceptable syncretism, and proposing baseless new revelations with esoteric knowledge and practices. The term cult also implies various abnormalities, including a high degree of centralized authority and hierarchical control, isolation from outside influences, and excessive demands on time and resources. If an NRM is unrelated to any mainstream religion, it is simply considered made-up, often dismissed as a mere business scheme. In particular, the Anti-Cult Movement (ACM), allied with mainstream religions, often describes cult-related issues as "economic," "political," or "psychological" when publicly criticizing them, to avoid grouping NRMs with traditional religions.[9] In other words, once labeled as a cult, NRM, according to Lewis, "loses their chance at a fair hearing."[10]

Third, the existence of NRM itself is often criminalized. It means that not only are the NRMs viewed as dangerous in public perception, but they also experience various unfair treatments in legal and institutional dimensions. For instance, despite the opposition from the Senate, France has recently passed an anti-cult law, which embraced the idea of "a new crime of psychological subjection." The new law mandates up to three years' imprisonment and a €375,000 fine for placing individuals in psychological or physical subjection through serious or repeated pressure or techniques likely to impair their judgment, resulting in severe deterioration of their health or actions prejudicial to them.[11] Due to the subjective nature of interpreting and applying this law, which largely hinges on the dominant or mainstream view, the religion most likely to be impacted would

[9] Wilson and Cresswell, *New Religious Movements, Challenge and Response*, 105. For the definition of ACM, see Paul J. Olson, "The Public Perception of 'Cults' and 'New Religious Movements'," *Journal for the Scientific Study of Religion* 45, no. 1 (2006): 97–106, https://doi.og/10.1111/j.1468-5906.2006.00008.x, 98.

[10] James R. Lewis, *Legitimating new religions* (New Brunswick, NJ: Rutgers University Press, 2003), 206.

[11] "France Passes New Anti-Cult Law Against Senate's Opposition." EU Reporter, April 13, 2024, accessed June 28, 2024, https://www.eureporter.co/world/france-world/2024/04/13/france-passes-new-anti-cult-law-against-senates-opposition/.

undoubtedly be NRMs. This new law originated from reports by *saisines* from MIVILUDES, the governmental anti-cult agency, whose legal foundation and primary function are specifically tasked with monitoring sectarian movements that might harm public well-being, making it highly controversial. It is extremely challenging for the government to establish criteria for cults and sectarian groups and to avoid the legal challenges associated with its agencies' monitoring of classified groups, as shown in other similar examples such as Germany's Federal Office for the Protection of the Constitution (BfV) and Belgium's Centre for Information and Advice on Harmful Sectarian Organizations (CIAOSN).[12] NRMs face numerous other disadvantages due to public criminalization, including discriminatory legislation targeting them, lack of due process, and sensationalized media influence, making it difficult for them to compete with other mainstream religions on a level playing field.

3 Public Perception of NRMs as *Idan* and *Saibi*

3.1 Mainstream Religions' Perceptions

As previously outlined in the theoretical overview, three negative approaches—derationalization, cult-labeling, and criminalization—are prevalent in the public perception of NRMs in Korea. Notably, cult-labeling and criminalization are predominant attitudes among mainstream religions. Their general perception can be immediately sensed from the 2022 Research Report on the Definition of and Guidance against *Idan* and *Saibi* by the Presbyterian Church of Korea (PCK). This report outlines the church's definitions of *idan* and *saibi* (NRMs), drawing on the dictionary meanings mentioned earlier, and critically examines the theological doctrines and religious practices of major NRMs by comparing them with orthodox beliefs. The problem is that the church's criteria for defining "deviance" and "essential difference" are based on its own perspective and judgment.[13] At the outset of this report, the PCK asserts that

[12] United States Department of State, "2009 Human Rights Report: China (includes Tibet, Hong Kong, and Macau)," Refworld, 25 February 2010, accessed June 28, 2024, https://www.refworld.org/reference/annualreport/usdos/2009/en/70690.

[13] Presbyterian Church of Korea, "*Idansaibi Chonghoe Juyo Gyeol-ui: Idan Saibi Jeong-ui wa Pyojun Jichim-e Gwanhan Yeongu Bogoseo* (Resolution of the General Assembly: 2022 Research Report on and Guidance Against *Idan* and *Saibi*) (Resolution on *Idan* and *Saibi* hereafter)," accessed June 29, 2024, http://new.pck.or.kr/bbs/board.php?bo_table=SM02_18_06&wr_id=73.

NRMs, identified in Korea as *idan* and *saibi*, pose threats to true Christianity. While recognizing the relatively mild biblical connotation of the term *idan*, signifying deviation from truth and righteousness, the PCK underscores that this distinction is crucial as it represents a fundamental departure from both the origin (*cheoeum*) and the end (*kkeut*). According to the PCK's definition, *idan* refers to those who "deny or significantly distort, forming a faction, any of the fundamental doctrines of Christian faith, which constitute the basis of doctrine and agreement among parties, namely, God, Jesus Christ, the Holy Spirit, the Trinity, the Bible, the Church, and faith concerning salvation."[14] The definition of *saibi* is not significantly different from that of *idan*, but more general. *Saibi* are individuals who "create factions and either deny or distort key doctrines essential to the foundational teachings of the Christian faith." These two words are interchangeable, though the latter evokes more negative connotations. It is noteworthy, though, that the PCK's official policy on *idan* and *saibi* is deeply doctrinal, showing no concern for Non-Christian New Religious Movements. Article 4 of the Guidelines for Penalty provides definitions of *idan* and *saibi* based specifically on Biblical interpretation.[15] The ten criteria for identifying *idan* and *saibi* all reflect orthodox theological perspectives. It is common to hear churches use *idan* to refer to Christian-related NRMs. However, the term *saibi*, similar to the English concept of cult, is widely applied to non-Christian NRMs. Thus, the fact that the PCK put these terms together in its penalty guidelines is confusing.

An important point to note here is that despite the official stance of the Korean church and its relatively mild tone toward NRMs in the policy manual, individual church communities often exhibit strong hostility toward them. For example, the document related to *idan* posted on the website of Handong University's Chaplain's Office, the most prestigious Christian university in Korea, clearly demonstrates a cult-labeling and criminalization attitude toward NRMs, reflecting the generally hostile tone of Korean mainstream religions' perception highlighted at the beginning of this section. This document originated from The General Assembly of the Presbyterian Church in Korea's (GAPCK) countermovement effort to NRMs, shared by numerous church communities. In this document,

[14] Resolution on *Idan* and *Saibi*.

[15] General Assembly of the Presbyterian Church of Korea, "*Chonghoe Ollain Gyujeongjip* (Online Policy Manual of the General Assembly)," Presbyterian Church of Korea, accessed June 29, 2024. https://new.pck.or.kr/ruleContents/rule_view.php?cate1=1&cate2=15.

idan is used as a cult-labeling for both individuals and organizations that present doctrinal teachings different from those found in the Bible and traditional church confessions of faith. S*aibi*, which aligns more closely with our understanding of NRMs, refers to "the unethical individuals or groups that disrupt society for their own benefit, rather than serving a positive religious function inherent to their beliefs."[16] This perspective is in harmony with the old consensus reached by leading Korean church denominations, the Christian Council of Korea (*Hangichong*) and the Council of Presbyterian Churches in Korea (CPCK), during their 2004 summit on countering the rise of NRMs. NRMs, exemplified here by *idan* and *saibi*, not only "espouse beliefs deviating from orthodox Christianity" but also "pose threats with their anti-social and immoral practices."[17] Here we observe the negative impact of the ambiguous connection between *idan* and *saibi* in public discourse. These concepts are often conflated, leading to the belief that one necessarily entails the other, thereby implying that deviations from orthodox Christian beliefs and practices are viewed as threats to society as a whole, which is, in principle, problematic in societies with a separation of church and state.

Seoul Church, one of the mega-churches in Gangnam, which is the wealthiest region in Korea, also shares the above-mentioned GAPCK document on its website, highlighting Christian NRMs' perceived threats to families and society. It accuses Shincheonji Church of Jesus, the Temple of the Tabernacle of the Testimony (SCJ), of causing family breakdowns and juvenile runaways, citing its controversial covert and invasive mission strategies. Beloved Church, formerly known as Keunmideum Church, is criticized for its detrimental influence on youth and for engaging in an unclearly defined, morally questionable ministry. Despite the document's relatively detailed explanation of their unorthodox beliefs in biblical interpretation, soteriology, spirit possession, prophecy, and glossolalia, it does not clearly articulate how their religious beliefs translate into social threats.

[16] Handong University Chaplain Office. "*Idan* Related Information (*Idan Gwallyeon Jeongbo*)," accessed June 29, 2024, https://church.handong.edu/main/sub.html?pageCode=68.

[17] "*Hangukgyohoe Idansaibi Gyujeonggijungwa Yongeo Tongil* (Korean Church's Unifying Terms and Definitions of *Idan* and *Saibi*)," The Christian Council of Korea, accessed June 29, 2024, http://www.cck.or.kr/chnet2/board/view.php?id=118&code=intro05b&cate=&start=&category=&word=&viewType=&category_id=. Also see "Unifying terms of *idan* and *saibi*," iGoodNews, accessed June 29, 2024, https://www.igoodnews.net/news/articleView.html?idxno=6763.

International Youth Fellowship (IYF), called *Guwonpa*, and the World Mission Society Church of God, formerly known as Ansanghong Jeunginhoe, receive the same cult labeling and criminalization. They are both depicted as snaring people with deceptive programs such as domestic community services and humanitarian activities in foreign lands. Jehovah's Witnesses (JW) and the Family Federation of World Peace and Unification (FFWPU), formerly known as the Unification Church, face even harsher criticism. For Jehovah's Witnesses, behaviors deemed anti-social and anti-state—including refusing blood transfusions, evading military service obligations, refusing compulsory residence registration, renouncing occupations, rejecting compulsory education, opposing the national system as Satanic, and refusing to salute the national flag and anthem—are highlighted, while the FFWPU is particularly criticized for instances of financial fraud and exploitation. Similarly, Daesoonjinrighoe, mentioned in Handong University's version but omitted in Seoul Church's, is criticized for pressuring members to relinquish their property and education to devote themselves more fully to the church.

In other words, NRMs are often collectively and indiscriminately perceived as wolves disguised as sheep—angels on the outside but Satan inside—possessing massive moral flaws and constantly preying on the vulnerability of people within communities. They are considered cults not because they exhibit some special characteristics of religion but due to their deviation from the beliefs and practices of mainstream religions, particularly the Protestant Christianity in this chapter. This unfavorable or hostile religious view of NRMs often leads to portraying them as a potential danger to society, without substantiation.

3.2 Public Media's Perceptions

The way public media in Korea handles NRMs is unfortunately perfectly aligned with the tone of mainstream religions, characterized by denigrating and defamatory language, fear-mongering rhetoric, unfounded accusations, alarmist perspectives, and a dismissive and condescending attitude. It is often hard to detect even a minimum effort to meet general standards of good journalism, including accuracy and precision, objectivity and fairness, and investigative rigor. Of particular concern is the propensity for derationalization, as observed in mainstream religious discourse. While fully acknowledging the necessity of addressing and criticizing criminal activities within some NRMs, I find the media's excessively sensationalist tendencies troubling, particularly in their ambiguous and indiscriminate use of terms such as *idan* and *saibi*. This concern is not solely due to the inappropriate alarmism directed toward problematic individuals and organizations but due to the questionable foundations upon which their labeling and criticisms are predicated. Their criteria are, most of the time, based on the beliefs and practices of established mainstream religions and the views from the concerned families, defectors, and Anti-cult Movements (ACMs). The main reason for this is that, as discussed earlier, Korean journalists *otherize*, more specifically, derationalize NRMs. Since the public media collectively believe that the practices of mainstream religions represent the orthodoxy of what it means to be a religion, they cast suspicion on anything that differs from them. If a religion deviates from these norms, it is immediately labeled as a cult. Once labeled as such, it is not subjected to rational conversation. Instead, it needs to be publicly shunned; its members should be immediately rescued and sent to rehabilitation, or, in the worst expression, deprogrammed.

Thus, most journalists tend to avoid consulting individuals who could provide a broader perspective, such as academics and members of NRMs themselves, whose viewpoints often diverge from their sensationalist objectives. They do not bother to consider why their subject religion or social group should be classified as *saibi*. Nor do they feel the need to define *idan* and *saibi*, setting aside their occasional failure to provide substantial evidence for their sometimes magnified accusations and hyperbolic assertions. A recent article by a religion correspondent from *Hankyoreh*, a national newspaper in Korea, introducing a *saibi* detection technique to its readers is a case in point.[18] Reflecting on *In the Name of God*, a Netflix documentary that recently gained widespread popularity, Hyun Jo, a journalist known for his expertise in religion, offers a typical write-up, reminding readers of the heinous crimes committed by major problematic NRMs in Korea's modern history, including JMS, Agadongsan, and Youngsaenggyo. Highlighting the various crimes of these NRMs, which range from economic fraud, sexual crimes, and exploitation to homicide and family estrangement, Jo warns of the devastating harms of *idan* and *saibi*. His criticism extends to other problematic groups such as the Unification Church, SCJ, and Mamin Jungang Church. His discourse

[18] Hyeon Jo, "*Naneun Sinida Oechimyeon…Saibi Jonggyo Gambyeolbeop Allyeodeurimnida* (Claim that I am God…Tips to Detect *Saibi*)" *Hankyoreh*, accessed July 1, 2024, https://www.hani.co.kr/arti/culture/culture_general/1082793.html.

clearly demonstrates the aspect of derationalization, coupled with cult-labeling. As I articulated earlier, even before presenting his warning about *idan* and *saibi*, Jo already has his own understanding of them but does not lay it out for the reader. Like most other journalists, he jumps into his task of bashing the problematic NRMs with massively confusing and grossly generalized ideas of *idan* and *saibi*. Unfortunately, the criteria he applies are the beliefs and practices of mainstream religions, which he calls *jeong-tongjonggyo* (orthodox religion). The NRMs discussed in the article are all considered cults simply because their teachings and practices violate the norms of mainstream religions. For instance, according to Jo's line of thought, founders of religions should not claim to be God, as many leaders of NRMs do, because Jesus in Christianity did not claim to be God. Similarly, the True Buddha would not claim to have supernatural powers to promote material blessings, as the Buddha in Buddhism did not do so. It is questionable, however, whether the founder's self-proclamation of divinity and supernatural powers for blessing can be considered a criterion of a false or harmful religion. If it can, no faith community on earth would be free from this cult labeling.

Due to this convenient practice of labeling cults, journalists often fail to uphold rigorous journalistic standards. For them, the mere exposure of a criminal incident within an NRM seems sufficient to explain everything, including even the legitimacy of the group as a religion, which may not necessarily be relevant. Thus, as Barker notes (1989), when covering NRMs, the public media tends to seek experts who can speak against cults rather than genuine experts with specialized academic training and unbiased objectives. Instead of consulting a sociologist specializing in NRMs, for example, Jo of Hankyoreh sought advice from a theologian of a mainstream Christian church, such as Jeong Bae Lee, a Methodist pastor. Even more concerning is his mention of the criteria for cult leaders that he shares with readers. Jo references Sylvia Browne's *End of Days*. Browne, a psychic and medium, is known for her intellectual claims and spiritual prophecies that have been debunked multiple times for their inaccuracy.[19] In her 2022 article for Chosun Ilbo, Korea's largest national newspaper, *Eunju Park*, also consulted Jiwon Tark, a prominent anti-cultist, whose father, Meyonghwan Tark, was a well-known trailblazer of ACM, to gain insights on *idan* and saibi. According to Tark, NRMs represented by *idan* and *saibi* inevitably lead to negative situations such as susceptibility to

[19] Hyeon Jo, "*Naneun Sinida Oechimyeon…Saibi Jonggyo Gambyeolbeop Allyeodeurimnida.*"

manipulation, labor exploitation, becoming targets for infiltration, and deception through hidden multi-level marketing.[20] The 2023 article by Gieun Yun from the Kyunghyang Shinmun similarly suffers from ambiguity in her use of *idan* and *saibi*.[21] Warning of the invasive, strategic evangelism of *saibi* groups on college campuses, Yun does not specify what types of faith communities qualify for that problematic category. Her professional consultation comes solely from the anti-cultist activist Tae Ryeong Gwon, Director of Recovery from Cults and the Human Rights Alliance. Although alerting to the fact that some college clubs on campuses are *idan* and *saibi* in the guise of Bible study or faith meetings and that a blacklist of them is circulating, there is no further discussion about her source or who made the list and by what criteria.

To sum up, in Korea, media perception portrays NRMs represented by *idan* and *saibi* as hateful, inferior, dangerous, immoral, deceptive, exploitative, and anti-social sub-cultural groups. Regardless of the nature of their religious efforts and expressions, whether in old or new shape and forms, these movements are considered dysmorphic or mutated due to their dissociation from established religions and their competitive stance in the religious market, which contrasts with the established frames of operation. The media frequently transcribes rhetoric from mainstream religions regarding NRMs for convenience, emphasizing themes of immorality and criminality in their news coverage. Thus, recognizing the shared elements of religion and religious practices between NRMs and mainstream religions, while distinguishing them from immoral and criminal acts, consistently falls outside the media's focus.

3.3 Government's Perceptions

The perception of the government in Korea of NRMs seemingly differs from that of mainstream religions and media. Within the modern

[20] Eunju Park, "*Jiokboda Ttokttokan Urigyeotui Saibi* (*Saibi*, close to us, smarter than Hell)," *Chosun Ilbo*, December 3, 2021, https://www.chosun.com/national/national_general/2021/12/03/2E3JTBLBPBCNNO3TTRJCFWSFFU/. Tark made this statement during Park's special interview on NRMs, which was explicitly designed to highlight their societal problems.

[21] Gi Eun Yun, "*Eoseong·Saenaegi·Jibang Haksaeng… 'Gatja Sin'i Norinda*" (*Women, Freshmen, and Regional Students… 'Fake Faith' Spreads*), *The Kyunghyang Shinmun*, accessed February 23, 2025, https://www.khan.co.kr/article/202303092136035/?utm_source=google&utm_medium=news_app&utm_content=khan.

democratic framework, under the condition of church and state separation, the government must, in principle, remain neutral with no establishment and try to guarantee religious freedom in public spaces while upholding a secular policy framework. However, as in many other countries, the Korean government's approach to NRMs is far from ideal. If summarized in a single descriptor, its treatment would be "non-presence," meaning that NRMs are mostly nonexistent in their various activities to promote religious education and tolerance, including workshops and seminars related to religious diversity and inclusion training, legislative and policy education, surveys and feedback, and community engagement. While this may not actively endorse the hostile sentiments discussed earlier, such as derationalization and cult-labeling, it could be interpreted as a tacit agreement to prevent public unease. Its overall tone is defensive and ignorant.

For example, the early government documents, such as the 1999 Statistics of Religious Affiliation, do not present any data on NRMs.[22] The overview on religions in Korea in 2018, Religious Statistics in Korea notes that the government adopts a somewhat defensive stance toward the notion of the freedom of religion. It states that the principle of church and state separation restricts public religious education, where learning about religions generally occurs through subjects like history, albeit in a fragmented and unsystematic manner.[23] This problem is rooted in the selective emphasis on the latter part of Article 20 of the Constitution, which states, "All citizens enjoy freedom of religion. No state religion shall be recognized, and there shall be a separation of religion and politics."[24] Although the report points out that three major religions—Buddhism, Protestantism,

[22] Ministry of Culture, Sports and Tourism, "*Jonggyobyeolgyosehyeonhwang* (Statistics of Religious Affiliation)," accessed July 2024, https://www.mcst.go.kr/kor/s_policy/dept/deptView.jsp?pSeq=129&pDataCD=0408010000&pType=.

[23] The Ministry of Culture, Sports, and Tourism, "2018 *Hanguk Jonggyo Hyeonhwang* (2018 Religious Statistics in Korea)," 5, accessed February 23, 2025, https://www.mcst.go.kr/kor/s_policy/dept/deptView.jsp?pCurrentPage=2&pType=03&pTab=01&pSeq=1731&pDataCD=0406000000&pSearchType=01&pSearchWord=.

[24] Article 20, Sections 1–2, *Gukga Beomryeong Jeongbo Senteo*, accessed February 23, 2025, https://www.law.go.kr/lsLinkProc.do?lsClsCd=L&lsNm=%EB%8C%80%ED%95%9C%EB%AF%BC%EA%B5%AD%ED%97%8C%EB%B2%95&lsId=prec20070629&joNo=002000&efYd=20070629&mode=11&lnkJoNo=undefined. "1. *Modeun gukmin eun jonggyo ui jayureul gajinda* (All citizens have freedom of religion). 2. *Gukgyo neun injeongdoeji anmyeo, jonggyowa jeongchi neun bunlida* (A state religion is not recognized, and religion and politics are separated)."

and Catholicism—are currently receiving preferential treatment,[25] a more serious concern is the lack of meaningful recognition of NRMs, not only as legitimate candidates for religious status in society but also as subjects of conversation related to social problems. While the report includes statistics on NRMs, its coverage is notably limited in both breadth and depth. This statistical data does not capture the population of NRMs that have splintered from established religions. Moreover, while it acknowledges relatively larger and well-known groups such as Won Buddhism, Confucianism, Cheondogyo, Daejonggyo, and Daesun Jinrihoe, it overlooks NRMs that may be concealed within other groups. In other words, NRMs were not originally seriously considered in the design of these statistics. The 2012 study on enhancing religious and cultural education, conducted by the Ministry of Culture, Sports, and Tourism, shows a minimal or negligible presence of NRMs. *Sosu Jonggyo*, a term comparable to NRMs, is mentioned only once in the 189-page report—briefly in the literature review—with little to no discussion.[26] Similarly, sinheung jonggyo appears just once on page 45, not as part of a substantive analysis but merely to clarify terminology.[27]

The Cyber Education Program for Public Officials on Preventing Religious Discrimination, available on the website of the Religious Affairs Office (*Jongmusil*) since 2012, neglects to acknowledge NRMs.[28] This educational material aims to prevent religious discrimination among public officials. While it covers various examples and situations, it notably lacks specific instances addressing NRMs, which not only cause conflicts in

[25] The Ministry of Culture, Sports, and Tourism, "2018 *Hangukjonggyohyeonhwang*," 6. The government favors major religions in state-sponsored funerals, allowing only three religions to conduct services in the military and police. It also restricts participation in the National Prayer Breakfast to mainstream religions.

[26] The term *Sosu Jonggyo* in this report carries two meanings: one as a reference to minority religions and the other as a general term for a few religions, regardless of their size or societal impact.

[27] Ministry of Culture, Sports, and Tourism, "*Jonggyo Gyoyanggyoyuk Hwalseonghwa Bangan Yeongu* (*The 2012 Study on Enhancing Religious and Cultural Education*)," accessed February 23, 2025, https://www.mcst.go.kr/kor/s_policy/dept/deptView.jsp?pCurrentPage=4&pType=03&pTab=01&pSeq=1422&pDataCD=0406000000&pSearchType=01&pSearchWord=.

[28] Ministry of Culture, Sports and Tourism, "*Gongjikja Jonggyochabyeol Yebang Saibeogyoyung Peurogeuraem* (The Cyber Education Program for Public Officials on Preventing Religious Discrimination)," accessed July 2, 2024, https://www.mcst.go.kr/kor/s_policy/dept/deptView.jsp?pSeq=1430&pDataCD=0406000000.

society but also face significant discrimination and prejudice. This training is theoretical and abstract, lacking practical relevance, and does not mention NRMs at all. Another government study with a similar title, Research on the Role of Religion in Promoting Optimal Multicultural Community, overlooks NRMs.[29] In pursuit of a robust, healthy multicultural society, the study emphasizes the importance of educating about the role of religion. However, it omits any reference to issues or potential concerns related to NRMs. The religions predominantly mentioned center on mainstream faiths such as Catholicism, Protestantism, Buddhism, Won Buddhism, and Islam. The Case studies on Interreligious Harmony and Its Effectiveness, conducted in 2011, do mention NRMs a few times.[30] However, their evaluation is not constructive. Notably, while highlighting that most positive efforts for religious harmony were carried out through larger denominational cooperation among major faith communities, the study casts a cautious eye on interreligious engagement outside these networks, specifically referring to NRMs and suggesting that such engagements can appear questionable. In particular, when it states, "Non-denominational interreligious engagement might cause a drawback that could give the impression of being a new religious movement," the document presumes that NRMs do not even qualify for contributing positively to society.[31] It assumes the inherent danger of NRMs without elaborating on it. And it prompts questions about the government's operational definition of religion, the criteria by which a self-proclaimed religious group can qualify as acceptable or legitimate, and the basis of the government's moral judgments regarding religion. The 2012 Case Study on Improvements in Religious Education Systems in Foreign (Anglophone) Countries briefly mentions NRMs but does not engage in discussing ways to enhance understanding or address conflicts related to them.[32]

[29] Ministry of Culture, Sports and Tourism, "*Baramjikan Damunhwa Gongdongche Hyeongseongeul Wihan Jonggyoui Yeokal Yeongu* (Research on the Role of Religion in Promoting Optimal Multicultural Community)," accessed July 2, 2024, https://www.mcst.go.kr/kor/s_policy/dept/deptView.jsp?pSeq=1429&pDataCD=0406000000&pType=.

[30] Ministry of Culture, Sports and Tourism, "*Jonggyogan Hwahapsaryewa Hyogwayeongu* (The Case studies on Interreligious Harmony and Its Effectiveness)," accessed July 2, 2024, https://www.mcst.go.kr/kor/s_policy/dept/deptView.jsp?pSeq=926&pDataCD=0406000000&pType=03.

[31] Ministry of Culture, Sports and Tourism, "*Jonggyogan Hwahapsaryewa Hyogwayeongu*," 136.

[32] Ministry of Culture, Sports and Tourism, "*Oeguk(yeongmi)ui Jonggyogyoyukjedo Gaeseonsarye Yeongu* (The 2012 Case Study on Improvements in Religious Education Systems in Foreign (Anglophone) Countries)," accessed July 2, 2024, https://www.mcst.go.kr/kor/s_policy/dept/deptView.jsp?pSeq=926&pDataCD=0406000000&pType=03.

3.4 Academic Perception and Discourse

If one examines how academics have treated *idan* and *saibi*, or NRMs, particularly in the past decades, the public's ambiguous and indiscriminate hostile treatment of them would be better understood. Serious academic attention to NRMs already began in the early 1990s. Chong-suh Kim, a leading sociologist of religion, initiated a concise theoretical discussion on NRMs in his 1994 work *Hyundae Sinjongyoui Ihae* (Understanding Modern New Religions), addressing the problematic terminology commonly used by the public. Prior to his full discussion, Kim critically examined terms related to NRMs, such as *sinheung jonggyo* (newly emerged religions), *yusajonggyo* (pseudo-religions), *saibijonggyo* (cultic religions), minjung-mijok jonggyo (*people-nationalist* religions), and *jubyeon* jonggyo (quasi or peripheral religions), arguing that these labels are often inadequate or insufficient for objective academic analysis.[33] Significantly, Kim's work introduced a broader concept of "newness" frequently associated with NRMs, emphasizing not only the negative notion of deviation or defiance but also the positive notion of innovation.[34] In doing so, he cautioned against the unfounded and overly negative public perceptions of NRMs. Despite this foundational contribution, scholarly discourse on NRMs has made little headway in the years that followed. The lack of research on *idan* and *saibi* in Korean academia is one issue. Moreover, even when they are studied, the treatment often neglects their sociological dimensions, which is a more significant concern today. Hyun-Beom Jo's exploration of *saibi*-religiousness in 1994 stands out, especially when compared to more recent works with *saibi* in their titles, for its broad-stroke yet nuanced discussion of the term's elusive nature, which fluctuates with Korea's historical vicissitudes.[35] He notes that what determines *saibi* or *saibi-religiousness* is the social context and public perception responding to it, rather than any inherent qualities, as exemplified in his discussion of the new historical waves such as Western scientific reason and the religion's controllability and utility for regimes, including those of Japanese colonialism and subsequent Korean governments, both civilian

[33] Chong-suh Kim, *Hyundae Sinjongyo Ihae* (Understanding Contemporary Religions), (Seongnam: Hanguk Jeongsin Munhwa Yeonguwon, 1994): 4–5.

[34] Chong-suh Kim, *Hyundae Sinjongyo Ihae*, 5.

[35] Hyun-beom Cho. 1994. "*Saibijonggyorone Daehan Seongchal-Jinjja Jonggyo, Gajja Jonggyo* (Reflections on 'Saibi' and '*Saibi* Religiousness'-True Religion, False Religion)," *Hangukjonggyoyeonguhoehoebo* 5, (1994), 4.

and military. Other studies since 2014 are either not directly related to my current theme of exploring public perceptions or are anti-cultist works primarily conducted by Protestant theological communities, including their affiliated cult-watch groups.

Jeong Eun Lee's article titled Features of "Sa-i-bi Discourse Reinforced by Protestant I-dan-sang-dam" is noteworthy at least for its relevancy to my theme.[36] Although her discussion of the Protestant community's counseling efforts on *idan* and its development as a deprogramming scheme is significant, the question of what *idan* and *saibi* mean to the public and the problems surrounding them is, however, not within her scope. For academic research specifically addressing *saibi* in their titles, little has been explored except for the two most recent works: Yeon Sang Roh's "Current Status and Countermeasures of the Crimes of Pseudo-Religious Cults" and Seungjin Hong's "Public Philosophy: Covid-19 and Shincheonji." Unfortunately, both discussions are grounded in an anti-cultist perspective that assumes the criminality of NRMs. Roh presents diverse statistics on crimes related to *saibi* religions and discusses corresponding countermeasures. Like other public views previously discussed, Roh considers *saibi* religions to be pseudo-religions that deviate from mainstream beliefs and "contradict common societal norms."[37] Not only is his operating definition of *saibi* ambiguous, but the information regarding where he obtained the crime reports specifically tagged with *saibi*-religion is also unclear.[38] Hong's short essay echoes a similar sentiment. As suggested by its subtitle, "Saibi-Religions Encroaching upon a Deficiency of Sacredness," certain aspects of religious experience are deemed essential, which NRMs are perceived as unable to fulfill, unlike mainstream Christian practices. This biased and tangential discussion is exacerbated as he attempts to emphasize his point by linking the SCJ's early involvement in the spread of COVID-19 to its theological unorthodoxy.[39] The

[36] Jung Eun Lee, "*Gaesingyo Idansangdamgwa Saibi Damnonui Gwangye Gochal* (Features of *Sa-i-bi* Discourse Reinforced by Protestant I-dan-sang-dam)," *Jonggyoyeongu* (The Journal of the Korean Association for the History of Religions) 83, no. 3 (2023): 85–118.

[37] Yeon Sang Roh, "*Saibi Jonggyobeomjoeui Hyeonhwanggwa Daechaek* (Current Status and Countermeasures of the Crimes of the pseudo-religious crime)," *Inmunsahoegwahagyeongu29*, no. 2 (2021): 36–59, 39.

[38] Yeon Sang Roh, "*Saibi Jonggyobeomjoeui Hyeonhwanggwa Daechaek*," 43.

[39] Seungjin Hong, "*Gonggongcheolhang: Korona-19wa Sincheonji, Sinseongui Gyeolpibeul Pagodeun Saibi* ([Public Philosophy] Covid-19 and *Shincheonji*: Pseudo-religions encroaching upon a deficiency of sacredness)," *Wolganonggongjeongchaek* (Monthly Public Policy) no. 177 (2020): 76–81.

majority of anti-cultist studies within theological and missiological communities, of course, express a militant stance toward NRMs, purportedly to safeguard orthodoxy and rescue what they perceive as kidnapped or enslaved members. Refer to recent titles such as Dohoon Choi's "*Counterfeits, Idan and Saibi*," and The Christian Holiness Church of Korea's official document titled "*Heresies and Cults Defined by the Holiness Church*."[40] They all portray NRMs as the worst threat to the church's growth and as leading its members astray. The titles with *sinheungjongyeo* are in the same vein. Relatively most recent works within that category, such as Ji-il Tark's "The Pathological Phenomenon of the Korean Church and New Religious Movements" and Geum Jae Lee's "Spiritual Discernment of Contemporary Trends in New Religious Movements and Identification of Heretical Religions," diagnose the root cause of the thriving of NRMs in Korea from the internal problem of the mainstream Protestant churches.[41]

In the meantime, research featuring *sinjonggyo*—the Korean term for NRMs—maintains a clear, unbiased tone. Most researchers are trained in religious studies, viewing NRMs as a significant academic subject requiring rigorous investigation and fair treatment alongside established religions. There is no place for unfounded accusations, emotional criticism, or stigmatization against NRMs. However, a comprehensive discussion on *idan*, *saibi*, and public perceptions has not been attempted in Korean religious studies and sociology of religion. Although Chae Young Kim's work on *sinjonggyo* may be the closest to my theme in terms of discussing ways to enhance its understanding, his discussion is more focused on the psychological aspect than the sociological, suggesting that we update our traditional cognitive framework of mental problems and well-being to highlight attention to the vertical dimension of religiousness rather than the horizontal, which is social and historical.[42] The primary focus of most

[40] Choi Dohoon, "*Jjaktung, Idangwa Saibi* (*Sallineun Saem*) (Counterfeits, Heresies, and Cults (the Saving Spring))," *Hwalcheon* 836, no. 7 (2023): 28.

[41] Ji-Il Tark, "*Hangukgyohoeui Byeongnihyeonsanggwa Sinheungjonggyoundong* (The Pathological Phenomenon of the Korean Church and New Religious Movements)," *Christianity and History in Korea*, no. 48 (2018): 123-153; Geum Jae Lee, "*Idan Jonggyowa Yeongjeok Sikbyeol*) *Sinheungjonggyoui Hyeondaejeok Donghyange Daehan Yeongjeok Sikbyeol* (*Idan* Religion and Spiritual Discernment: A Study on the Contemporary Trends of New Religious Movements)," *Samokjeongbo* 8, no. 3 (2015): 38–42.

[42] Chae Young Kim, "*Sinjonggyo Insikgwa Jeongsingeongang Damnon* (Perceptions of the New Religious Movement and the Discourse on Mental Health)," *Seoganginmunnonchong* (Sogang Journal of Humanities) 43 (2015): 271.

other studies has similarly centered on theoretical aspects, covering, for instance, field research findings, doctrinal and historical explanations, typological characteristics, phenomenology, and denominational developments. Cho's 2020 work, titled "A Sociologist's Study on New Religions and the Sincheonji Group," points out the lack of academic, particularly sociological, engagement with recent religious phenomena, such as the COVID-19 incident involving SCJ. However, he did not elaborate on the potential benefits that a sociological approach to NRMs could offer to the public, and on the fact that our understanding and articulation of them has been deficient.[43] Taeyeon Kim's critical historical reflection on the term *sinjonggyo* focuses specifically on its conceptual evolution from national religion, minjung religion, and periphery religion to cult, as well as its broader implications for understanding religion. Nevertheless, it does not delve into what it means that the public has a specific word and definition of NRMs in a better understanding of the relational dynamic between religions and various social groups.[44] Other notable studies by Park and Ahn offer meaningful insights into *Sinjonggyo*, or NRMs, focusing on the role of changes in the religious market terrain and their various strategic responses to the COVID-19 pandemic, respectively.[45] In these discussions, NRMs are seen as market players significantly impacted by various external factors. They experience, metaphorically speaking, a sort of semi-monopolies due to government intervention, discriminatory pricing derived from the public's prejudiced view of their compensators, barriers to entry caused by the established power structure, and subsidies resulting from political favoritism. Like other mainstream religions, NRMs, as Ahn suggests, also adopt a variety of rational responses to best accommodate the crisis for their own ends. Some spiritually internalized

[43] Sung Youn Cho, "*Sahoehakjaui Sinjonggyo Yeonguwa Sincheonji* (A Sociologist's Study on New Religions and Sincheonji Group)," *Jonggyowamunhwabipyeong* (The Critical Review of Religion and Culture) 37, (2020): 358–368.

[44] Taeyeon Kim, "*Sinjonggyo yeongue daehan bipanjeok seongchal: sinjonggyo gaenyeom munjereul jungsimeuro* (A Critical Review on Researches about 'New Religions': Focused on the concept of 'New Religion')," *Jonggyowamunhwabipyeong* (The Critical Review of Religion and Culture) 31, (2017): 288–322.

[45] Seung Gil Park, "*Jonggyosijangjeok Jihyeong Sogui Sinjonggyoundonggwa Jonggyojihyeong Byeonhwa* (New Religious Movements in the Religious Market and their Topographical Mutation)," *Hangukjonggyo* (Korean Religions), 40 (2016): 3-42; Shin Ahn, "*Wideukorona Sidaee Hanguk Sinjonggyoui Insikgwa Daeeung* (New Religions in the Era of WITH-COVID-19: Their Perceptions and Responses)," *Jonggyoyeongu* 81, no. 2 (The Journal of the Korean Association for the History of Religions): 85–104.

it, some took advantage of it to innovate their religious practices, including mission strategies, some utilized it for both internal solidarity and external outreach, and others outright challenged its existence to bolster their spiritual fight against the secular. In all these cases, the task of breaking into the public perception of *idan* and *saibi*, otherwise known as NRMs, was not part of their interests.

4 Reevaluation of NRMs in the Rational Choice Theory of Religion (RCTR)

4.1 Principle of RCTR

I have so far demonstrated examples from different sectors of Korean society to show the persistently hostile view toward NRMs, as represented by *idan* and *saibi*. Although the list is, of course, not exhaustive, I believe my point about the abnormality remains valid. Recognizing these cognitive and epistemological flaws regarding NRMs, I propose in this section a new frame of perception that would help establish a rational and moral grounding to promote peace and harmony among diverse social groups and institutions, if properly applied, while also allowing for effective criticism of disruptors. To have a fair legal and moral judgment on any social group, particularly NRMs in this discussion, our evaluative frame needs to be based on reason, the standard criterion for modern society that has embraced the secularization thesis separating church/religion and state. This means that the public acknowledges and respects their unique reasons for existence and functions, thereby applying different frames of assessment for their values. In the following discussion, I suggest that we make a clear distinction in the evaluative criteria, particularly concerning secular/social and religious practice, to avoid the unintentional misuse or, more often, intentional abuse of incorrect applications. I argue that the only logically and morally defensible criterion for evaluating the value of a religion or an NRM, particularly concerning public benefit, should be secular and rational.

As defined by its constitution and affirmed by the general public's consensus, Korean society is a democratic society that upholds fundamental principles such as the rule of law, civil liberties, human rights, pluralism, and more. These principles are integral parts of the legacy left by humanity's long and illustrious historical struggles, including numerous cultural and political revolutions such as the Protestant Reformation, followed by the Peace of Westphalia, which established the political landscape of secularization and state sovereignty, along with the American and French Revolutions that historically solidified the separation of church and state to ensure religious freedom, and the Industrial Revolution and Enlightenment, which accelerated the differentiation of roles among various social institutions. Upon this long and deep historical legacy of secularization, most modern societies have established a shared idea that the essential function of religion deals primarily with ultimate questions of life, including its mysterious origin, profound meaning, and its purpose and direction within and beyond life. The truth and efficacy of a religion should be thus measured by its internal logic and the shared faith of its community, not in the gaze of outsiders who see but do not know. The grounds on which we can base our criticism should be the rational horizon, where every social group, including mainstream religions and NRMs, is considered on equal footing—not as groups with distinct spiritual natures and functions but as groups operating under shared expectations and legal and moral accountability. Drawing from Rawls's original position and the veil of ignorance, every social group needs to be stripped of its respective particularities, such as wealth, status, strength, skin color, age, and faith. The criteria of reason should dictate the process of assessing the legal and moral stance of each social group. Among the range of theoretical frameworks, I personally believe that the rational choice theory of religion (RCTR) would best demonstrate fair handling of NRMs, particularly their challenging interactions with mainstream religions and the public in general.

Derived from the innovative thinking of twentieth-century sociology and economics, the RCTR understands religious practices, particularly in the social dimension, through the principle of rational calculations of costs and benefits to maximize one's interests. According to the RCTR, individuals and groups in society are generally rational in their decision-making, barring mental illness. People select a university, choose a career path, invest in stocks, buy a home, and make ethical decisions. They are rational not because their choices are always right and beneficial for themselves, but because they are individuals who consistently calculate costs and benefits in their lives. Under this principle, every individual stands on an equal footing. All individuals possess the capacity for rational action, assuming they maintain sanity. They have the right to enjoy equality. This principle can be applied to all human activities, including ethics, economy, politics, and even religion.

When the rational choice theory is applied to religion, just as it is for every individual and social group, conventionally important questions about its validity and efficacy—such as the veracity of doctrines, rituals, and other spiritual expressions—become irrelevant. It's not that they are no longer important within their own faith community, but rather that they are not directly related to the secular, social evaluation of its legal and moral stance. Every religion, whether mainstream or dominant religion or an NRM, is a player in the religious market of a society. Like typical market players in the economy, religions advertise, recruit, educate, collaborate, expand, retain members, and monitor trends in economic terms. Like Microsoft Philanthropies and Google for Non-Profits, which work to solve various global challenges, religions also engage in social services.[46] In the public sphere, religions are, as per RCTR, conceptualized in purely rational terms using the market metaphor. Each religion is viewed as a participant on equal footing, eliminating the need for prejudice, bigotry, or suspicion. Similar to suppliers such as manufacturers, farmers, retailers, and service providers in a market economy, religions offer religious services and commodities. Like clients, users, and shoppers, religious adherents consume these products to fulfill their spiritual needs. What sets religious providers and consumers apart from market players in the economy is the distinct quality of the connection that actually links them together. It is the religious reward or commodity characterized as a "compensator" by Rodney Stark and William Sims Bainbridge (1987). Unlike the tangible benefits and values of commodities in the regular marketplace, a religious compensator is a psychological, social, and spiritual benefit, some aspects of which cannot be externally grasped in reality and may be acquired after death, such as salvation in heaven and liberation from the cycle of birth. Regardless of the verifiability and empiricability of the religious commodity offered, devoted individuals embrace it within their cognitive framework of rationality and plausibility, particularly in their acts of choice. Given the established principle of church and state separation that I have outlined as foundational to my discussion, society—encompassing

[46] "Everything You Need to Know About Microsoft Philanthropies," *Powernet*, accessed July 3, 2024, https://power-net.com.au/blog/everything-you-need-to-know-about-microsoft-philanthropies/; "Google for Nonprofits," accessed July 3, 2024, https://www.google.com/nonprofits/.

the general public, the media, other religions, and the government—has no obligation to verify the distinctive spiritual claims of any specific faith community. This is not only because these claims are, in principle, beyond outsiders' understanding, but also because our current system safeguards religious freedom.

In this market metaphor and perception, all religions are considered equal in that they offer their respective religious services and compensators. There is no orthodoxy or heresy, nor superiority or inferiority among them. Just as Pickard illustrated in 2006 article, a religion acts as a supplier providing what its believers demand. If it successfully meets these demands, more members will join, and its institutional size will increase. A similar situation can occur with other religious providers. As the number of religious organizations and participants grows, there will be a heightened need for additional services. Religious institutions will expand their offerings not only to meet this demand but also to attract new members, thereby fostering a continuous cycle of increasing membership and service provision, which is a "self-perpetuating feedback loop."[47] In this setting, all religions are providers, all members are consumers, and the government is a major arbitrator for market supervision and regulatory oversight specifically to maintain order and stability.

4.2 RCTR Handling of NRM Malefactors

Now, the important question is how to handle the negative perception of *idan* and *saibi*, and what should be done about troublemakers such as Myung Seok Jung, Gyeong Yeong Heo, and Jaerok Lee, who have committed heinous acts of rape, sexual exploitation, and financial fraud. Given that the RCTR primarily focuses on market activities, any negative judgments regarding NRMs, especially those concerning spiritual matters, should be excluded from public discourse. The compensators that each religion claims to offer are internal and subjective, making them irrelevant for public debate. Just as it would be absurd to criticize the Christology of Christianity in public discourse due to the lack of empirical evidence, it is unfair to attack the supernatural aspects of an NRM's faith and practice. While individuals can choose not to believe in its magical and mystical

[47] Joseph G. Pickard, "What's in It for Me? Rational Choice Theory and Religion," *Journal of Religion & Spirituality in Social Work: Social Though* 24, no. 4 (2006): 39–54, 44.

aspects, they cannot extend this disbelief to deny its existence without potentially affecting all religions equally.

Religious troublemakers, particularly NRM malefactors, should be understood within this rational framework of the religious market, alongside the principle of consistency that requires equality of treatment, objectivity, and fairness. Just as specific business products, philosophies, and marketing strategies are not inherently evil as long as they comply with legal regulations, neither is any religion inherently evil. Individuals may perceive some religions as good/true and others as bad/false, similar to how consumers perceive wines and artisan cheese. However, there should not be a blanket negative view toward a particular religion simply because it differs from the most popular brands. Sociological research has shown that the diversity of religions within a society is a positive factor for the overall health and growth of religion, similar to how diversification of products in the market stimulates consumption. While the self-messianic claims and belief in supernatural powers attributed to Man-hee Lee, Jaerok Lee, and Myeong Seok Jung by their followers may appear ludicrous and unacceptable to devoted members of mainstream Christian churches, these beliefs are considered legitimate within their respective communities. Mainstream Christians have the right to reject and ridicule these beliefs within their own community but cannot bring these criticisms into public discourse to influence the presumably fair conditions of the religious market.

Following the general rules of surveillance in the economic market, the public can critique and control NRM malefactors based on four criteria: legality, transparency, fair competition, and social responsibility. In the public sphere, like other social organizations and mainstream religions, NRMs should comply with constitutional and legal requirements, including both criminal and civil laws such as non-profit charitable laws, employment laws, tax laws, health and safety laws, and contractual laws, just as any other social institution and group. The aforementioned NRM leaders were all prosecuted and are under investigation not because of their bizarre and unorthodox religious teachings and practices, but because of their criminal acts. However, they are not obligated or expected to do more than others, as is currently happening in Korean society. As in commercial exchange, NRMs can be also subjected to criticism or, if necessary, prosecuted if they violate the rule of transparency. A good market prohibits false advertising, misleading labels, quality deception, bait-and-switch tactics, safety hazard, phony reviews, etc. If an NRM intentionally and systematically deceives a prospective member of its religious services and products, it deserves public blame and an investigation, as in the 2018 civil lawsuit against the SCJ.[48] Fair competition is another hallmark of a healthy market. One of the aspects of fair competition, particularly relevant to NRM malefactors in Korea, would be the deliberate dissemination of false information about their competitors, including the government. In regular markets, such actions constitute defamation, false advertising, and trade libel, leading to civil and criminal lawsuits. Similarly, NRMs' consistent and systematic spread of misinformation about mainstream religions or other societal entities can result in moral and legal consequences. For example, NRMs promoting conspiracies such as government cover-ups like the New World Order and hidden technologies, as well as medical misinformation such as suppressed cures and vaccine misinformation, and stigmatization of conventional medical practices, can lead to legal repercussions. This criterion, however, applies equally to all religions. Finally, NRMs can be morally evaluated, particularly in terms of their social responsibility. Even though church and state separation are the norm and there is freedom within religion, there remains a significant public expectation of religion, similar to that of corporate business entities. This goes beyond the legal dimension. Just as in the regular market, business entities strive to uphold high standards of Corporate Social Responsibility (CSR) not only to maintain positive public perception and employee morale but also to ensure long-term sustainability. NRMs are expected to coexist

[48] The Supreme Court of South Korea recently adjudicated that Shincheonji Church of Jesus, the Temple of the Tabernacle of the Testimony (SCJ), under the leadership of Lee Man-hee, bears no legal responsibility for damages in a case centered on allegations of deceptive proselytism, which masked its activities under the pretext of cultural and biblical study centers. Originating in 2018 and termed the "Youth Return Lawsuit," the litigation was brought forth by former members seeking restitution for their time and experiences within Shincheonji. While lower courts acknowledged Shincheonji's misleading recruitment tactics and their implications on religious liberties, the Supreme Court reversed aspects of these decisions. It acknowledged societal censure of Shincheonji's actions but determined that they did not surpass reasonable limits. The court highlighted that plaintiffs were aware of their involvement with Shincheonji at some point in time yet continued doctrinal studies. Despite recognizing deceptive practices during proselytism, the court concluded there was insufficient evidence of significant financial or personal harm to the plaintiffs during their affiliation. See "*Daebeobwon, Sincheonji Yesugyo, Gyoyugwon Seongyo Jeokbeop* (Supreme Court Rules on Shincheonji Church of Jesus, Legal Validity of Educational 'Proselytism')," *Nyuseuaenjoi*, accessed July 3, 2024, https://www.newsnjoy.or.kr/news/articleView.html?idxno=304616.

harmoniously with their competitors, neighbors, and society in general. Even if a bizarre religious practice of an NRM may not draw legal scrutiny due to the principle of freedom of religious expression, it is still subject to moral scrutiny if perceived to harm the overall well-being of society. No entity in the religious market can simply ignore this expectation. NRMs, like other social communities, face pressure to align with societal norms at any given time. If they fail to do so or experience setbacks, criticism, and negative public perception, even if not persecution or oppression, may be justified on rational grounds. Heaven's Gate's toxic belief in and practice of UFO-apocalypticism, Aum Shinrikyo's and the Branch Davidians' delusional theology of government conspiracies and end times, and the Children of God's lascivious sexual liberty are notable examples. These beliefs were part of their religious expressions, which were legally protected but also became triggers for their downfall.

5 Conclusion

Idan and *saibi* are representative terms for NRMs in Korea. The former is used primarily within the Protestant church community, while the latter is used more broadly to refer to any individual or organization perceived to deviate from accepted societal norms. The main problem I have highlighted in this chapter is that, due to the ambiguity of these terms and their exclusive use by mainstream religions, particularly Korean Protestant churches, once a religion is labeled as *idan/saibi* in public discourse, it faces significant and often irreversible ramifications. NRMs labeled as *idan* or *saibi* are seen as public enemies in Korea not because of substantiated wrongdoing, but because of the collective irrationality formulated by major stakeholders in society, including the media, the government, mainstream religions, and some academics. In the current discourse, which is fraught with negative frames such as cult-labeling, derationalization, and criminalization, it is very challenging to initiate a constructive public discussion on NRMs, particularly regarding the problems they may trigger. I have suggested that we place this subject matter on rational ground, where everyone stands on equal footing. Drawing from the rational choice theory of religion (RCTR), I suggest the metaphor of a religious market, in which religions and practitioners act as suppliers and consumers of religious commodities, some of which are characterized as compensators. In this framework, the status of every participant is considered equally, functioning in the shared role of providing religious services, and assessed for their faults by the rational criteria expected for a good market, such as transparency, legality, fairness, and social responsibility. Each individual possesses the freedom to assess religions independently—they may choose to appreciate, support, and believe in, or question, disdain, and criticize any religion according to their personal convictions. However, their expressions in the public sphere and discourse, involving fair treatment and policymaking, application, and interpretation of the law, should be based on rational grounds. I believe that discussing NRMs through the frame of the RCTR would help us disentangle from misunderstandings and prejudices and better equip us to evaluate their social and moral issues.

References

Ahn, Shin. 2021. *Wideukorona Sidaee Hanguk Sinjonggyoui Insikgwa Daeeung* (New Religions in the Era of WITH-COVID-19: Their Perceptions and Responses). *Jonggyoyeongu* (*The Journal of the Korean Association for the History of Religions*) 81(2): 85–104.

Barker, Eileen. 1986. Religious Movements: Cult and Anticult Since Jonestown. *Annual Review of Sociology* 12:329–346.

Barker, Eileen. 1989. *New religious Movements: A Practical Introduction*. London: Her Majesty's Stationery Office.

Beckford, James A. 1985. *Cult Controversies: The Societal Response to the New Religious Movements*. London and New York: Tavistock.

Beckford, James A. 1999. The Mass Media and New Religious Movements. In *New Religious Movements: Challenge and Response*, ed. Bryan Wilson and Jamie Cresswell, 103–119. London: Routledge.

Cho, Sung Youn. 2020. *Sahoehakjaui Sinjonggyo Yeonguwa Sincheonji* (A Sociologist's Study on New Religions and Sincheonji Group). *Jonggyowamunhwabipyeong (The Critical Review of Religion and Culture)* 37:358–368.

Choi, Dohoon. 2023. *Jjaktung, Idangwa Saibi* (*Sallineun Saem*) (Counterfeits, Heresies, and Cults (the Saving Spring)). *Hwalcheon* 836 (7): 28.

Daebeobwon. *Sincheonji Yesugyo, Gyoyugwon Seongyo Jeokbeop* (*Supreme Court Rules on 'Shincheonji Church of Jesus, Legal Validity of Educational 'Proselytism*). *Nyuseuaenjoi* (News & Joy). https://www.newsnjoy.or.kr/news/articleView.html?idxno=304616. Accessed 3 July 2024.

Department of State, United States. 2009 Human Rights Report: China (Includes Tibet, Hong Kong, and Macau). *Refworld*, 25 February 2010. Accessed 28 June 2024. https://www.refworld.org/reference/annualreport/usdos/2009/en/70690.

Everything You Need to Know About Microsoft Philanthropies. Powernet. Accessed 3 July 2024. https://power-net.com.au/blog/everything-you-need-to-know-about-microsoft-philanthropies/.

France Passes New Anti-Cult Law Against Senate's Opposition. *EU Reporter*, April 13, 2024. Accessed 28 June 2024. https://www.eureporter.co/world/france-world/2024/04/13/france-passes-new-anti-cult-law-against-senates-opposition/.

General Assembly of the Presbyterian Church of Korea. *Chonghoe Ollain Gyujeongjip* (Online Policy Manual of the General Assembly). Presbyterian Church of Korea. https://new.pck.or.kr/ruleContents/rule_view.php?cate1=1&cate2=15. Accessed 29 June 2024.

Google for Nonprofits. https://www.google.com/nonprofits/. Accessed 3 July 2024.

Gukga Beomryeong Jeongbo Senteo. Article 20, Sections 1–2. https://www.law.go.kr/lsLinkProc.do?lsClsCd=L&lsNm=%EB%8C%80%ED%95%9C%EB%AF%BC%EA%B5%AD%ED%97%8C%EB%B2%95&lsId=prec20070629&joNo=002000&efYd=20070629&mode=11&lnkJoNo=undefined. Accessed 23 February 2025.

Handong University Chaplain Office. *Idan* Related Information (*Idan Gwallyeon Jeongbo*). https://church.handong.edu/main/sub.html?pageCode=68. Accessed 29 June 2024.

Hangukgyohoe Idansaibi Gyujeonggijungwa Yongeo Tongil (Korean Church's Unifying Terms and Definitions of Idan and Saibi). *The Christian Council of Korea.* http://www.cck.or.kr/chnet2/board/view.php?id=118&code=intro05b&cate=&start=&category=&word=&viewType=&category_id=. Accessed 29 June 2024.

Hong, Seungjin. 2020. *Gonggongcheolhang: Korona-19wa Sincheonji, Sinseongui Gyeolpibeul Pagodeun Saibi* [Public Philosophy] Covid-19 and Shincheonji: Pseudo-religions Encroaching Upon a Deficiency of Sacredness. *Wolgangonggongjeongchaek (Monthly Public Policy)* 177:76–81.

Jo, Hyeon. *Naneun Sinida Oechimyeon…Saibi Jonggyo Gambyeolbeop Allyeodeurimnida* (Claim That I am God…Tips to Detect Saibi). *Hankyoreh.* https://www.hani.co.kr/arti/culture/culture_general/1082793.html. Accessed 1 July 2024.

Kim, Chong-suh. 1994. *Hyundae Sinjongyo Ihae (Understanding Contemporary Religions)*. Seongnam: Hanguk Jeongsin Munhwa Yeonguwon.

Kim, Chae Young. 2015. *Sinjonggyo Insikgwa Jeongsingeongang Damnon* (Perceptions of the New Religious Movement and the Discourse on Mental Health). *Seoganginmunnonchong (Sogang Journal of Humanities)* 43:271–317.

Kim, Taeyeon. 2017. *Sinjonggyo yeongue daehan bipanjeok seongchal: sinjonggyo gaenyeom munjereul jungsimeuro* (A Critical Review on Researches About 'New Religions': Focused on the Concept of 'New Religion'). *Jonggyowamunhwabipyeong (The Critical Review of Religion and Culture)* 31:288–322.

Lee, Geum Jae. 2015. (*Idan Jonggyowa Yeongjeok Sikbyeol*) *Sinheungjonggyoui Hyeondaejeok Donghyange Daehan Yeongjeok Sikbyeol* [*Idan* Religion and Spiritual Discernment: A Study on the Contemporary Trends of New Religious Movements]. *Samokjeongbo* 8 (3): 38–42.

Lee, Jung Eun. 2023. Gaesingyo Idansangdamgwa Saibi Damnonui Gwangye Gochal (Features of Sa-i-bi Discourse Reinforced by Protestant I-dan-sang-dam). *Jonggyoyeongu* 83 (3): 85–118.

Lewis, James R. 2003. *Legitimating New Religions.* New Brunswick, NJ: Rutgers University Press.

Melton, J. Gordon. 1999. Anti-cultists in the United States: An Historical Perspective. In *New Religious Movements, Challenge and Response*, ed. Bryan Wilson and Jamie Cresswell, 217. New York: Routledge.

Ministry of Culture, Sports and Tourism. *Jonggyobyeolgyosehyeonhwang* (Statistics of Religious Affiliation). https://www.mcst.go.kr/kor/s_policy/dept/deptView.jsp?pSeq=129&pDataCD=0408010000&pType=. Accessed July 2024.

Ministry of Culture, Sports, and Tourism. 2018 *Hanguk Jonggyo Hyeonhwang* (2018 Religious Statistics in Korea). https://www.mcst.go.kr/kor/s_policy/dept/deptView.jsp?pCurrentPage=2&pType=03&pTab=01&pSeq=1731&pDataCD=0406000000&pSearchType=01&pSearchWord=. Accessed 23 February 2025.

Ministry of Culture, Sports and Tourism. *Baramjikan Damunhwa Gongdongche Hyeongseongeul Wihan Jonggyoui Yeokal Yeongu* (Research on the Role of Religion in Promoting Optimal Multicultural Community). https://www.mcst.go.kr/kor/s_policy/dept/deptView.jsp?pSeq=1429&pDataCD=0406000000&pType=. Accessed 2 July 2024.

Ministry of Culture, Sports and Tourism. *Jonggyogan Hwahapsaryewa Hyogwayeongu* (The Case Studies on Interreligious Harmony and Its Effectiveness). https://www.mcst.go.kr/kor/s_policy/dept/deptView.jsp?pSeq=926&pDataCD=0406000000&pType=03. Accessed 2 July 2024.

Ministry of Culture, Sports and Tourism. *Oeguk(yeongmi)ui Jonggyogyoyukjedo Gaeseonsarye Yeongu* (The 2012 Case Study on Improvements in Religious Education Systems in Foreign (Anglophone) Countries). https://www.mcst.go.kr/kor/s_policy/dept/deptView.jsp?pSeq=926&pDataCD=0406000000&pType=03. Accessed 2 July 2024.

Ministry of Culture, Sports, and Tourism. *Jonggyo Gyoyanggyoyuk Hwalseonghwa Bangan Yeongu* (The 2012 Study on Enhancing Religious and Cultural Education). https://www.mcst.go.kr/kor/s_policy/dept/deptView.jsp?pCurrentPage=4&pType=03&pTab=01&pSeq=1422&pDataCD=0406000000&pSearchType=01&pSearchWord=. Accessed 23 February 2025.

Ministry of Culture, Sports and Tourism. Program for Public Officials on Preventing Religious Discrimination). https://www.mcst.go.kr/kor/s_policy/dept/deptView.jsp?pSeq=1430&pDataCD=0406000000. Accessed 2 July 2024.

Park, Seung Gil. 2016. *Jonggyosijangjeok Jihyeong Sogui Sinjonggyoundonggwa Jonggyojihyeong Byeonhwa* (New Religious Movements in the Religious Market and Their Topographical Mutation). *Hangukjonggyo (Korean Religions)* 40:3–42.

Park, Eunju. 2021, December 3. *Jiokboda Ttokttokan Urigyeotui Saibi* (*Saibi*, Close to Us, Smarter Than Hell). *Chosun Ilbo.* https://www.chosun.com/national/national_general/2021/12/03/2E3JTBLBPBCNNO3TTRJCFWSFFU/.

Pickard, Joseph G. 2006. What's in It for Me? Rational Choice Theory and Religion. *Journal of Religion & Spirituality in Social Work: Social Though* 24 (4): 39–54.

Presbyterian Church of Korea. *Idansaibi Chonghoe Juyo Gyeol-ui: Idan Saibi Jeong-ui wa Pyojun Jichim-e Gwanhan Yeongu Bogoseo* (Resolution of the General Assembly: 2022 Research Report on and Guidance Against Idan and Saibi) (Resolution on Idan and Saibi Hereafter). http://new.pck.or.kr/bbs/board.php?bo_table=SM02_18_06&wr_id=73. Accessed 29 June 2024.

Roh, Yeon Sang. 2021. Saibi Jonggyobeomjoeui Hyeonhwanggwa Daechaek (Current Status and Countermeasures of the Pseudo-religious Crime). *Inmunsahoegwahagyeongu* 29 (2): 36–59.

Stark, Rodney and William Sims Bainbridge. 1987. *A Theory of Religion* (p. 27). New York: Peter Lang Inc.

Tark, Ji-Il. 2018. *Hangukgyohoeui Byeongnihyeonsanggwa Sinheungjonggyoundong* (The Pathological Phenomenon of the Korean Church and New Religious Movements). *Christianity and History in Korea* 48:123–153.

Unifying Terms of *Idan* and *Saibi*. *iGoodNews.* https://www.igoodnews.net/news/articleView.html?idxno=6763. Accessed 29 June 2024.

United States Department of State. 2009 Human Rights Report: China (Includes Tibet, Hong Kong, and Macau). *Refworld*, February 25, 2010. https://www.refworld.org/reference/annualreport/usdos/2009/en/70690. Accessed 28 June 2024.

Wilson, Bryan, and Jamie Cresswell. 1999. *New Religious Movements, Challenge and Response.* New York: Routledge.

Yun, Gi Eun. *Eoseong·Saenaegi·Jibang Haksaeng… 'Gatja Sin'i Norinda*" (Women, Freshmen, and Regional Students… 'Fake Faith' Spreads). *The Kyunghyang Shinmun.* https://www.khan.co.kr/article/202303092136035/?utm_source=google&utm_medium=news_app&utm_content=khan. Accessed 23 February 2025.

CHAPTER 6

Constructing K-Multicultural Space from Below: A Case of Little Manila and Korean Catholic Church

Hyunjoo Jung

1 Introduction

One of the greatest changes and challenges facing South Korean society in the twenty-first century is the transition to a multicultural society. South Korea, which achieved rapid economic development while maintaining the myth of a homogeneous nation as an ideology for national integration, is now facing new challenges in the midst of globalization and mass immigration. The rapid integration of the global economy and culture after globalization, along with the movement of populations, has ushered in the age of "mass migration" (The Economist 2023), and as Korea emerged as a rising power in Asia while becoming an OECD member, it could not escape these global trends. For a long time, Korea was an

H. Jung (✉)
Department of City Planning, Seoul National University,
Seoul, Republic of Korea
e-mail: Jung0072@snu.ac.kr

© The Author(s), under exclusive license to Springer Nature Singapore Pte Ltd. 2025

Y. Yoo, S. C. Lee (eds.), *Reimagining Korea*, Palgrave Series in Contemporary Korean Studies,
https://doi.org/10.1007/978-981-96-6990-5_6

emigration-sending country with a large diaspora;[1] however, entering the twenty-first century, it transitioned into an immigration-receiving country and found itself experiencing reverse migration from the diaspora.

After experiencing the economic crisis and IMF restructuring in the late twentieth century, Korea rapidly transformed from a protectionist economy to an open export-driven neoliberal economic model. From the 1990s onward, with the relocation of domestic small and medium-sized manufacturing companies abroad and a rapid decline in the working-age population, the country faced structural changes akin to those of advanced nations. This neoliberal shift created the need to bring in large-scale, low-skilled foreign labor to maintain the competitiveness of domestic manufacturing and industries that are increasingly confronted with difficulties in recruiting domestic labor.

Like Japan and Taiwan, which were in similar situations, Korea joined the ranks of late immigration countries and adopted strict regulative migration regime, often framed under the discourse of "Developmental Migration State" (Chung et al. 2024). Unlike Europe, which introduced multiculturalism as a new governance ideology and tool for coexistence of different ethnic groups, based on long histories of colonial rule and world wars that fostered population movements and cultural exchanges, Korea introduced immigration as a post-developmental strategy in the era of deindustrialization and declining working-age populations. As a result, the migration regime in Korea has focused on economic revitalization and addressing the lack of labor force, rather than issues of citizenship rights or social integration of migrants. This led to a government-driven, top-down migration regime characterized by selective exclusionary governance based on non-settler programs.

The most representative example of this characteristic is the Employment Permit System (EPS), which unintentionally became "Korea's first immigration program" (Jung et al. 2024). Replacing the Industrial Trainee System, EPS is a low-skilled foreign labor recruitment policy overseen by the Ministry of Employment and Labor, aimed at small and medium-sized businesses (with fewer than 300 employees) in mostly root industries, agriculture, and other sectors requiring strategic consideration or protection. Under this Government to Government (G2G) model, the central

[1] Three are 7.32 million (7,325,143 as of 2021) overseas Koreans, consisting of 4,813,622 foreign nationals (citizens) and 2,511,521 Koreans staying abroad (Overseas Koreans Agency n.d., https://oka.go.kr/oka_en/about/history/).

government signs memorandums of understanding (MOUs) with 17 countries and sponsors labor provision to Korean employers. The foreign workers are matched to jobs through Local Employment Centers in Korea. EPS issues two types of working visas, H-2 and E-9, both of which are granted for an initial period of three years, extendable twice up to a maximum of four years and ten months each time, based on the employer's recommendation. The H-2 visa is given to ethnic Koreans, allowing them to work in diverse low-skilled sectors such as caregiving, housekeeping, serving, and construction while the E-9 visa is provided to foreign nationals for work in manufacturing and agriculture (no service industries with a few exceptions).[2]

These foreign workers (E-9) are guaranteed the same minimum wage as domestic workers but are subject to strict management and regulations, including their assignment to a specific business through a standard contract signed before arrival, with limitations on changing workplaces. Recently, to prevent concentration in Seoul Metropolitan Area, the contract has added clauses restricting movement to this region from other provinces. Through this system, the government closely monitors and governs the employment of foreign workers based on quarterly adjustments made by the Foreign Labor Policy Committee and the Human Resources Development Service of Korea, responding flexibly and efficiently to the country's economic and labor needs.[3]

As of November 2024, EPS workers from the 16 countries with MOUs represent 43% of the total 2.64 million foreign nationals in Korea, including 336,858 workers with E-9 visas and 94,382 with H-2 visas. They form the second-largest group, after overseas Koreans (F-4 visa holders, numbering 560,000). Since most low-skilled foreign workers enter through EPS, their distribution tends to be centered around small and medium-sized industrial cities and rural areas, especially in regions that are dense with small businesses, while large cities like Seoul and Busan, where manufacturing activities are limited, essentially restrict their residence. Only overseas Koreans who are allowed to work in service industries and to hold renewable visas, as a result, reside in large cities like Seoul alongside skilled workers, creating a dual spatial governance system where other low-skilled

[2] Ministry of Labor EPS website, https://www.eps.go.kr/index.jsp

[3] This strict governance by the central government, including severe restriction on socio-spatial mobility and the principles of no dependents and no settlement, differentiates the EPS from other low-skilled immigration programs, such as EB-3 in the United States.

foreign workers are largely assigned to small to medium-sized cities and some rural areas (Jung 2020).

In contrast to long-established immigrant-receiving countries such as United States and Canada, that have created ethnic enclaves in downtown areas of large cities, the selective and controlling nature of Korea's K-migration regime has led to a different ethnic landscape, where various (mostly from developing countries in Asia) ethnic groups, granted the status of low-skilled migrant workers, are dispersed across small and medium-sized industrial cities or rural areas. On Sundays, these workers gather in the old towns of these small cities to shop, interact, and participate in religious activities, giving rise to the pockets of "multicultural spaces" nationwide (Jung and Song 2011; Kim and Jung 2018; Kim 2019). However, as the number of migrants increases, such spaces are also emerging in large cities like Seoul, albeit different from general multicultural spaces that are detached from Korean residents' areas. These multicultural spaces in large cities function as sub-areas where diverse groups encounter each other. Unlike the segregated multicultural spaces in small and medium-sized cities, they utilize the resourceful social-cultural as well as physical infrastructure of large cities and exhibit immersive characteristics with indistinct boundaries. A representative example of this is Little Manila, a multicultural space created around the Hyehwa-dong Cathedral in the center of Seoul, where Filipino migrants and others form a weekend sanctuary. With the dedicated support of the Seoul Archdiocese, Little Manila has been established around Hyehwa-dong Catholic Church. Every Sunday, Filipinos gather here to attend Mass in Tagalog, and a market and other facilities emerge around the church, offering Filipino food and daily necessities. Little Manila has become a vital community hub for Filipino migrant workers, attracting not only other migrants but also Koreans who visit as volunteers, workers, customers, and tourists. The strategic location of Hyehwa-dong Cathedral, along with its extensive networks and resources, has provided unexpected opportunities to cultivate a culturally rich and diverse space. Situated in Daehangno, the former location of Seoul National University's main campus and now one of Seoul's most vibrant cultural districts known for its arts and theater scene, Little Manila exemplifies how the collaboration between religious institutions and urban infrastructure can foster multicultural coexistence. This chapter explores how, within the top-down controlled migration governance in Korea, civil society institutions like the Catholic Church have intervened and influenced the creation and operation of multicultural spaces from below. It aims to examine how religious institutions can act as resources that empower migrants. This study is based on fieldwork conducted from 2008 to 2010 and 2024 to 2025, including field observations, interviews,[4] and literature reviews.

2 Korean Migration Regime and "Unintended" Outcomes

2.1 *"Not Talking About Multiculturalism" but Advocating for "Orderly Immigration"*

The characteristics of Korean-style multiculturalism have already been the subject of much critical research. In summary, South Korea has implemented an assimilationist population policy under the guise of multicultural family support policies, rather than pursuing multiculturalism that guarantees the civil rights of migrants (Kim 2011, 2013; Lee 2023; Oh 2010). Two main criticisms are embedded in these claims: first, that these policies aim to support assimilation into Korean culture rather than guaranteeing the right to cultural difference, and second, that they are distorted forms of multiculturalism limited to marriage migrants (particularly women). These mean that so-called multiculturalism only applies to marriage migrants while excluding the large portion of other immigrants such as labor migrants. The latter is only considered as temporary guests not falling into potential residents and target for social integration. Such arguments consistently criticize the Korean government for failing to implement proper multiculturalism.

Looking back, this implies that South Korea has never genuinely practiced multiculturalism. In various government and local government documents and policies, the term "multiculturalism" is hardly mentioned. While academia, the media, and civil society engage in diverse discussions about transitioning to a multicultural society, the government has never declared South Korea a multicultural society or announced the adoption of multiculturalism.

This situation is similar to that of the Japanese government, which officially does not recognize multiculturalism but permits various foreigner-related policies by local governments under the term

[4] All names are pseudonyms.

"multicultural coexistence" (Choi 2011). Like Japan, the Korean government still predominantly uses the term "foreigner" instead of immigrants or migrants. Even the term "immigration policy" itself appeared for the first time in the *4th Master Plan for Immigration Policy* (2023–2027).[5]

This hesitancy to readily embrace the term "multiculturalism" highlights the government's deliberate caution. In an era where the foreign population has reached 2.64 million (5.2% of the total population),[6] the decreasing working-age population and regional depopulation have made it more urgent to bring in foreign labor and long-term residents. However, instead of adopting Western-style multiculturalism, South Korea has sought a different approach—one that minimizes societal misunderstandings and prejudice.

The concept of "orderly immigration" is particularly notable. According to Yoon (2008), a leading Korean migration scholar, "orderly immigration" refers to "effectively managing the scale and qualifications of immigrants and their status within the host country to minimize harm to nationals and contribute to societal development" (JoongAng Ilbo 2022.9.27). This political rhetoric essentially replaces Western-style multiculturalism's emphasis on guaranteeing immigrants' civil rights and rights to difference. Instead, it attempts to maintain economic development strategies while gradually accepting foreigners as needed, paying minimal social integration costs. The frequent use of this term in government documents and discussions surrounding the establishment of an immigration office suggests it is a rhetorical device for seeking an alternative to K-multiculturalism without explicitly endorsing multiculturalism.

[5] A comprehensive, five-year, government-wide master plan finalized in December 2023. The five key policy objectives in this plan were as follows: promote economic and regional development through immigration, ensure a safe and orderly society, foster social integration between nationals and immigrants, respect immigrants' human rights and values, and establish an immigration administration that aligns with global standards. As these objectives suggest, the "foreigner policy" traditionally adhered to was officially replaced by an "immigration policy" for the first time. The plan also outlined a specific direction emphasizing "orderly" immigration and "social integration" (Korea Immigration Service 2024a, 2 July).

[6] Ministry of Justice, *Immigration and Foreign Policy Statistics Monthly Report*, November 2024.

2.2 *Paradox of Multicultural Coexistence Arising from a Top-Down Migration Regime*

The adoption of "orderly immigration" instead of multiculturalism has led to the establishment of a functionalist migration regime based on selective, top-down, and socio-spatial mobility control (Jung 2020). This approach has resulted in a disregard for the civil rights and coexistence of migrants. While appearing to symbolically endorse Western-style multiculturalism, South Korea's migration regime lacks a discourse on citizenship (Kim 2011). Instead of implementing comprehensive multiculturalism across society, it has produced selectively limited spaces of multicultural coexistence.

Government-led immigration programs such as EPS have created unique Korean-style multicultural spaces, distinct from Western-style ethnic enclaves (Jung et al. 2024). Western ethnic enclaves are socio-spatial outcomes reflecting migration history, where ethnic groups arriving at different times establish survival spaces in response to discrimination and exclusion from the mainstream society (Portes and Manning 1986). Examples include Chinatowns and Koreatowns, often linked to urban decline and suburbanization (e.g., white flight) in Western cities.

In Korea, however, ethnic-specific spaces like Incheon's Chinatown and Seoul's Yeonbyeon (Yanbian) Town are rare. Outside of these two examples, most ethnic spaces are not exclusively occupied by single ethnic groups. Instead, they tend to be temporary shared spaces reflecting the precarious status of foreign low-skilled migrants under strict immigration control in Korea.

The government-led, top-down migration regime enforces rigorous socio-spatial mobility control and a principle of non-permanence, which prevents the bottom-up formation of organic migrants' spaces. Furthermore, the functionalist stratification of migrants based on skill level (Chung 2020) discourages separation by ethnicity or religion. For instance, Muslims, Christians, and Buddhists can be randomly assigned to work and share spaces together unless the employers cautiously arrange them.

For EPS workers, who typically work six days a week, Sundays are their only day off, during which they engage in routines like socializing, shopping, and sending remittances. Markets that cater to these workers often emerge in areas where EPS workers gather, functioning as spaces of multicultural coexistence that are multinational, multiethnic, and multicultural in character.

3 Multicultural Spaces

3.1 *Why Discuss Multicultural "Spaces" Instead of Multiculturalism?*

The concept of multicultural space was first academically introduced by Choi Byung-Doo (2009). It refers to the spatial conceptualization of multicultural processes arising from transnational migration in the context of glocalization. This concept is based on the premise that multiculturalism is not universal but is rather a regionally selective and spatially discriminative process. Choi (2009) criticized Western multiculturalism for being almost synonymous with policy and overly focused on rights discourse, which can neglect the inequality in distribution and struggles for recognition. He proposed multicultural space as a conceptual tool to capture multiculturalism from the below and its multi-scalar processes (Choi 2009).

Following Choi's suggestion for a spatialized approach to multiculturalism, many Korean scholars have applied this concept to explain transnational migration into Korea and its impact (Cha 2014; Kim 2019; Kong 2013; Jung and Song 2011). Most of these studies have utilized the concept as a tool to narrate a story or describe changes in specific sites resulting from transnational migration. In this context, space is understood as a physical entity, a unit of analysis, or a background for subjects—separate from the social processes or agency that produce it. This flat understanding of space, often referred to as an absolute perspective on space, aligns with the Euclidean and Newtonian views that treat space as a mere container for social processes. However, this perspective limits a deeper understanding of the dynamics occurring in and around multicultural spaces. Alternative perspectives that have emerged since the spatial turn in social sciences—often under the name of the relational approach—propose a different understanding. Rather than viewing spatiality as a fixed, physical entity separate from social processes, the relational approach sees space as an integral part of these processes, emerging from the relationships between things. While the former approach considers space as a static or bounded entity, the latter conceptualizes spatiality as fluid, multi-scalar, networked, and, most importantly, socially constructed.[7]

[7] Inspired by Henri Lefebvre's theory on the production of space, the intertwined understanding between spatiality and social processes—termed socio-spatial dialectics—has evolved through extensive debates in political economy and critical geography. For some key texts and summary, refer to works by Lefebvre (1974/1991), Harvey (1973), Soja (1980), Massey (2005), and Sheppard (2019), among others.

Building upon the relational approach to space, I aim to expand the conceptual utility of multicultural space as a tool to capture the characteristics of what I may call "K-multiculturalism."[8] In essence, I attempt to conceptualize multicultural space as a social construct that emerges out of transnational migration and related processes. In other words, multicultural space refers to a socio-space that mediates the ontological phenomenon of coexistence of difference in a specific place through the multiscale processes of migration, rather than merely serving as a container for the institution of multiculturalism (Jung et al. 2024).

The rationale for adopting a spatial approach is twofold: first, as Choi (2009) asserts, it addresses the spatial selectivity inherent in multicultural processes; second, it seeks to explore alternatives to Western multiculturalism theories. Developing a Korean model of multiculturalism requires integrating locally embedded, socially mediated, and historically path-dependent characteristics alongside universal principles. In the absence of an established model and terminology to describe it, adopting the concept of "multicultural space" from a relational perspective offers flexible frameworks to capture the emergence of spatially selective multicultural coexistence. This phenomenon is driven by Korea's (post) developmentalist migration governance within the context of uneven regional development, and the resulting urban and social environments, such as the growing polarization between the Capital Region and others, and rich sociocultural infrastructures in large cities, all of which contributed to constructing unique conditions for the emergence of Little Manila. Through this spatialized approach, I propose examining the interplay between the universal process of transnational migration and the locally specific process of multicultural coexistence.

[8] For theoretical expansion and application of multicultural space, see Jung (2010), and Jung et al. (2024). Jung (2010) explored the glocal composition of multicultural spaces, asserting that while transnational mobility created a transnational social field called Little Manila, the local contingency and the unique urban spatiality of Korea made Little Manila locally embedded. Jung et al. (2024) demonstrated that multicultural spaces are not only glocally constructed but also formed from the bottom-up through everyday encounters and practices, using Gimhae as a case study.

Whether a society like Korea—where transnational migration is rapidly increasing but multiculturalism is not fully embraced as a governance ideology—can be called a multicultural society remains ambiguous. Simply having more foreigners does not make a society multicultural. Depending on how efforts to coexist with foreigners evolve, concepts like multicultural transformation, multicultural coexistence, and social integration might be used, and something beyond multiculturalism might even be devised. The concept of multicultural space may offer useful insights into cases like Korea, where transnational migration leads to geographically selective multicultural interactions rather than a comprehensive shift toward multiculturalism.

Multicultural space can also be refined theoretically as an accumulation strategy and governance technology of post-developmentalist states that employ neoliberal migration regimes, characterized by stratification of migrants (Chung 2020; Jung 2020) and socio-spatial mobility control. This study seeks to explore the Korean application and expansion of multicultural space using Little Manila in Seoul as a case study in this theoretical context.

3.2 *The Strangers Who Appeared on the Street of Culture and Arts in a Global City*

Korean-style multicultural spaces appear in two main types. Heo (2021) proposed two types of foreigner aggregation areas, one born out of the geopolitical context of colonialism and post-colonialism, especially in Korea during the Cold War and post-Cold War periods, and the other born out of the foreigner aggregation areas created by the EPS and subsequent migration governance. The first includes the first-generation multicultural spaces such as Itaewon, which developed around US military bases, and Incheon Chinatown, which served as a treaty port. The second includes the second-generation multicultural spaces created by low-skilled foreign workers and marriage migrants that emerged recently. In addition to this historical classification, I propose to divide Korean multicultural spaces into permanent and temporary (weekend) ones to capture the dynamic of the second case, the majority in Korea. Permanent multicultural spaces include historical multicultural spaces formed during the colonial and post-colonial periods as well as former temporary multicultural spaces that have become permanent. A representative example is the Korean Chinese enclave in the Daerim 2-dong, often called as Yanbian Town, in southwest Seoul. The ethnic town is expanding to places like *Yanggokchi* (Lamb skewer) Street in Jayang-dong in Seoul, and growing cities like Bucheon and Siheung with large stock of affordable housing outside Seoul. Up to now, the only multicultural space that has transitioned from temporary to permanent and is monopolized by a specific ethnic group is the Korean Chinese Town. The Korean Chinese community is the largest foreigner group in the country. As of November 2024, Korean Chinese people account for 24% of all foreign residents in Korea, totaling 642,846 individuals out of 2,692,359 foreign residents (Korea Immigration Service 2024b.11).

Due to their high language proficiency and cultural adaptability and the stability granted to them in terms of residence, Korean Chinese are more empowered and have higher socio-spatial mobility than any other foreign groups. There is no dispute that the Korean Chinese are the only ethnic group with a permanent ethnic space in Seoul. However, ironically, their space is often perceived as a space of discrimination and exclusion, truly seen as an “enclave” (Bark and Jung 2023). It is very similar to the process of creation and operational mechanism of Western ethnic enclaves, which were established by invading low-cost housing areas that became hollowed out and slum-like after the removal of the old industrial district. Their space was naturally created by an ethnic group with relatively high autonomy and socio-cultural resources, largely unaffected by the hierarchical governance of the Korean migration regime.

Except for the spaces of the Korean Chinese, most of the spaces for migrants in Korea are temporary and non-permanent, although with some becoming permanent. This latter type reflects the influence of the Korean migration regime. Unlike the ethnicized and segregated first type, the second type is multiracial, with unclear boundaries, and temporarily occupies existing urban facilities. This reflects the result of the Korean migration regime’s unintended promotion of multiracial/multinational coexistence by stratifying migrants based on their skills, rather than segregating them by race and ethnicity. The controlled placement of migrants in different industries and regions through EPS led to their isolation in small and medium-sized industrial cities, away from the center of large cities. This means that the placement was not a process of voluntary settlement but was strongly influenced by top-down arrangements.

In the midst of this process, weekend-type multicultural spaces that temporarily occupy the old city center are increasing. The "Borderless Village" in Ansan, which has been repeatedly mentioned as a residence for foreign workers in Korea, is a representative example of a temporary settlement that has become permanent. However, not in the industrial city of Ansan, located near the Banwol Industrial Complex, but in the costly global city of Seoul, a group of strangers, mainly Filipino workers, have temporarily occupied one of Seoul's major cultural spaces: the so-called Hyehwa-dong Filipino community. Their space, also called Little Manila, is one of the few foreigner settlements in Korea that is based on ethnicity.

3.3 *Religious Institution That Facilitated Uneasy Coexistence: Catholic Church and Daehangno*

Little Manila is located at the edge of Daehangno (meaning University Avenue), one of Seoul's representative "cultural and artistic streets" or "cultural districts"[9] (Fig. 6.1). Since being designated as a "Cultural and Artistic Street" in 1985, this area, which stretches from the Jongno 5-ga intersection to the Hyehwa Rotary, was designated as the second "Cultural District" in 2004, after Insa-dong.[10] The reason Little Manila emerged here is because of Hyehwa-dong Cathedral (Fig. 6.2). In 1996, the Archdiocese of Seoul established Tagalog Masses for Filipino migrants at Hyehwa-dong Cathedral, which led to the emergence of related service facilities in the surrounding area. Every Sunday afternoon, a multicultural space for the Filipino community was formed around the cathedral. The reason why, every weekend, the edge of Daehangno, filled with young Koreans, became crowded with another group of young people, Filipino migrant workers, is because Hyehwa-dong Cathedral is located at the end of Daehangno (Fig. 6.1).[11]

[9] Jongno District Office (n.d.), https://tour.jongno.go.kr/tour/tour/indvdlz/view.do?nttId=34102&viewType=BODY&dongCode=1111016900&setCategory=1. According to Encyclopedia of Korean Culture (n.d.), a "Cultural District" is a legal and policy term created to protect and nurture specific areas rich in cultural resources (https://encykorea.aks.ac.kr/Article/E0067979).

[10] Jongno District Office, *Ibid.*

[11] Hyehwa-dong Cathedral is located at the Hyehwa Rotary, at the boundary between Hyehwa-dong and Seongbuk-dong, just about 100 meters from Exit 1 of Hyehwa Station on Subway Line 4.

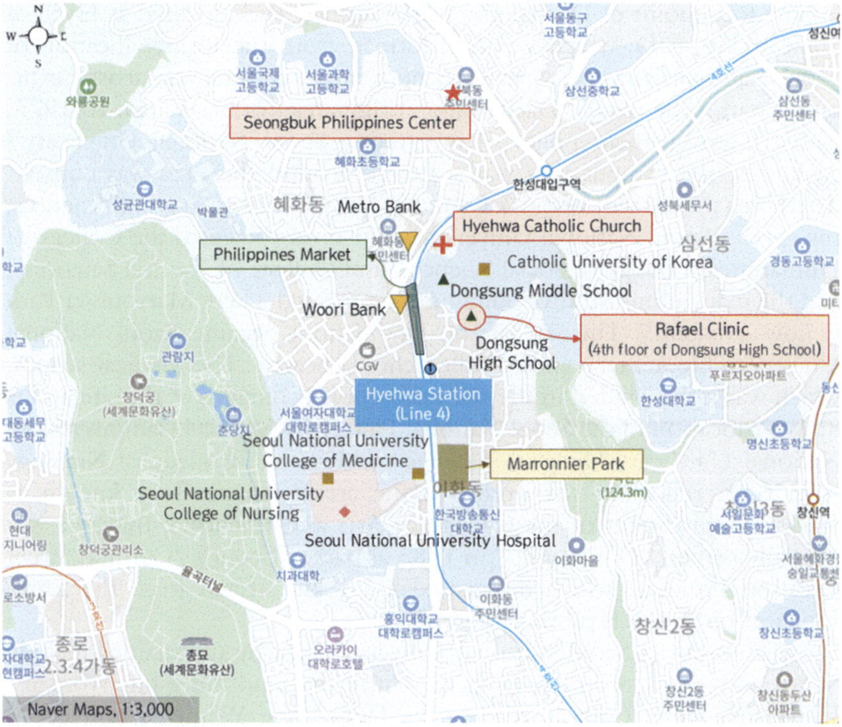

Fig. 6.1 Map of Little Manila

Fig. 6.2 Hyehwa-dong Cathedral (left, 2024.11.) and after Mass (right, 2010.11.)

The focal point of Daehangno is Marronnier Park, located at Hyehwa Station (Fig. 6.1), which was transformed from the former location of Seoul National University's main campus into a cultural and artistic exhibition park. The name "Daehangno" originates from this area. In 1975, with the government policy of integrating Seoul National University's campuses, the campus that was scattered around this area was consolidated into the current Gwanak Campus. The College of Arts and Sciences, the core of Seoul National University (now diversified into the College of Humanities, College of Social Sciences, and College of Natural Sciences), and the main administrative building were located where Marronnier Park is now situated.[12] The site of the Law School became Seoul National University Elementary and Middle Schools nearby. The medical school, which was not included in the relocation policy, remains at the site and is now the location of the Seoul National University Medical Campus (Seoul National University Hospital, College of Medicine, College of Nursing) (Fig. 6.1), reflecting the origin of the area's name. Once known as Munridae-gil (Street of the College of Arts and Sciences), this area was officially named "Daehangno" in 1985 as part of Seoul's "Cultural Street Creation Project," which designated a 1.1 km stretch from the Ehwa Intersection to the Hyehwa Rotary.[13]

In addition to Seoul National University, nearby universities include Sungkyunkwan University, Hanshin University, and Sungshin Women's University, while Catholic University, Deokseong Women's University, and Seoul Women's University also have campuses in Daehangno, maintaining the image of the area as a university district. Even after the relocation of the Seoul National University campus, this area developed into a cultural and artistic street, becoming the center of small theaters, performances, and exhibitions, thus maintaining a vibrant, youthful, and open cultural atmosphere. Despite being officially part of Hyehwa-dong and having Hyehwa Station, most Koreans still refer to this area as Daehangno due to its historical and cultural significance.

While the area is commonly known as the cultural district of Hyehwa-dong or Daehangno, another lesser-known feature is its

[12] In the center of Marronnier Park, old campus sculptures remain, and on the right side is the former main building of Seoul National University, now used as the building for the Arts Council (SBS 2008.11.21.).

[13] Jongno District Office, https://tour.jongno.go.kr/tour/tour/indvdlz/view.do?nttId=34102&viewType=BODY&dongCode=1111016900&setCategory=1).

proximity to Seongbuk-dong, which is often referred to as "Korea's Little Rome"[14] or "Korean Vatican." Located across from the Hyehwa Rotary at the end of Daehangno, Seongbuk-dong (near Hanseong University Station) is home to the Seongbuk-dong Cathedral, which was separated from Hyehwa-dong Cathedral, and over 20 Catholic institutions clustered around it (Parantar, 2008, Interview; recited from Jung 2010, 36).

The Filipino Catholic community, which moved to Hyehwa-dong Cathedral in 1996 from Jayang-dong Cathedral, has been renting a four-story villa for free since 2001 from the Filipino Ministry Center under the Archdiocese of Seoul (Seongbuk Philipppines Center in Fig. 6.1). This building, located just 10 minutes from the cathedral, serves as a center for Filipino migrant workers, a women's shelter, offices, and a rectory (Catholic Peace Weekly 2006.5.24). The Hyehwa-dong Cathedral is surrounded by Catholic institutions such as Catholic University Sungshin campus, Catholic Catechetical Institute, and Catholic schools (Dongseong Middle and High Schools) (Fig. 6.1). The Filipino community's relocation from Jayang-dong to this area was not merely about moving a place of worship but also about gaining better access to the Korean Catholic network and securing a material foundation to tap into the social and cultural capital of Daehangno. Through this movement, the location of Daehangno's cultural and artistic street and the religious significance of "Korea's Vatican" have been connected via the Filipino community, creating a multicultural space that is inclusive, free-spirited, and youthful. This combination may be a historical coincidence, but the force mediating this coincidence is the religious institution of the Korean Catholic Church. Moreover, the coexistence of high culture in Daehangno's cultural street and the subculture of migrant workers is accepted because of the shared openness and inclusiveness of both the Korean Catholic Church and the university district culture.

4 The Origins and Operation of Little Manila

4.1 *The Origins of Little Manila*

The origin of Little Manila dates back to the era before the present-day Hyehwa-dong, going back to the time of Jayang-dong. Filipino migrants began arriving in South Korea around the time of the 1988 Seoul

[14]The Catholic Times (2013.4.16). https://www.catholictimes.org/article/201304160023279

Olympics, making them part of the first generation of foreign workers who began settling in Korea before the introduction of the EPS (2004) and the establishment of diplomatic relations with China (1992). Many of them entered as tourists and worked in small factories that were operating in the northern areas of Seoul. In 1980, due to the Metropolitan Area Readjustment Planning Act, which aimed to prevent overcrowding in the capital area, the establishment of new factories and the reconstruction of existing ones were prohibited in Seoul, and the remaining factories were relocated to the outskirts of Seoul, such as in Gyeonggi Province.

Filipino migrants, who are over 80% Catholic, tend to form communities centered around churches in their new societies as well. At that time, Jayang-dong Church was not only relatively close to the workplaces of Filipino workers but was also the church where Sister Marian, who had dedicated herself to supporting Filipino migrant workers, was based (Kim 2010). In addition to Sister Marian, Mexican missionaries from the Guadalupe Foreign Missionary Society and priests from the Maryknoll Foreign Missionary Society helped form a transnational Catholic network centered around Jayang-dong Church. This network played a key role in organizing the first Filipino community in South Korea, "Jayang-dong Filipino Community" (Kim 2010, 54–55).

The Jayang-dong Filipino Community, formed in 1992 by Jayang-dong Church and Filipino workers, organized its activities with the Philippine Ministry Center next to the church as its base. The Philippine Foreign Missionary Society (MSP) began sending priests around this time to support Overseas Filipino Workers (OFWs). Under the cooperation of both the South Korean and Filipino Catholic Churches, Filipino migrant workers began building a voluntary community to address poor working conditions, living difficulties, and language barriers. The Philippine national sport, basketball, was replicated by creating a league for OFWs in Korea, and they even began publishing a newsletter named after the Philippine national flower, "Sampaguita" (Kim 2010, 56–57). In addition to community activities, the Jayang-dong Filipino Community, with the help of Jayang-dong Church, started offering general migration services, including remittances, free legal consultations, and job placement services. At that time, there was no official migrant worker program in Korea, and ethnic communities, apart from the Korean Chinese community, were almost non-existent. Therefore, there was virtually no infrastructure to support migrants. In the absence of such migration infrastructure, the

Catholic Church filled the gap and helped establish a community where faith and labor merged, relying on the dedication of priests and community members.

However, as the number of workers increased, the Jayang-dong community reached its limits in accommodating the growing population. Hearing about this situation, Cardinal Stephen Kim Sou-hwan (the Archbishop of Seoul at the time) arranged for the community to relocate to Hyehwa-dong Church, where he himself attended. Under the support of the Seoul Archdiocese, the community relocated in 1996, where they resumed the Tagalog-language mass. With the arrival of Father Glenn Giovanni Jaron, the second priest of the MSP, in 1998, the "Hyehwa-dong Filipino Catholic Community (HFCC)" was established. When they moved, the community had about 800 members, but by around 2010, it had grown to over 2000 members, and the community served as the center for Filipino migrant workers across Seoul and the surrounding metropolitan area. Since the 25th anniversary ceremony in 2017, the community has changed its name to "Seoul Filipino Catholic Community (SFCC)" and continues to thrive.[15]

Unlike most migrant communities that are centered in industrial cities like Ansan and Hwaseong in Gyeonggi Province, the Filipino migrant community established its base in the heart of Seoul, an area without factories, relatively early on, due to the support of the Catholic Church.

4.2 *Transnational Operation and Local Embeddedness of Little Manila*

With transnational support from both the South Korean and Filipino Catholic Churches, the Filipino community that settled in Hyehwa-dong absorbed local resources from both the Korean Catholic Church and the area of Hyehwa dong itself, thereby becoming embedded in the local multicultural space. The evolution of Little Manila from an enclave exclusive to a specific ethnic group to a multicultural space can be understood through the combination of transnational deterritorialization and local reterritorialization processes (Kwon 2005; Jung 2010).

The transformation of Little Manila into a multicultural space, rather than an exclusive ethnic enclave, occurred because it was initially

[15] Seoul Archdiocese Migrant Ministry, http://www.seoulmigrant.net/load.asp?subPage=312

supported by a specific religion, Catholicism, but leveraged the transnational nature of this religion to create a space with a multicultural, multiethnic character. It evolved into a space that was not closed off from other groups but rather became an open venue for various people (including non-Catholics and non-Filipinos). Additionally, the vulnerability of the space, as temporary in nature, that is "borrowed" every weekend, contributed to its flexibility and fluidity, which prevented the formation of exclusionary boundaries. Instead, it shared the existing urban infrastructure and created a flexible multicultural space that was neither ethnic-exclusive nor an enclave. This transnational migration process and Catholic missionary work combined with the local specifics of South Korea's migration governance and Hyehwa-dong's assets, resulting in a temporary multicultural space where various races and cultures coexist without being exclusively occupied by any one group.

As a multicultural space, Little Manila is both transnational and contains elements of local contingencies. The transnational and local configuration of Little Manila operates through several key mechanisms. Among them, two representative physical infrastructures are the street market and the Raphael Clinic.

4.2.1 Filipino Street Market

A visual marker of Little Manila is not actually Hyehwa-dong Church, but rather the Filipino street market. Located between Hyehwa-dong Church and Exit 1 at the Hyehwa subway station, the Filipino market is a temporary weekend market that opens on Sunday afternoons to coincide with the Tagalog-language mass. This market sells a variety of goods needed by Filipino migrants, such as daily necessities, food, ingredients, small items, souvenirs, and services (Fig. 6.3). Although it flourished until around 2010, reaching its peak just before the COVID-19 pandemic, it has since become somewhat quiet with fewer customers.[16] The market was once introduced in various blogs as a unique experience space and a place to experience Filipino food, with most of the store owners being Filipino marriage migrants and their Korean husbands, while most of the

[16] The decrease in Filipino gatherings in Little Manila is likely due to a combination of factors. The COVID-19 pandemic directly contributed to the decline by prompting many Filipinos to return home (refer to Fig. 6.5). Additionally, changes in Korea's migration geography, including the emergence of more migrant centers elsewhere, have also played a significant role.

Fig. 6.3 Filipino street market (Left, 2009.12., Right, 2024.11)

customers were Filipino migrant workers. While some customers come to the market after attending mass, many others who do not attend Hyehwa-dong Church also gather here, and the space functions as a meeting place or a sort of haven.

Many of the goods sold here are imported from the Philippines, but some are brought in through domestic distribution networks and peddlers (Kwon 2005; Jung 2010). Before smartphones became widespread, international calling cards for the Philippines were a key service offering, but since then, the market has shifted to offering services such as tailored mobile phone plans for Filipinos in Korea, as well as selling the latest phones, and, more recently, promoting remittance apps (Fig. 6.4). Filipino food and necessities attract not only Filipino migrant workers but also Filipino students and marriage migrants, and serve as a draw for non-Filipinos, including both Koreans and tourists, thereby creating a cultural space of the Philippines, or Little Manila, within South Korea. This "translocality" (Kwon 2005; Jung 2010; Greiner and Sakdapolrak 2013) functioning within the transnational network connecting the Philippines and South Korea was initially created through religious practices related to Catholicism, but has since evolved into a place of encounter where diverse people meet, not limited to Catholics.

Fig. 6.4 Change in cutting edge products from the 2G phones with a carrier (left, 2009. 11.) to a remittance app (right, 2024.11.)

For example, David, a Protestant who attends a different church, identifies himself as part of the Hyehwa-dong community despite not being a Catholic. He works as a vendor at the market, selling hats, and sees the market as a space of safety and familiarity for Filipino migrant workers, as he feels that it provides an inclusive environment for marginalized individuals like himself.

> I feel at ease when I come here. It feels like “Little Manila,” almost like home. ... As undocumented migrants like us, we feel safer among Filipinos. There’s a priest here for us, a church, and we can speak freely in Tagalog. ... It’s a place for Filipinos. I’m not a Catholic, but I consider myself part of the Hyehwa-dong community. (David, Interview, 2009; quoted from Jung 2010, 308)

Rosy, a former Filipina student who graduated from a college in Korea and now works for a platform company in Korea, regularly visits the Filipino market to promote a new financial app her company launched. She markets the app as a service that can not only facilitate remittances but also handle international payments (see Fig. 6.4 right). She noted that the response to this service has been very positive (Interview, 2024.11.24). Compared to the days when people had to wait in long lines at Sunday bank branches to send remittances, she feels that the twenty first-century digital revolution has brought about a fundamental innovation in the mobility and access to information and resources for migrant workers. Most of the migrant workers are young and have rapidly adopted this digital transformation, which is expected to significantly change the elements and formation of multicultural spaces in the future.

4.2.2 Raphael Clinic

Along with the Filipino market, the Raphael Clinic is another iconic location in Little Manila. The Raphael Clinic began as a free medical service for migrant workers shortly after the formation of the Hyehwa-dong Filipino Catholic community. It started on April 13, 1997, at the Hyehwa-dong Church's Baek Dong-gwan makeshift clinic and later expanded to Dongseong High School, a private school belongs to Korean Catholic Church, where it continues to operate today. After the success of the 1st Raphael Clinic in Hyehwa-dong, it opened branches in Dongducheon and Cheonan and recently started medical services for multicultural families. In the meantime, Raphael International was established, expanding its operations to Mongolia, Laos, Nepal, Myanmar, and the Philippines (Raphael Clinic n.d.).[17]

The growth story of the Raphael Clinic, which has become a large and systematic medical institution, is truly miraculous, akin to the "loaves and fishes" story. It all began in a prayer meeting at Seoul National University College of Medicine (SNUCM). Professor Ahn, Curie (Sohwa Teresa, Seongbuk-dong Catholic Church), a member of the association of Catholic Professors at SNUCM, along with four students from the Catholic Student Association (CASA) and their mentor, Professor Kim Jeon, decided to provide medical services to migrant workers near Hyehwa-dong Church (Maeil Business Newspaper 2017.5.30.). The inspiration for this decision was largely influenced by Cardinal Kim Souhwan, Ahn's lifelong mentor (*The Catholic Times* 2014a.6.8.). In 1996, Cardinal Kim came to know about the poor human rights conditions of migrant workers after hearing the case of Pakistani death-row inmates.[18]

[17] http://raphael.or.kr/ko_KR/

[18] In 1993, two Pakistani migrant workers, Mr. Aziz and Mr. Jamil, were convicted of the alleged murder of fellow Pakistanis and sentenced to death by a Korean court. They sent a

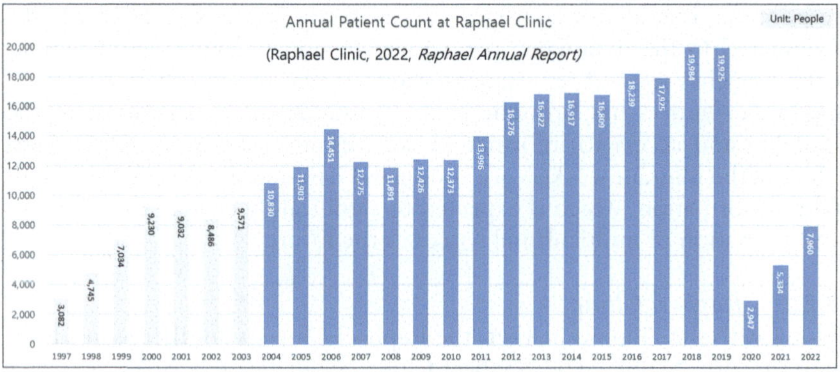

Fig. 6.5 Annual number of patients in Raphael Clinic

This awareness led the Archdiocese of Seoul to become actively involved in migrant workers' rights advocacy. Following Cardinal Kim's request, Professor Ahn, who had visited the two Pakistani migrant workers on death row, decided to leverage her medical expertise to serve migrant workers (Maeil Business Newspaper 2017.5.30.; Chosun Ilbo 2016.2.27.).

With the active support of Cardinal Kim and the Archdiocese of Seoul, the Raphael Clinic, which started as a street clinic with Ahn and several colleagues, grew into a hospital that treats over 300 patients weekly and has accumulated over 300,000 patients (Fig. 6.5). It now offers over 20 medical specialties and collaborates with 36 hospitals across Korea. It also expanded internationally with Raphael International, a medical service organization for underdeveloped countries, and Raphael Academy, which trains medical volunteers, and the Raphael Sharing Foundation, which provides medical welfare for marginalized groups (The Catholic Times 2023.7.18.). Curie Ahn, who was the founder of Raphael Clinic, expanded her role internationally as the chairwoman of Raphael International and the Raphael Sharing Foundation (*The Catholic Times* 2014b.6.3.). As a result of these efforts, Raphael Clinic has won prestigious awards such as

letter to Cardinal Stephen Kim Sou-hwan, asserting their innocence and stating they were unjustly denied proper legal assistance due to language barriers and lack of understanding. In response, Cardinal Kim entrusted the Catholic Human Rights Committee with investigating the case and sought cooperation from international Catholic institutions (The Catholic Times 2011. 4.14. https://www.catholictimes.org/article/201104140006672). This initiative led the Archdiocese of Seoul to become one of the earliest advocates in Korea for the human rights of death-row inmates and migrant workers.

the Korea Human Rights Award, the Asan Award, and the POSCO Cheongam Award, presenting a groundbreaking model for migrant workers' healthcare (Maeil Newspaper 2016.4.3.).

Raphael Clinic's reputation spread quickly, and it became a free clinic not only for Filipino migrants but for many other foreign nationals. One migrant worker from China, who regularly uses the clinic, even noted that despite having several free clinics for overseas Koreans, she prefers Raphael Clinic because it is renowned for having "Seoul National University doctors."

> You have to come here to see Seoul National University doctors. It's famous for being effective. ... There's a bigger hospital in our neighborhood, and it's free, but they don't have Seoul National University doctors. (Interview with a Chinese migrant worker, December 2009)

In fact, the clinic's users represent a wide range of nationalities, with Filipinos making up only about 30% of the clientele. As of 2019, patients came from as many as 97 countries, and in 2022, this number had decreased slightly to 65, due to the pandemic (Fig. 6.6). While the first migrant worker clinic was established as a result of the settlement of Filipino migrant workers at Hyehwa-dong Church, Raphael Clinic has

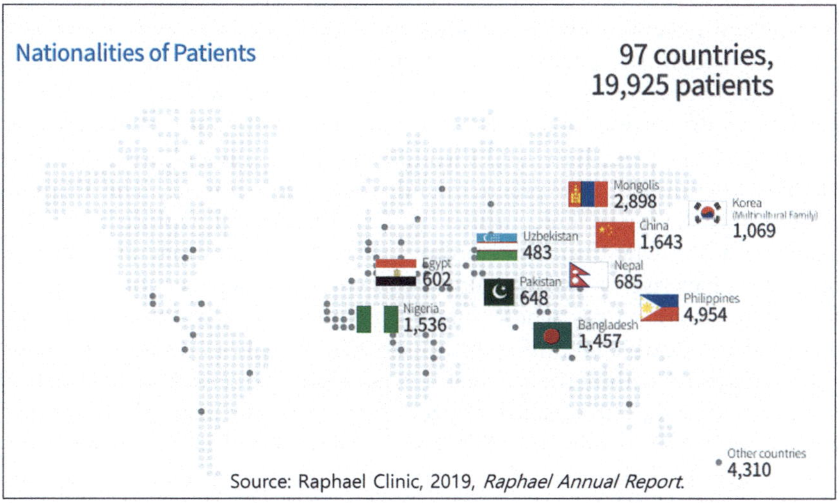

Fig. 6.6 Nationalities of Raphael Clinic patients

since become a crossroads where countless foreigners, beyond just Filipinos and Catholics, are welcomed and encounter each other. This intersection, which began in Hyehwa-dong, has expanded to Dongducheon and Cheonan, and through Raphael International, it is connecting to Mongolia and many other parts of Asia. The birth and miraculous growth of the Raphael Clinic involved many coincidental events, people, and circumstances, but the key element that brought all of these together was the religious organization of Hyehwa-dong Church and the Archdiocese of Seoul, with Catholicism as the unifying faith that inspired commitment and solidarity among many people. In addition to key figures like Cardinal Kim and Professor Ahn, there were people both within and outside of the Catholic Church who contributed. Most notably, the Archdiocese of Seoul played a significant role by providing free use of Dongseong High School after Hyehwa-dong Church. The success of Raphael Clinic has significantly contributed to the maintenance of Little Manila's weekend community for nearly 30 years. This case demonstrates that religious institutions, with their faith, networks, and diverse resources operating on both local and international levels, serve as passionate and effective mediators in supporting transnational migrants. This positions them as well-suited agents to facilitate multicultural spaces.

4.3 Contact Zone: Place of Encounter

If transnational composition and local rootedness are key mechanisms that create multicultural spaces, a crucial element that defines these spaces is the "place" where encounters are mediated. In other words, what distinguishes multicultural spaces from other spaces is that heterogeneous encounters take place here, and through the repetition and normalization of these encounters, new practices and ways of life emerge. The Filipino market and Raphael Clinic, which we have previously explored, are the frontline places where such encounters are realized. Homogeneous crossbreeding gives rise to exclusive enclaves, whereas heterogeneous encounters create open spaces where internal diversity coexists, thus fostering inclusive and flexible identities. Although ethnic enclaves do have diversity and exceptions within them, they are generally perceived as segregated places because they are exclusive spaces formed by the principle of homogeneity rather than diversity. What sets multicultural spaces apart from ethnic enclaves is that even if a specific ethnic group represents the space, they do not exclusively occupy it. Little Manila is claimed by the Filipino community, but in reality, it holds only limited occupancy, temporarily borrowing the space of the mainstream group, the indigenous Koreans. This vulnerability places them not as rulers but as co-users. In Little Manila, Filipino migrant workers and indigenous Koreans regularly encounter each other, sometimes helping one another or clashing, leading to mutual learning.

While Filipino migrant workers are in a subordinate position as factory laborers during the week, they appear as guests, worshipers, and patients in Little Manila on Sundays. Unlike the Catholic Church, which hosts them with the fundamental principle of hospitality based on religious faith, Koreans they encounter in commercial spaces or on the streets often show prejudice and coldness toward them. A typical example is when Koreans who welcome them as guests feel uncomfortable with the sudden reversal of power dynamics.

One employee at a bar, which had become a regular hangout for Filipino migrant workers, expressed the following:

> I'm not sure what the merit is in having so many Filipinos come. ... Honestly, they don't really order but do a lot of running around. They even bring their own food. They only order beer. ... Since they are foreign workers, the sales per table are much lower. Our boss doesn't like it. ... And the food they bring is so greasy, cleaning up afterward is really tough. (Korean part-time worker in his 20s, Interview, July 26, 2009)

The young male employee, who had to serve Filipino migrant workers whom he considered inferior to himself, referred to them as "those kids" or "Filipino kids" in a derogatory manner but paradoxically described the business as "multinational" and "global," recognizing it as possessing culturally superior assets due to the uncomfortable nature of dealing with these customers, which set it apart from other restaurants.

> I heard the previous owner was on good terms with people from the extremes, so they treated foreigners kindly, and a lot of them started coming. ... Since the new owner took over two months ago, the store has become known as cultural and global, so people keep coming. ... On Sunday afternoons, it's totally multinational and global here. (Ibid.)

While some are reluctantly serving "global" customers, others actively try to attract them. The Woori Bank branch across from Hyehwa-dong

Church was designated as a "foreign worker remittance-specialized branch" and began offering remittance services for Filipino workers every Sunday starting in June 2006 (The Hankyoreh Newspaper 2006.6.22.). The deputy branch manager who strongly led this service stated, "The actual profit margin is negative, but we are investing for the future," and expressed excitement about the promotional effect, saying, "In the Philippines, it become so famous that people think Woori Bank is the only one in Hyehwa-dong" (Interview, December 6, 2009). He also opened a "Filipino Workers Library and Rest Area" on the second floor, transforming the space not just for remittance services but as a place for culture and relaxation, with a vision to make it a one-stop service portal for all matters related to the Philippines (Interview, December 6, 2009).

> Thinking back to the past, the current overseas Koreans must have been like this at first. … I see the library as a business from a corporate culture perspective. … Since opening, high-ranking officials such as Father Alvin Parantar, the Woori Bank president, and the Philippine ambassador have visited. … This branch was so well-known during the Commercial Bank days that it became a landmark, even being associated with the major financial scandals like the 1982 Daegu economy scandal involving Jang Yeong-ja and Lee Cheol-hee. It was famous enough that if you wanted to become a bank president, you had to go through it. … It was a landmark branch, not because of its sales, but because it had symbolic significance. (In 50s, deputy branch manager, Interview, December 6, 2009)

As a prominent elite of the Baby Boomer generation, a key figure in Korea's dramatic industrialization and democratization, this deputy branch manager, despite low profits, showed a business-oriented perspective on the importance of attracting potential customers, while understanding foreign workers through a nationalist lens, expressing empathy by saying, "We too struggled in the past." This perspective shows a shift from a superior nationalism to a more compassionate view. Meanwhile, like the bar employee, the expectation of economic contributions from "immigrants from poor countries" is low, but they are symbolically recognized as contributing to the "global" or "multicultural" vision of future Korea, reflecting an ambivalent and contradictory view of foreigners.

This "ambivalent and contradictory" view represents the current state of K-multiculturalism, which has neither been independently established nor has followed Western pathways. As discussed earlier in this chapter, it clearly reflects a developmentalist legacy, shaped by a functionalist and neoliberal migration regime. In this context, immigration is welcomed as a developmental strategy in response to depopulation and regional decline. As demonstrated by statements such as the Korean server's reference to a "multinational and global" hip place and the elite banker's mention of "symbolic significance," multicultural spaces and the presence of foreigners are often positively framed as markers of advancement or future development. However, these perspectives tend to overlook concrete measures or in-depth discussions on the social costs of coexistence, reducing the complexities of the issue to racial prejudice (as in the Korean server's case) or nationalism (as in the banker's case). Therefore, these encounters must be sustained and integrated into everyday life so that real issues can be meaningfully addressed.

As the number of migrants in Korean society increases, certain spaces, especially universities and global franchises, tend to normalize multicultural mixing as an everyday occurrence. The area in front of Exit 1 of Hyehwa subway station plays a role as a gateway where such encounters frequently occur (Fig. 6.7). On weekend afternoons, the Starbucks in front of Exit 1 is filled with Filipino customers, creating a scene that resembles a foreign café. One part-time worker at this Starbucks, who was unaware of why they came every Sunday, had become so accustomed to the presence of foreign visitors that it was an ordinary part of their work

Fig. 6.7 Contact zones: Street food stalls, crosswalk, and coffee shops (2024.11.24)

routine (Interview, November 24, 2024). Similarly, at the street food stalls in front of Hyehwa Station, Filipino migrant workers are often seen choosing Korean street food stalls despite the nearby Filipino market. One Filipino migrant worker shared that eating *tteokbokki and odeng* (popular Korean street food) among Koreans on Sundays had become a small, cherished happiness (Interview, November 24, 2024). These individuals are becoming agents who occupy and negotiate their coexistence by utilizing and consuming the various facilities of Hyehwa-dong on Sunday afternoons.

5 Conclusion

In the previous sections, I sought to examine the current and future state of K-multiculturalism by using multicultural spaces where this recent challenge and phenomenon of multicultural transition in Korean society is concretely manifested as a testbed. Modern Korea, with its distinct path dependence, has established a state-driven developmental and neoliberal migration regime, which has resulted in selective and hierarchical forms of governance over migrants. This has produced a socio-spatially uneven multiculturalism, leading not to multiculturalism as an overarching governance ideology or institution but to the coexistence of intermittent diversity through exceptional spaces such as multicultural spaces. Although Korea has moved beyond the myth of a homogenous nation in the era of 2.6 million foreigners, the social consensus on how to coexist with these outsiders is just beginning.

In contrast to top-down rhetorical multiculturalism, self-organizing multicultural spaces are also being created from the bottom up, and one of the key mechanisms in this process is religious institutions. This study focused on the role of the Catholic Church in Korea, not only through its organizational structure and resources but also through the dedication and solidarity of Catholic believers, creating exceptional spaces of coexistence. Through the Hyehwa-dong Filipino community, I explored how the Catholic Church established a transnational solidarity that supported Filipino migrant workers in Korea, in line with the universal faith and community ideals of Catholicism (derived from the Greek word katholikos meaning universal). Since the 1960s, the Catholic Church in Korea has been deeply involved in labor rights movements through labor pastoral work, accumulating civil societal tradition and capacity. This background enabled swift and exceptional hospitality and support for migrant workers. According to *Seoul Archdiocese Labor Pastoral 50 Anniversary* (2008), Catholic priests and organizations have dedicated to resist labor rights violations since the 1960s. Long before the EPS program, they were investigating human rights violations against undocumented workers and industrial trainees and advocating on their behalf. The Catholic Labor Pastoral Committee was among the first to denounce the inhuman aspects of the EPS program (Seoul Archdiocese Migrant Ministry n.d.). Cardinal Kim, Sou-hwan's attention to migrant workers' human rights, and Professor Ahn, Curie's awakening leading to the establishment of the Raphael Clinic in 1996, were pivotal moments, sparked by petitions for the human rights of migrant workers, including a case involving a Pakistani death-row inmate in the Seoul Archdiocese.

Under this support from the Catholic Church, Filipino migrants in Korea gained better access to resources compared to other migrant groups and were able to form multicultural spaces while sharing in the cultural streets of Seoul. Hyehwa-dong Church, located in what is known as Korean "Vatican," used various Catholic resources to lay the foundation for the growth of Little Manila. Additionally, as seen in the case of the Raphael Clinic, which started at Seoul National University medical school, Hyehwa-dong's location and accessibility, combined with Catholic resources, created a multicultural space that empowered Filipino migrants.

This case study explored the conditions that allowed the reconstruction of values and identities in contemporary Korean society and how these were made possible. Over the past half-century, Korea has achieved simultaneous industrial growth and democratization, yet it now faces the limitations of the myth of homogeneity that underpinned its growth and development. It must now confront the challenge of pioneering new growth through the coexistence of diversity and a global civic identity. Unlike Western multiculturalism, which was presented as an alternative to racial discrimination and assimilationism, Korea, having experienced colonialism rather than being a colonial power, seeks to implement multiculturalism that avoids the failures seen in Western countries (Mitchell 2004). This approach, which could be tentatively called K-multiculturalism, requires exploration of the forces that make it possible. This study is an initial attempt at such an exploration.

While the top-down development model driven by the government boosted efficiency and led to rapid growth, civil society supplemented the gaps left by this growth and played a key role in Korea's democratization by cultivating values from the bottom up. The Hyehwa-dong Little Manila case, introduced in this chapter, demonstrates how civil society, centered around the Catholic Church, filled the gaps left by the top-down, instrumental migration regime and embarked on a journey to find keys to coexistence with migrants from below.

References

Bark, Hyehyeon, and Hyunjoo Jung. 2023. Selective Inclusion and Exclusion of Ethnic-Spatial 'Differences': Neoliberal Discourses and Policies in Local Governance of Daerim-dong 'Chinatown'. *Contemporary Society and Multiculture* 13 (4): 1–38. (in Korean).

Cha, Chul Wook. 2014. Formation of Leisure Space for Immigrants in Gimhae and Reconstruction of Locality: Focusing on Restaurants. *The Journal of Localitology* 12: 85–110. (in Korean).

Choi, Byung-Doo. 2009. Multi-cultural Space and Glocal Ethics: From Cultural Space of Transnational Capitalism to Space of Recognition Struggle. *Journal of the Korean Association of the Regional Geographers* 15 (5): 635–645. (in Korean).

Choi, Byung-Doo. 2011. The Socio-Spatial Transformation Process Towards Multicultural Society and Limitations of 'Multicultural Coexistence' Policy of Japan. *Journal of the Korean Association of the Regional Geographers* 17 (1): 17–39. (in Korean).

Chung, E. A. 2020. Creating Hierarchies of Noncitizens: Race, Gender, and Visa Categories in South Korea. *Journal of Ethnic and Migration Studies* 46 (12): 2497–2514.

Chung, E. A., Darcie Draudt, and Yunchen Tian. 2024. The developmental migration state. *Journal of Ethnic and Migration Studies, 50*(3), 637–656.

Greiner, Clemens, and Patrick Sakdapolrak. 2013. Translocality: Concepts, Applications and Emerging Research Perspectives. *Geography Compass* 7 (5): 373–384.

Harvey, David. 1973. *Social Justice and the City*. London: Edward Arnold.

Heo, Kwon. 2021. A Critical Analysis on the Political and Spatial Changes in Ansan. *Space and Environment* 31 (3): 304–337. (in Korean).

Jung, Hyunjoo. 2010. Reading 'Little Manila' along Daehangno: Exploring the Conceptualization of Transnational Spaces. *Journal of the Korean Association of the Regional Geographers* 16 (3): 295–314. (in Korean).

Jung, Hyunjoo. 2020. Civic Stratification and Spatial Division of Immigrants in Korean Migration Policy: Differentiation of Migrant Workers' Visa Status Based on Ethnicity, Class and Gender. *Journal of the Association of Korean Geographers* 9 (3): 567–585. (in Korean).

Jung, Byoungho, and Doyoung Song, eds. 2011. *Multicultural Spaces in Korea: Searching for Social Spaces of Multicultural Migrants in Korea*. Seoul: Hyunamsa. (in Korean).

Jung, Hyunjoo, Ilhong Ko, Woojin Shim, and Jungseob Kim. 2024. Rethinking Multicultural Space from a Mega-Asian Perspective: Using Gimhae City's Foreigner Street as an Example. *Journal of Humanities* 81 (4): 383–424. (in Korean).

Kim, Sun-Im. 2010. A Study on the Community Formation Process of the Philippine Migrant Workers: Focusing on Hyehwadong Community and Catholicism. *Journal of Religion and Culture* 14, June:46–82. (in Korean).

Kim, Jungsun. 2011. The Critical Study of 'Korean Style' Multiculturalism as Welfare Policy Excluding Citizenship. *Economy and Society* 92: 205–246. (in Korean).

Kim, Hee-Kang. 2013. The Paradox of Multiculturalism. *Discourse201* 16 (4): 67–95. (in Korean).

Kim, Yoon Young. 2019. Making Identity of Multicultural Space and Discursive Discourse: The Case of Two Small Public Libraries, Damunhwa and Modoo in Wondok-dong, Danwan-gu, Kyounggi-do, South Korea. *Space and Environment* 29 (4): 242–270. (in Korean).

Kim, Yeong-Hyun, and Hyunjoo Jung. 2018. Promoting and Controlling Labor Migration: South Korean State's Intervention for Control in the Temporary Migrant Worker Program and Its (Un)intended Outcomes. *Journal of the Korean Geographical Society* 53 (2): 229–246.

Kong, Yoon-Kyung. 2013. The Dualistic Viewpoint and Discrimination Towards Multi-Cultural Spaces. *Journal of Koreanology* 48: 183–214. (in Korean).

Korea Immigration Service. 2024a. *The 4th Master Plan for Immigration Policy.*

Korea Immigration Service. 2024b.11. *Monthly Report on Foreign Nationals and Immigration Statistics.*

Kwon, Jong-hwa, 2005, *The Formation and Experiences of Philippine Migrant Community in Korea from a Translocal Perspective*, MA Thesis, Yonsei University. (in Korean)

Lee, Byoungha. 2023. The Nexus between Population Policy and Immigration Policy in South Korea: From a Perspective of Migration State. *Discourse201* 26 (1): 7–36. (in Korean).

Lefebvre, Henry. 1974/1991. *The Production of Space.* Oxford: Blackwell.

Massey, Doreen. 2005. *For Space.* Sage.

Mitchell, Katharyn. 2004. Geographies of Identity: Multiculturalism Unplugged. *Progress in Human Geography* 28 (5): 641–651.

Oh, Kyung Seok. 2010. Rethinking Multiculturalism in Korea. *Lingua Humanitatis* 12 (2): 447–478. (in Korean).

Portes, Alejandro, and Robert D. Manning. 1986. The Immigrant Enclave: Theory and Empirical Examples. In *Competitive Ethnic Relations*, ed. Susan Olzak and Joanne Nagel, 47–55. Academic Press.

Seoul Archdiocese Labor Pastoral Committee. 2008. *Seoul Archdiocese Labor Pastoral 50 Anniversary*. Seoul: Korean Catholic Press. (in Korean).

Sheppard, Eric. 2019. Sociospatial Dialectic. In *The Wiley Blackwell Encycloopeida of Urban and Regional Studies*, ed. Anthony M. Orum. Wiley & Sons.

Soja, Edward. 1980. The Socio-Spatial Dialectic. *Annals of the Association of American Geographers* 70: 207–225.

Yoon, In-Jin. 2008. The Development and Characteristics of Multiculturalism in South Korea with a Focus on the Relationship of the State and Civil Society. *Korean Journal of Sociology* 42 (2): 72–103. (in Korean).

The Hankyoreh Newspaper. 2006.6.22. Woori Bank Hyehwa Branch Offers International Remittance Services on Sundays https://www.hani.co.kr/arti/economy/finance/135043.html. (in Korean)

Newspaper, Broadcasting, and Websites

Catholic Peace Weekly, 2006.5.24. United Neighbors in Asia, and the World 2—Philippines (Part 1), http://news.cpbc.co.kr/article/189321

Chosun Ilbo. 2016.2. 27. One Day a Week … Devoting One-Seventh of Life to Medical Volunteer Service. (in Korean)

Encyclopedia of Korean Culture. n.d.. https://encykorea.aks.ac.kr/Article/E0067979.

Jongno District Website. n.d.. https://tour.jongno.go.kr/tour/main/contents.do?menuNo=400167

Joongang Ilbo, 2022.9.27. The Solution to the Population Cliff: An Immigration Agency Dedicated to 'Orderly Immigration' Is Urgently Needed. https://www.joongang.co.kr/article/25104696. (in Korean)

Maeil Business Newspaper. 2017.5.30. 'Life Is About Happily Owing Each Other,' Said Professor Ahn Curie of Raphael Clinic, Recipient of the Ho-Am Prize in Social Service. (in Korean).

Maeil Newspaper, 2016.4.3. [Kim Byung-jun Interview] Professor Ahn Gyu-ri, CEO of Raphael Clinic. (in Korean)

Overseas Koreans Agency. n.d.. https://oka.go.kr/oka_en/about/history/.

Raphael Clinic. n.d.. http://raphael.or.kr/ko_KR/

SBS. 2008.11.21. Ode to Daehangno: The Origin of Daehangno. (in Korean)

Seoul Archdiocese Migrant Ministry. n.d.. http://www.seoulmigrant.net/load.asp?subPage=312

The Catholic Times. 2011.4.14. Pakistani Death Row Inmates Send Petition to Cardinal Kim. (in Korean)

The Catholic Times. 2013.4.16. Seongbuk-dong, Seoul: 'A Little Rome in Korea'. (in Korean)

The Catholic Times. 2014a.6.8.

The Catholic Times. 2014b.6.3. Professor Ahn Curie, CEO of Raphael Clinic. (in Korean)

The Catholic Times. 2023.7.18. Interview with Ahn Curie, Chairperson of the Raphael Sharing Foundation. (in Korean)

The Economist. 2023.5.28. A New Wave Of Mass Migrationhasbegun.

PART II

New Flows of Value and Identity in Contemporary Korea

CHAPTER 7

The Cosmopolitan Vernacular: Korean Shamans (Mudang) in the Global Spirituality Market

Liora Sarfati

1 Introduction

Cosmopolitanism has often been used to discuss religions that had been institutionalized, canonized, and then transmitted globally through premodern cultural flows. In the west, this mostly applies to Christianity and its migration from the Mediterranean to much of the world. In East Asia, Buddhism brought its belief system along with its arts, texts, and practices from India to China, and then to Korea and Japan (Baker 1994). In contrast, vernacular religions have maintained their local uniqueness in terms of pantheons, belief systems, practices, and ritual objects—even into the twenty-first century. Similar to other cases where hypermodernity and the

An Earlier Version of This Article Was Published First in Religions 2023, 14(2), 189. https://doi.org/10.3390/rel14020189

L. Sarfati (✉)
Department of East Asian Studies, Tel Aviv University, Tel Aviv, Israel
e-mail: lsarfati@tauex.tau.ac.il

© The Author(s), under exclusive license to Springer Nature Singapore Pte Ltd. 2025

Y. Yoo, S. C. Lee (eds.), *Reimagining Korea*, Palgrave Series in Contemporary Korean Studies,
https://doi.org/10.1007/978-981-96-6990-5_7

internet have become an inseparable part of vernacular traditional expressiveness, here too "folklore is empowered by its diversity" (Blank 2009, p. 7). As lived religions are unofficial local traditions (Primiano 1995), we must be cautious when examining the cultural and societal conditions that have enabled the vernacular traditions of Korean shamanism (musok) to travel globally in real and virtual worlds. In order to begin such an exploration, we need to seriously consider what musok practitioners say, feel, and experience, even when their reflections do not fit common scholarly distinctions. By conducting such inductive research, we can observe how individual religious creativity has enabled vernacular concepts and acts to reach all corners of the Korean Peninsula and expand outside the national borders.

One of the most emphasized features in scholarship about Korean shamanism has been that it is vernacularly rooted in local traditions and regionally defined. These religious beliefs, practices, and practitioners (mudang) were described and documented before and during the colonial period in the early twentieth century (Akamatsu and Akiba 1938; Choe 1978).[1]

Some folk religious practices have been gathered and titled musok (shamanistic customs—i.e., vernacular religion) as a historical consequence of Japanese imperialism when the Japanese declined to incorporate Korean deities into their own vernacular pantheon (Kim 2013b). Moreover, while vernacular religions in Korea have links with Daoism and Buddhism, the research produced by colonial folklorists distinguished mudang as unique local practitioners.

Extensive urbanization since the mid-twentieth century has introduced changes to this tradition and has created a new kind of musok practitioners who are cosmopolitan in their cultural interests, as well as their geographic movements, and who perform spiritual rituals outside Korea and for non-Korean spirits and clients. This innovative trend began in the late twentieth century and was accelerated with the advent of internet communication in the twenty-first century. It is an outcome of hypermodern cultural flows, where cosmopolitanism has become a perspective and a manner of constructing meaning rather than a description of movement in space (Hannerz 1990, pp. 238, 239).

Elsewhere I explained how practitioners of musok fit significant aspects of this concept, even without physically leaving Korea (Sarfati 2024). The case of cosmopolitan mansin challenges the conventional definition of

[1] Mudang is often translated as shaman. It is used here for both the plural and single forms. Other parallel terms used in Korean are mansin (literally 10,000 spirits, for possessed shamans) or bosal (literally Boddhisatva—a Buddhist entity).

cosmopolitanism as primarily associated with intellectual men of the bourgeois sector (Thompson and Tambyah 1999, p. 221). While this term often reflects a dialectical tension between masculinized meanings of travel and feminized meanings of dwelling, many female practitioners of Korea's vernacular religion have successfully adapted to accelerated globalization. This success stems in part from the open-minded attitude required from a practitioner who navigates between the human world and supernatural cosmologies. I analyzed the mansin's transition between these realms as structurally akin to intercultural experiences that is at the core of cosmopolitanism. The cosmopolitan's perspective requires an understanding that a person's daily life constituted only a small part of the universe, in contrast to what Hannerz calls locals, who live "purely within the structure of the locality" (1990, p. 237). Moreover, "the perspective of the cosmopolitan must entail relationships to a plurality of cultures understood as distinctive entities" (ibid., p. 239). Therefore, cosmopolitanism is not a mere globalized movement; rather it includes a stance toward diversity itself, and an incorporation of the coexistence of cultures in the individual experience.

This chapter follows the cosmopolitanization of musok and addresses the reasons for its occurrence. The hypermodern environment of the global spiritual market is explained and analyzed through ethnographic observations and interviews with four main informants who are cosmopolitan spiritual mediators. The selection of four cases of cosmopolitan mudang includes two that could be considered traditional practitioners who have extended their clientele and location of practice globally, a Korean-American mudang, born and raised in New York who was initiated there by a Korean mudang and caters to both ethnic Koreans and others, and a European mudang, who has no ethnic or family ties to Korea, but was initiated in Korea by the most famous mudang, Kim Geum-hwa. This choice broadens the scope of scholarly discourse on the subject and effectively illustrates how musok is transcending its traditional local boundaries, facilitated by digital and communication technologies that connect practitioners and clients across the globe.

I interviewed the featured mudang several times, mostly within participant observations of ritual preparations, ritual practices, home visits, and other shared experiences. Most interviews and observations were conducted during my anthropological fieldwork visits in Seoul in 2007–2008, 2014, 2019, and 2022. During the COVID-19 pandemic, I began to "meet" the mudang through online video conference tools as well. Over the years, I documented and analyzed their online activity.

Since the 1990s, urban lifestyles have required mudang to shorten their rituals—which used to last several days—and to learn to practice without the traditional residence apprenticeship with a spiritual mother (sineomeoni) that was prevalent in the slower-paced villages (Guillemoz 1992). Most mudang now practice in the cities, but they still name and relate their musok traditions according to the place from which their particular ritual style originated. This has also been the common practice of Korean scholars who study this vernacular religion and the government offices that have supported the preservation of shamanic ritual elements within programs of heritage preservation. Although all of the practitioners of Korean spiritual mediation are colloquially referred to as mudang, the peninsula has been characterized as geographically divided between Northern shamanism—which is charismatic, ecstatic, and involves spirit possession trances (Hogarth 1998; Lee 1990)—and Southern shamanism, which is hereditary, priesthood-centered, and does not require possession trances (Yang 2004b). In terms of regional ritual (gut) styles, the most commonly discussed have been Seoul or Hanyang gut (Seo 2002) and Hwanghaedo gut (Hong 2006) in the Northern style (Fig. 7.1), and Jindo gut (Park 2003) and Eastern Coast Donghae gut (Mills 2007) in the Southern traditions. Urbanization, the decline of desire to be a hereditary mudang, and the acknowledgment of the artistic value of gut dance, song, and music have contributed to creating mediatized and staged musok performances that have been referred to by critical observers as "fusion style."

Then came the international spread of Korean shamanism, as a part of the hypermodern process that Korea's culture has been undergoing, and these divisions and distinctions became more blurred. Hypermodern society has evolved in the era of global capitalism and advanced communication technologies, which create more easily accessible networks of cultural distribution. Such "contemporary complex cultures," as Ulf Hannerz (1991, p. 6) terms them, enable a new scale of intercultural interactions that had been available in previous societies for only a few travelers. They flourish where technology, people, and cultural trends become inseparable, as observable in contemporary South Korean urbanity. Within this complexity, individual practitioners of musok need to interpret their religious experiences in a manner that can harmonize with a globalizing, technology-dependent, media-saturated society. Their lived religion is

Fig. 7.1 Mudang Yi Hae-gyeong (Lee Hae-kyung) performing a Hwanghaedo gut ritual while being filmed by a documentary film production team. July 2022, the photograph was taken by the author with consent from the people depicted

constructed in reaction to and in interaction with changing cultural and social conditions.

Vernacular in nature, musok enables flexible adaptations. Mudang alternate their practices as fits their various life contexts, without having to bargain such alterations with official religious organizations or hierarchies. However, in contrast with more eclectic new religions or religions of the new age, the practice of transnational mudang is rooted deeply in Korean traditional spirituality. Even the term mudang, which used to be disliked by the practitioners because of the stigma it carried, has been more widely accepted and used because of its extensive appearance in the media.

In the first part of this chapter, I discuss the evolution of mudang's image in the media over the past 50 years, and I then address the manner in which four spirit-possessed mudang have become media celebrities and examine how they used social media in 2019–2022. The four cases that I chose to present here offer insights on different aspects of the globalized hypermodern conditions where contemporary mudang practice their traditional religion. After introducing the four practitioners' work and lives, I draw conclusions on the roles and meanings of mediated shamanism in the twenty-first century. Such spiritual vernacular practices have not ceased to exist with urbanization and societal changes; rather, the practitioners have implemented vernacular qualities such as flexibility and openness to personal interpretations. The Korean case offers insights into the mediatization of popular religious leaders, the processes by which they become celebrities, and their global activities as innovative means to maintain spiritual practices in a technology-saturated culture.

2 Media and Shamans in Korea: From Social Outcasts to Media Celebrities

Local shamans who have become celebrities in Korea are often called Kun Mudang, which can be translated as big mediators with the spirits.[2] This often means that they have been nominated by the state as Holders of Intangible Heritage Assets (i.e., the traditional arts that they perform), and are often referred to as Human Cultural Treasures (ingan munhwaje)—people who receive recognition and stipends to keep important traditions alive (Howard 1998; Yang 2004a). However, mudang can make a decent if not luxurious living by practicing spiritual mediation for healing, divination, and blessings, even without the government's help (Bruno 2002; Harvey 1979).

The first media celebrities among mudang emerged in the late 1980s and were extensively documented by mainstream media and scholars. The most famous among them was Kim Geum-hwa—a mudang who underwent initiation in her late teens in what is now North Korea and then fled to the south during the Korean War. She was the first to receive official recognition, be filmed, and travel abroad for public performances of gut. It took the Korean government approximately 20 years from the beginning of the cultural property preservation program in the 1960s before they decided to include mudang in it. This delay resulted from the general disdain toward the work of mudang, who used to be mostly women from lower social strata (Harvey 1979; Kendall 1988). Moreover, their practice has included behaviors considered immoral, such as dancing and singing

[2] Mu (巫) means spiritual mediator, while dang (堂) refers to the practitioners' role as a home for the supernatural entities that possess them. Dang also means shrine, as in sindang (神堂)—a shrine for the spirits.

in public (even when performed to appease angry spirits), meeting men in private (even when done for spiritual consultation), and bargaining fiercely for their fees.

Adherents of other religions and ideologies in Korea—mainly Confucianism and Christianity—tended to view mudang as deviant, dangerous members of society (Grayson 1998). Confucians worried that such women, who challenged the accepted gendered behavior boundaries, might destroy social hierarchies where learned men are expected to be dominant in all social situations. Christians never accepted the polytheistic nature of musok (Oak 2010). The negative view of mudang was represented in the traditional media from the 1960s–1980s, mainly in film and television. Mudang were most often depicted as relics of old customs, colorful and beautiful but no longer central components of Korean society.

For example, such a stance is taken in the famous film Ieodo by the acclaimed director Kim Gi-yeong. In this masterpiece from 1977, the mudang is an evil scheming person who, in an extreme moment, forces her apprentice to have sexual intercourse with a corpse. Such a scene fits the general depiction of the mudang protagonist who lives on a remote island outside the small community that inhabits it. She also objects to any attempt to modernize the island through tourism and modern sea agriculture (see similar cases discussed in Sarfati 2021, pp. 63–66). The advent of new media—and especially the broad availability of internet platforms in Korea since the late 1990s—has resulted in the self-promotion of mudang, which has shaken the hierarchy between male experts (scholars/producers/directors) and female protagonists (actresses/mudang). The internet has created a new cultural arena with innovative options and norms for musok representation (Kim 2003). Mudang began to discuss their media representations with the professionals who produced them, as can be observed in many productions of the 2000s—for example, the docudrama Mansin, featuring Kim Geum-hwa as herself and several younger actresses as Mudang Kim in the earlier stages of her life. As the mudang have been increasingly depicted in positive ways, movies that include shamanism as central to the plot—such as *Fortune Salon* (*Cheongdam Bosal*, Kim 2009) and *Man on the Edge* (*Baksu Geondal*, Cho 2013)—no longer depict the mudang as a danger to society.

In the view of potential clients of mudang, media coverage is similar to endorsement by scholars and the government designation program. Most Koreans do not read academic research articles, and when they learn that a mudang has been considered proficient by scholars, it is usually through the media. Clients who I have met during rituals performed by celebrity mudang usually decided to consult with these practitioners after learning about them from newspapers, online forums, or documentary films. In the hypermodern society of Seoul, there is an excess of information that, combined with the lingering rumors about mudang who are fake and greedy imposters (rather than honest mediators with the supernatural), makes potential clients suspicious. When they watch television coverage of a mudang, with a scholar's commentary of her work, they feel safe to contact that individual for help. As an extension of this trend, many mudang self-promote through social media and upload films, free divinations, and contact information to online platforms.

However, the clients are aware that such self-declarations and testimonies of abilities might be fake. This general perspective was recently depicted in the successful television drama *Café Minamdang* (Go 2022). The plot centered around a young, handsome police detective who was falsely accused of corruption and fired (Fig. 7.2). He opens a private office and deciphers crimes through a sophisticated computer lab. The twist is that the office used to belong to a mudang, and the first clients mistook him for one. Ever since, he continued to deliver the information that he discovered about crimes as if this had been communicated to him

Fig. 7.2 *Café Minamdang*, Promotional poster and main characters. 2022, image KBS2

supernaturally. He collaborates with police investigators, who believe that he learns secret truths from spirits and gods. In the series, mudang in general are depicted in a degrading manner. For example, in episode 7, the detectives stumble upon a gut ritual, and as the mudang spot them they impersonate gods and the mudang buy into it and are afraid of them. Such a scene implies that mudang cannot really tell people from spirits.

Indeed, the mudang that I met in 2022 were not happy that this series became so popular. In their view, their sincere efforts to help people were being mocked and their belief in gods and spirits was presented as fraud. One mudang said, "The manner in which the clients of this fake detective are depicted makes my clients feel stupid for trusting me." In episode 9, a mudang who is depicted as a true spiritualist stabs a photograph of a candidate for mayor, and at the same time he suffers a heart attack during his election campaign. This scene portrays the mudang as a powerful person with supernatural abilities, but her intentions are driven by greed and evilness. In episode 11, in a gathering of shamans, the audience learns that the other practitioners consider the evil mudang to be unworthy of the vocation and decide to cut their ties with her. This scene represents the shared statement of mudang that they practice only for the good of their clients, without causing harm to others.

The depiction of mudang in mainstream media, combined with the increasing global popularity of Korean popular culture, referred to as hallyu—the Korean Wave (Kim 2013c)—has contributed to the globalization of musok. Many Korean Americans who grew up in Christian families and environments have taken an interest in musok after learning about it from the media, especially films and television dramas. They search for practitioners in the United States, thereby contributing to the success of mudang in diasporic communities. Such transnational mudang tell of communication with spirits and gods who are not Korean, and of helping people of various nationalities and ethnicities. Korean mudang have been traveling abroad to conduct rituals since at least the 1980s, and many specialize in performing for clients of Korean origins in Japan.[3] The innovativeness of hypermodern international mudang is that they also work with people of non-Korean origins and communicate routinely with spirits and gods who are not within Korea's traditional pantheons.

Following the mainstreaming of musok culture and mudang gut rituals, the practitioners who have become media-savvy have harnessed various

[3] For an extensive discussion of the Korean diaspora in Japan see Ryang (1997).

media platforms to become famous and influential. They no longer consider themselves victims of the system, nor do their clients view them with pity. Many of them have managed to accumulate significant wealth—for example, Kim Geum-hwa, who passed away in 2019. Recently, her many houses and assets have become the center of inheritance wars between her spiritual children and distant relatives (she did not bear children). Two of the mudang who are discussed below were initiated by Kim: one is a senior Korean woman who has been depicted and self-promoted through various media in the past 20 years; her story demonstrates how crucial media success is in contemporary Korea. The other is a German woman who became the first European to be initiated as a mudang; her story shows how this traditional vernacular belief and practice has managed to transcend ethnic and national boundaries. The two others discussed later have been apprentices of other mudang: one used to be a fashion model, became a mudang, and works with many non-Korean clients thanks to her online presence and English language skills; her case shows how media celebrity culture is prominent in different kinds of industries—in this case, fashion and religion. The fourth is a Korean American who was initiated in New York and works mainly with American clients; her success as a famous practitioner despite her relatively young age shows how the media can promote international awareness of traditions that used to be local and community-based. The order of appearance of the four cases below represents the chronological order of their initiation.

2.1 *Age Is No Limit to Media Publicity: The Story of Mudang Yi Hae-gyeong*

In her 60s, Yi Hae-gyeong (also transcribed as Lee Hae-kyung) is a very successful mudang who has maintained an online presence in a personal blog and on social media since mid-2005. I emphasize this chronology because it is not obvious that a middle-aged woman in Korea can master different kinds of media outlets to her benefit, and it is even less so when such a woman has been busy since her late 30s with spiritual mediation, healing, and divination (Fig. 7.3). Yi was initiated after apprenticeship with Kim Geum-hwa in the early 1990s, which makes her now one of the most knowledgeable and acclaimed practitioners of the Hwanghaedo style of gut since the passing of the older master in 2019. She has been acknowledged by Korean film directors as an important mudang, as she was featured in the opening scene of the documentary *Mudang: Reconciliation*

Fig. 7.3 Mudang Yi Hae-gyeong instructing an American visitor how to arrange his costume for a mugam dance during ritual. July 2022, the photograph was taken by the author with consent from the people depicted

Between the Living and the Dead (*Yeongmae: Sanja wa Jugueunja eui hwahae*, Bak 2003), and was the main protagonist of the film *Between* (Saieseo, Yi 2006). Both documentaries were screened in theaters with unprecedented success.[4] She has created a promotional website, which she has maintained since the 1990s.[5]

On her website, Yi lists her public gut performances, which attest to being legitimized by the government, museums, and municipal bodies who have hired her services for such public events. Another page on the

[4] *Mudang* was one of the top grossing documentaries in Seoul's history, with 13,474 admissions, while *Between* had over 24,000 admissions (Documentaries (2019)).

[5] This website has been less active since 2014, as she became more engaged with social media www.mansin.co.kr (accessed on January 25 2023).

website has live links to her media appearances since the year 2000; for example, several news articles that are linked to this page describe her joint performance with techno music DJs at the international Aurasoma music festival that was held in Seoul in August 2000. During the shooting of *Between*, she shared her experience in a blog that was uploaded on her website as an artistically designed production with black-and-white photographs along with long, emotional texts that she wrote.

In 2008, she redesigned her promotional website, and she opened a Facebook page in 2009 with 784 followers, and a Twitter account in 2010 with 447 followers. This chronology fits the changing popularity and incorporation of different internet outlets in Korea. On her Twitter account, she describes herself in Korean as "the person who performs Hwanghaedo gut, called shamanlee (this hashtag is in English)." In this first statement, Yi includes her regional gut style and her media name (shamanlee). She continues, "I am an artist, and was featured in the documentary Between." This second phrase summarizes her personal achievements as an artist and a media figure. In her third introductory sentence, she mentions her leadership as the person who founded and runs a musok shrine and a group of venerators, and who travels for consultation and rituals: "I am the leader of the Huibang sindang (the name of her countryside mountain shrine L.S) where gods, spirits, and people can communicate." This achievement ends the introductory passage of her Twitter account. The order of these sentences fits her life narrative: she was initiated into the Hwanghaedo gut style; she became a media figure; and in 2014, with her better economic standing, she purchased and constructed the mountain shrine where she now leads a small community of apprentices and clients. Her success as a practitioner and performer brought media attention which, in turn, extended her clientele and provided her with economic stability, which she has used for more grounded and extensive religious leadership. Although her Twitter account has more than 1000 tweets, she has not used it since the summer of 2021. Instead, she continues to post regularly on her Facebook page, which boasts a few hundred regular followers and clients.

Personal abilities, media engagement, and religious belief and practice combined to make Yi what she is today in the musok community. Yi likes to travel in Korea and internationally and shares photographs and ideas over social media. Her most popular posts are about pilgrimages and visits to holy mountains, springs, and shrines. She typically posts a few photos and videos and writes how good she feels being there. Such posts generate approximately 200 like/love reactions and a few dozen comments and shares. For example, on 18 June 2022, she posted about her visit to Stonehenge in England. She wrote that visiting this site of the ancestors brought her health and energy. A total of 256 like/love reactions were noted, and 39 comments—mostly in Korean—shared her excitement with phrases like "Wow! I envy you," "Ah! Wonderful traces of older times," "It's awesome in pictures but it's huge in person!!!," and "Wow~~Teacher, you went to a really cool place." She responded to many of the comments and questions, and she added a like reaction to most of them.

Although Yi does not speak any foreign languages, she has traveled to many countries to perform rituals—some public, or at research institutions; and others private, with translators. The main place to which she has traveled to perform for private clients is Japan. When I asked her about possession by non-Korean spirits in July 2022, she said that it was no problem at all. "Language is no barrier to communicating with ancestors and gods. I understand their message and tell it to the audience. I do not need to say things in words for the spirits to understand, nor do they need to speak in my language." When Yi insisted that she explain this point further, she chose to do so with another example: "It is the same as when a Christian worshipper prays in his own language to Jesus, and Jesus can hear and understand even though he never spoke that particular language while he was alive." There is no sense of difference or conflict between her and the Christian faith as far as she is concerned. "It is all about the supernatural communicating with people. The same as my work," she adds.

2.2 A Fashion Model Turned Shaman: The Story of Mudang Pang Eun-mi

For Pang Eun-mi (also transcribed as Bang Eunmi)—a Korean mudang in her 40s living in Ilsan near Seoul—the media is no stranger. She was a fashion model before being initiated as a mudang in the early 2000s. Her transition to spiritual mediation practice has been covered extensively in the media, and she has continued to be featured frequently on television and in fashion magazines, while also producing private media self-promotion via her active website and social media platforms (Fig. 7.4). Pang participated in several reality television shows after her transformation from fashion model to spiritual healer. In the television show *Job Stories* (Tvchosun 2012–2013), she received much appreciation from the audience when she declared that she had been possessed by Joan of Arc.

Fig. 7.4 Recent Korean magazines featuring Pang Eun-mi as their cover story. July 2022, photograph by the author

She keeps a specially ordered hand-painted musindo (god's painting) of her as a blue-eyed warrior in her home shrine.

Pang's website has a Korean version and an English version, and opens with a series of professional photographs of her presenting a talk to a non-Korean audience and performing a ritual in front of an altar laden with offerings.[6] On her Facebook account, she documents and uploads meetings that she has with foreign clients. Most of the Facebook photographs of her with clients in the shrine include non-Koreans. On 19 June 2022, her Facebook account posted a YouTube video produced by a channel called Creative Den, which is followed by almost 200,000 registered followers and creates content about Korean culture and society. The video shows Pang conducting divination in English for a Dutch YouTuber called Bart (with more than 100,000 followers), with the title "Skeptical

[6] The English version is in http://www.shamanpang.com/eng/ (accessed on January 25 2023).

Foreigner VS a Korean Shaman" (Creative 2022). In the video, she divines that he will have a boy and a girl within the next three years. She tells him that he has had a back problem since his teenage years and he declares that this is true. She advises him how to avoid major back pains through exercise. In the video, she describes her joy of acquainting non-Koreans with her spiritual practices and describes how it happened: "thankfully foreign reporters posted a lot of articles about me so there are people who search for me on Google and contact me." In January 2023, she advertised on her Facebook page an invitation to participate in a meditation session for English speakers, to be held in February at her newly opened café in Ilsan, a city at the outskirts of Seoul (Fig. 7.5). In the invitation she promised a short introduction to Korean shamanism, visit of her altar, meditation, and divination, along with tea.

On 1 May 2019, she posted a photograph of her seated in her home shrine with a Western-looking man. This post offered a long description of her meeting with a 26-year-old French martial artist.[7] She wrote how excited she was to discuss her vocation, and how fascinating she found his interest in spirituality. She ended the post by saying "There are many people who are prettier than flowers." The hashtags of this Facebook post were different in the Korean and English. In Korean, they included several with her name (Pang Eun-mi) and her town (Ilsan), and others related to shamanism, such as #musoksinang (Korean shamanism) and #sinjeom (divination). These were promotional words for Korean audiences. She also posted hashtags in English, for her foreign audience, including #Koreanshamanism, #godsofnature #spiritualtravels, and #Koreanheritage. These are more general terms, without mentioning her name or location, and aimed to attract people who search online for spirituality, Korean cultural heritage, and shamanism.

Our first meeting in 2019 was scheduled through online messaging correspondence that was coordinated by her personal manger—a young assistant who worked as a secretary and producer of her religious and media activity. In our first correspondence, he thought that I was a client who wished to have a spiritual consultation, and he explained to me the price and length of such a meeting. This seems to be a common kind of encounter that she has with non-Koreans. Less frequent intercultural exchanges have taken place at academic conferences, guest lectures in art

[7] https://www.facebook.com/photo/?fbid=2007234889399321&set=pob.100003384876407 (accessed on January 25 2023).

Fig. 7.5 Mudang Pang's invitation for foreigners to meditate. January 2023, the photograph is published with authorization from Pang Eun-mi

venues, and through media interviews. In our subsequent meeting in 2022, she told me how the COVID-19 pandemic has increased her reliance on the internet compared to our previous encounters in 2019. She gave examples of other successful mudang who have not spread their network to foreign audiences but still use the internet extensively. She said,

> "Now, the most successful mudang are YouTube figures, with a very active video channel. They post a new video every week or so, and these have to be interesting and well filmed and edited. They can be pieces of rituals with explanations, predictions for the coming week, or stories of successful healing."

She had tried to maintain such a channel for a few months but ceased, as it took too much time and effort to keep the content flowing. She has continued to post regularly on social networks, "meet" clients for screen-mediated consultations, and perform pilgrimages and rituals for clients, with a small number of apprentices and musicians.

The management of the pandemic in Korea did not involve the enforcement of complete lockdowns, but there were bans on indoor gatherings of more than 4–10 people for extended periods of time. This meant that no large-scale public rituals could be held for more than two years. Unlike Pang, the mudang that were less used to working through screen media found it difficult to adapt, but she did not view this as a hindrance. She had been performing online consultations for several years before the pandemic, and the problems of potential clients did not cease to create work for her during the crisis. Some COVID-19-related difficulties could be resolved with her help. Anxious ancestor spirits that needed comforting, spirits of people whose funerals were held with no audience because of the pandemic, gods of nature that were related to the general disharmonious conditions—all of these could be appeased through her work, and in return, much human anxiety could be diminished.

Nevertheless, she does not view COVID-19 as necessarily stemming from spiritual inflictions; rather, she believes that some people might be more prone to misfortune because they have been involved in complex supernatural tangles—for example, relatives of people who died in tragic circumstances without offspring. Such relatives might not find peace after their death because they might carry grudges toward the people whom they blame for their death—for example, a car driver who caused their fatal accident. Others might be restless because they have no offspring to take care of their ancestor rituals several times a year (Janelli and Janelli 2002). When such spirits hover around living people, it weakens them and might result in illness. In contrast, when a mudang asks the gods of nature to protect people, this might result in fewer illnesses and injuries. Thus, the help of mudang for purifying locations from angry spirits has been sought increasingly during the pandemic. The internet has enabled her to continue practicing her spiritual counseling for people in quarantine, or during restrictions on social gatherings.

2.3 A German Korean Shaman: The Story of Mudang Andrea Kalff

I first met Andrea Kalff because of the COVID-19 pandemic. I could not travel to Seoul to perform fieldwork and was looking for mediated ways in which to learn more about musok. I then began corresponding with several Korean shamans who were well-versed with media and had active presence on social networks such as Instagram and Facebook. One of them knew Andrea and thought that she also represented a media-centered self-promoted mudang. This was an interesting reference because, when I conducted my dissertation fieldwork in Seoul in 2007, Andrea was very well known there. She was featured in the mainstream media, including newspapers and television, soon after being initiated in 2006. She was the first well-known non-Korean to be a practicing mudang, and her spiritual mother Kim Geum-hwa was such a famous Kun Mudang that no one could doubt her choice to turn a German woman into a practitioner of traditional Korean spirit mediation. As in other cases where mudang conduct non-normative behaviors, here too Kim explained her choice of Andrea as an apprentice as a request from supernatural entities.

Andrea tells of her first encounter with Kim Geum-hwa:

> A friend invited me to a concert of Mongolian throat singing, and there were other spiritual performers there. After the show, a man approached me and said that his master wants to speak with me. She is a Korean shaman and has important information for my future. I was not interested, but after a phone call, decided to meet her. I traveled an hour to the place they stayed and she looked at me and said that I was very ill and I have to become a shaman, otherwise I might die. I felt fine, so I said I was not interested and went home. Six weeks later, I was diagnosed with advanced cancer [....]. I remembered the Korean shaman's word and contacted her [....] After a few weeks I traveled to Korea and stayed there for three weeks as her apprentice, and she initiated me as a shaman. She was afraid that I might not make it back because I was so sick [....] I had no idea that there was this big story behind everything. I just wanted to live for my daughters.

Andrea's story in many ways resembles the stories of other Korean practitioners of spirit possession rituals. The typical narrative includes severe illnesses diagnosed by a mudang, apprenticeship, self-healing, and transformation to a healer and diviner who can help others in trouble. The uniqueness of Andrea's case is that she is not Korean, and she did not intend to be diagnosed by the Korean practitioner. Her story could only have happened in hypermodern conditions, where Kim Geum-hwa was a famous media figure who was invited to many international gatherings all over the globe. Her performance in Germany was only one of many such events featured in her biography (Kim 1995). This might also be the reason Kim Geum-hwa initiated many more non-Koreans as mudang in the twenty-first century.

Andrea explains that Kim had a gift of seeing people's illnesses and problems after only a short glimpse, and that this capacity was not bounded by ethnicity or location of meeting. Thus, when observing local people in her audiences in Europe or the United States, she saw many who she believed needed her spiritual help and guidance. Furthermore, Andrea and other initiates outside Korea began practicing their newly acquired skills in their own countries, and they brought their patients to Korea when a complex ritual was required. Andrea tells that while Kim was alive she traveled to Korea almost every year, or invited Kim to Germany, in order to perform joint rituals for Andrea's clients. In Andrea's view, her meeting with the Korean mudang was a supernaturally induced event and might have happened even in premodern times, as people could travel in boats and over land before technology made such ventures common. However, there is no evidence that mudang initiated foreigners before the twenty-first century.

Andrea became a media celebrity in Korea almost immediately upon her arrival. Newspapers and television programs featured her story as "the first non-Korean mudang," and most scholars and musok practitioners that I met during my years of research had heard about her, although many had never met her in person. The local coverage in Korea did not result in a large Korean clientele; however, in the rituals soon after her initiation, many Korean audience members sought to hear her divinations (through a translator), because they believed that she had a unique kind of connection with the supernatural. Andrea has been working as a spiritual healer ever since (Fig. 7.6).

She was also featured in several television documentaries and programs in 2006–2007 on Korea's major television channels, such as SBS and KBS,

Fig. 7.6 Andrea Kalff in her home shrine in Germany, polishing brass bells in preparation for ritual. Behind her hang posters of documentary films featuring her. May 2022, the photograph was taken by the author with consent from the person depicted

in the documentary film *Andrea's Sky* (*Le Ciel D'andrea*, Nisic 2014), the mystery documentary *Rebirth* (*Wiedegerburt*, Schmelzer 2018), and documentaries that focused on Kim Geum-hwa such as *The Silk Flower* (*bidan kkotgil*, Kim 2013a) and *Mansin: Ten Thousand Spirits* (Bak 2014).

Recently, she began a medical research project in collaboration with an Austrian psychiatrist that will compare normative medical treatment of people with addictions, depression, and other mental illnesses with Andrea's treatments of similar cases. They have already published a book about the potential of shamanic healing (Kalff and Zachenhofer 2022). On her home page, Andrea describes herself as follows:

> As a shaman, I see myself as a bridge between life and death. I work with a wide variety of doctors, psychologists, and therapists around the world. In 2006 I was found by the world-famous master shaman Kim Keum Hwa from South Korea. She recognized my calling and the shamanic abilities and initiated me as the first European into Korean shamanism. Today I travel all over the world, mainly in Europe, Korea, Mexico, and Hawaii to help and support people in difficult life situations, psychological and physical problems and much more.[8]

She emphasizes her collaborations with medical practitioners and her worldwide travels, while at the same time using the term that became her nickname in Korean media, the first European initiated into Korean shamanism. Korean scholars of this tradition doubt that a mudang can practice without speaking Korean, but Kim Geum-hwa had been a well-respected professional, and it would be problematic to doubt her perception of Andrea as a Korean shaman (Fig. 7.7). One Korean scholar told me: "She might be a shaman but probably not a proper mudang. She can heal and divine, but not perform the ancient songs and chants."

Andrea's response to such criticism is that even Kim did not expect her to master the performance arts of musok; rather, she instructed her to use her hands and eyes to diagnose and heal. She views her place within musok in a manner that fits Hannerz's explanation: "the cosmopolitan may embrace the alien culture, but he does not become committed to it" (1990, p. 240). The scholarly definitions of musok practice and rituals might not include Andrea's work, because she has what Hannerz (1990, p. 246) calls "decontextualized cultural capital," but this capital stems from the fact that the most acclaimed traditional practitioner endorsed her. The media enabled her to create a broad base of international clientele, for whom such strict boundaries between ethnicities and spiritual

[8] Her website has English and German versions https://korherr-kalff.com/en/schamanismus/ (accessed on January 25 2023).

Fig. 7.7 Andrea Kalff clad in the outfit of a mythical General, Janggun. 2021, the photograph is published with authorization from Andrea Kalff

practices matter less than the efficacy of the treatment. I met and interviewed a pediatrician who brought her son to Andrea's home for treatment. She was very attentive to Andrea's explanation of spiritual disharmonies that affected her son's ability to walk straight, as well as her suggestions for actions that might reduce this disability. One of the main features of late modernity and hypermodernity is the deconstruction of boundaries, definitions, and regionalities; at the same time, in hypermodern conditions, new connections and networks are formed with the assistance of global media (Giddens 2011; Gottschalk 2018). In this way, Andrea is a hypermodern mudang.

2.4 *Spiritual Practices of a Korean American: The Story of Mudang Jenn*

I have been following and archiving mudang Jenn's Facebook page, which has 255 followers, since 2018. She has maintained this page since around the time of her initiation in the mid-2010s, and it has become a venue to express her beliefs and advocate against the stigma associated with shamanism. I found it fascinating that a mudang living in New York chooses to publish extensive English explanations about musok and her practice, and I wondered who her potential clientele were. We met in Seoul in July 2022 after more than a year of online Zoom interviews and chatting. Mudang Jenn (Jennifer Kim) works with different kinds of clients, as befitting her location in the hypermodern cosmopolitan metropolis of New York. Many of the clients she meets are of Korean American origins, but others are of various ethnicities, with significant success among Russian Americans. Being a first-generation American-born child of a Catholic family, Jenn's shamanic activity is not a family heritage; rather, she learned about it during her own search for spirituality. She was initiated by an elderly mudang living nearby, and the process was eased by Jenn's mastery of the Korean language. Unlike the case of Andrea Kalff, Jenn can learn the Korean scripts and texts, and she considers herself a traditional Korean mudang, while also being an American media-savvy person of her generation. Many of her writings throughout the years have included advocacy against the stigma associated with spiritual practices. She maintains an active website in English, where information about musok is provided, her personal initiation and beliefs are explained, and the various options of consultation meetings and rituals are listed.[9]

On 16 November 2021, she posted on Facebook a photograph of a nightly ancestor worship altar, with candles and offerings, and wrote, "Our ancestral and spiritual practice is demonized because it's used to empower people." The 54 love/like/care reactions and 26 comments were mostly from supportive non-Koreans. Other posts that generated many comments and reactions contained detailed explanations of musok

[9] https://www.shamanmudang.com (accessed on January 25 2023).

in general and her activities in particular. On 14 June 2021, she wrote, "Feeling that ceremonial itch. Almost time for another renewal Magi Gut." A more personal post from 23 February 2022 read:

> I'm Mudang Jenn.
> Weaver of heavenly and earthly.
> A Korean American shaman called mudang.
> My journey as a Korean mudang has been hard. The struggles I went through in silence and the financial hardship trying to support my kids and family.
> I spend nights and days in my shrine room doing bows and prayers-contemplating if I was on the right path and journey. Praying for prosperity, blessings, and abundance.
> My spirits said if they send all the blessings and abundance to me—I would reject it. I was uncomfortable with money, value and self-worth. Money is something that tore my entire family apart. My deeper issue was really self-worth. (I blame my Scorpio rising with Saturn in 1H 😂).
> And now I'm consulting and working on projects that feels OMG fucking amazing. I said in my workshop—your storytelling matters. I'm here to tell you that your voice and story has a place. Your spiritual art and practice is your storytelling.
> Thank you so much to everyone who supported me.

Her followers responded with 75 like/love/care responses and comments such as "Standing ovation for that from over here," "Thank you for sharing your story and for your beautiful message that our voices and stories matter," and "Grateful for you being here with us." Some of Jenn's posts include photographs of her children, or shares of news articles that are political or ethnic-related but not connected to musok. She handles her Facebook page as both a personal and professional platform (Fig. 7.8).

One of the things that mudang Jenn laments, as she observes the globalization of musok, is that some Koreans and non-Koreans think that they can practice musok without proper guidance. "Some people, who do not understand the depth of musok thought and practice think they are some kind of witches, but do not understand the true meaning of Korean shamanism. They begin taking clients to divine their future and cause harm instead of good." She explains, "Musok initiation should move slower, with more attention to proper understandings of the spiritual worlds." While she has no objections to foreigners being initiated, she distinguishes between different forms of initiation. Her case shows the different layers of cosmopolitanism performed by second and

Fig. 7.8 Altar for the ancestors. Screen capture from Mudang Jenn's Facebook page. March 2019, the photograph is published with authorization from Jennifer Kim

third-generation Koreans living outside the peninsula. They combine their family heritage and ethnicity as a unique marker of identity and a skill set, with their locational and cultural features as, in Jenn's case, being an American who can cater to non-ethnic Koreans easily.

In Jenn's perception, musok places of practice can change, but ritual basics must be maintained. She conducts pilgrimages to mountains in New York State for prayer and purifications, and she has several sacred locations that are close enough for her to visit regularly. Nevertheless, she finds Korea to be the center of her spirituality, and she travels there with her spiritual mother in most years for rituals and pilgrimages. She said that in some years they had stayed for weeks performing various rituals for clients who live in the United States. Sometimes the clients arrived in person, while in other cases they watched live broadcasts of the rituals they had sponsored. The main events in the rituals, according to Jenn, are the communications that she and her spiritual mother have with spirits and gods. Therefore, the physical presence of the clients is not mandatory. This is also the reason that she views conducting consultation meetings and simple divination through video chat as a viable option. In fact, she sometimes prefers them because, as a mother of two toddlers, her house and home shrine are sometimes too noisy and messy for clients to visit. She had offered such online meetings to her clients before the COVID-19 pandemic, but not all clients wished to proceed this way. Under the new conditions, even some of her elderly Korean patrons preferred not to leave their homes, and her practice became almost solely screen-mediated.

Jenn visited Korea in the summer of 2022 as a part of a project to teach an off-campus class on musok and musok arts for a college in Minnesota. The travel's goal was to plan and prepare for the students' visit. This was an innovative form of teaching a whole class of foreign students about musok while on an excursion in Korea, but unfortunately it did not materialize. Unlike most of her previous visits to Korea, this time Jenn was not accompanied by her spiritual mother. She did not conduct extensive rituals, and she visited places that could fit students' visits, such as the Museum of Shamanism (Fig. 7.9). The effort to hold such a unique field class fits

Fig. 7.9 Mudang Jenn during her visit in the Shamanism Museum in Seoul. July 2022, the photograph was taken by the author with consent from the people depicted

the double vocation that Jenn follows: being a practicing mudang, while also being a spokesperson and advocate for shamanic healing in the United States and in general.

3 Discussion

Not all Korean shamans work with foreigners—in fact, most do not. The ability to speak non-Korean languages in a manner that can enable direct communication between mudang and client is mostly lacking, as is the ability of foreign visitors and residents in Korea to speak Korean. While many tourists and temporary workers seek fortune-telling as an entertaining activity, only a few seek the advice of mudang regarding life-changing consultations. Nevertheless, those who have made musok available to non-Koreans have been using the media—and especially the internet—extensively as a means to reach global audiences who are potential clients and spiritual followers. Such international activity has become an easily achievable task in hypermodern conditions. Communication technologies that are within reach of billions have enabled the practical aspects of this cultural development, whereas cultural curiosity and the online search for spiritual guidance have increased the global awareness of such practices. Several million Koreans living in the diaspora, along with a few hundred Korean adoptees in the West, have also become the target audience of cosmopolitan mudang. The phenomenal success of Korean television dramas and films in the past 20 years has also played an important role in creating interest in mediated encounters of non-Koreans with musok. However, as mentioned above, not all Korean mudang practice with international clients.

In Seoul, people are constantly interconnected locally and globally through complex economic and cultural networks. As hypermodern South Korea has become more cosmopolitan, geographic national boundaries have become more blurred and local traditions have become more infused with practitioners and clients who are not necessarily Korean natives. In the hypermodern spiritual market, each practitioner can self-tailor their beliefs and market practices using contemporary means and artifacts.[10] Life in Seoul, as in other hypermodern societies, is full of "non-places," where the masses circulate, commute, and work with little personalized

[10] See Yun (2019, pp. 108–113) on how the Southern-style mudang of Jeju island discuss their fees with clients. See Kendall (2021) for a discussion of the material aspects of musok.

contact (Augé 1995). In terms of the geographic aspects of musok, this means that rituals and consultations are no longer performed only in the Korean Peninsula—and definitely not solely in the regions from which they originated. Sometimes they are conducted over the internet, with the mudang and clients in different continents.

In the worldview of the cosmopolitan mudang, spiritual mediation is an option for anyone rather than a nation-bound heritage. They can communicate with Korean and non-Korean spirits and gods and perform in Korea or abroad for Korean or non-Korean clients. The mudang that are discussed above are cosmopolitan both in their view of the human world and in that of the supernatural. They accept "the coexistence of cultures in the individual experience [and express] a willingness to engage with the other" (Hannerz 1990, p. 239). The transnational cultures in which cosmopolitans usually engage are most often in the realms of business and politics but, as explored above, can be extended to include the mudang, who are "systematically and directly involved with more than one culture" (ibid., p. 244).

When practitioners of musok began taking on the media as a crucial component in expanding their clientele base, they did not pause to explain what regional style they practiced or where their spiritual mother (i.e., the shaman who initiated them) learned spiritual mediation. They did not confine themselves to reside in a specific part of the country, nor necessarily to practicing a style connected exclusively with a certain place of origin. Some have increasingly relied on clients who are not Koreans, while others have immigrated and continued to practice abroad. The current situation is far from showing a general collapse of the old system as predicted by critical postmodernity (Augé 1995, p. 26); rather, hypermodern social structures, with their inherent quality of excess, allow for the old and the new to coexist in a vernacular, non-contradictory manner (ibid., pp. 29, 30; Gottschalk 2018).

Vernacular religion is a creative process, where no official script or rules prevail. Thus, shamanism is especially suited to correspond with changing circumstances. Spiritual mediators became media celebrities beyond the audience of their direct clients and, in the process, some have taken on the role of musok advocates and protectors of magical ways of thought and practice. In a workshop sold through the website of Mudang Jenn, one can take a class in New York or online, where she is "Teaching folk magic to empower your connection with the spirits of Korea."[11] Like the spiritualist mediums in the Victorian age discussed by Natale (2013, p. 95), contemporary mudang often present their rituals in theaters and public halls, and similarly, they mingle "entertainment with religious beliefs, and frequently offered some spectacular manifestations of spirit presence." They also charge fees for their performances and employ assistants and business managers. These features, together with the usage of media, allow for the discussion of contemporary mudang as a part of celebrity culture. Some mansin have been accused of being too media-oriented or derogatively called "superstar shamans," implying that they have neglected their religious quest to some extent (Choi 1987, p. 77). Nevertheless, the practitioners discussed above cannot in any way be denigrated as "phony" practitioners—"insufficiently inspired and badly trained" (Kendall 2008, p. 155). They dedicate most of their time and effort to appeasing angry spirits and helping suffering clients.

Mudang are different from celebrities in the entertainment industry, as they usually do not engage in commercial advertising of general consumer goods for transnational conglomerates. Nevertheless, their global engagement benefits from the same trends that Elliott and Boyd (2018, p. 14) have identified: "the more the global spread of communication networks and digital networks unfolds, the denser and more complex become patterns of cultural life." They might not be worth millions of dollars, but they perform the function of a curious persona, beyond the scope of everyday life. Celebrity mudang are venerated by their followers because "In an entertainment culture of manufactured hype and planned novelties, celebrities project an image of life beyond the routines of the everyday and thus one that is tantalizingly transgressive" (ibid., p. 21). This is similar to celebrity creation in other genres of popular culture in the Korean Wave (hallyu), as described by Kim (2013c).

The increased legitimization and acceptance of musok practitioners is a process of constant remodeling and reshaping of traditional culture to fit the new material and global conditions, while allowing Koreans to keep their sense of self and cultural uniqueness in the face of new ideas and practices. The blurry boundaries between objects and meanings—typical of hypermodern societies—are a given in musok, where the unseen spiritual realm is believed to coexist within the human world, and unforeseen

[11] Mudang Jenn's homepage has a section called "Workshop and Classes" https://www.shamanmudang.com/offerings (accessed on January 25 2023).

powers of nature and ancestral spirits interfere in the human experience at the micro level. Therefore, mudang are in full performance in the here and now, in various visible locations in and around Seoul, as well as in the rest of Korea. They advertise their work in signposted offices in downtown areas, perform noisy rituals at rental shrines on hills around the metropolis, provide artistic performances at festivals and official openings, and feature in various mass media depictions.

Many mudang became celebrities through mainstream media and have managed to bypass word-of-mouth promotion or endorsement by scholars and experts (Sarfati 2016). In more recent times, they have increasingly created their own image through internet platforms such as YouTube and social media. This does not mean that they have millions of followers or clients, but the numbers of people who know about them can reach many thousands, whereas their actual clientele is a few dozen. In this respect, mudang who become celebrities in their field undergo a process of magnification, and their global appeal is a part of the overall global celebrity production process that exists in various fields, from popular culture to politics and beyond (Elliott and Boyd 2018, p. 10). The mainstreaming of spiritual practices through the media is related to the socio-historical context, but without the active interest and actions of the cosmopolitan mudang, their transnational spiritual mediation would not be possible. Hypermodernity as a social condition that accelerates international flows of culture, excess in visual promotion, and the broad availability of technology-mediated experiences fits the work of global spiritual healing and divination, but also requires the exercise of personal agency by them and their clients. Cosmopolitan mudang are a type of new spiritual practitioners who are promoted and acknowledged mainly through their internet and media activity.

The four mudang introduced above demonstrate how specific circumstances and abilities have contributed to the internationalization of musok in each case. Yi Hae-gyeong—the oldest among them—is a Korean who likes Western music and arts, and she is famous thanks to her participation in major documentary films. Most of her clients are Koreans, but she also conducts consultations and rituals with Korean–Japanese clients and occasional foreigners. Pang Eun-mi is a younger mudang who had been immersed in the media industry before her initiation and can speak English, so she can easily seek Western clients via social media. However, her main clientele consists of Koreans living in Korea. Andrea Kalff is a German spiritual practitioner who was initiated and taught by the famous

Korean mudang Kim Geum-hwa and now caters mostly to European clients. Mudang Jenn—the youngest of the four—is a Korean American who works mainly with clients from the New York area—some of Korean descent, and others who found her thanks to her social media presence. The four became mudang through very different life circumstances, were initiated at different times and in different locations, and work with different kinds of clientele, but they share the same kinds of spiritual healing skills and religious beliefs.

A few statements are common to all four mudang: that spirits can communicate beyond spoken languages; that mudang clients do not have to be Koreans; that understanding of the Korean language is needed only for following the performance script and not necessarily for the spiritual work involved; that musok practice can be beneficial and should be open to global audiences; and that media depictions are a vehicle for making the practice available to more people in Korea and worldwide.

The lives of these spiritual mediators revolve around hypermodern technologies and mindsets, while their religion is ancient and linked to historic ancestors and spirits. They do not view this as a dichotomy; rather, they view their cosmology as eternal and universal, and their practice as beneficial to people in the contemporary urban clusters where they work. The manner in which they have adjusted their practices to the changing conditions have not, in their perspective, affected the essence of it. They can communicate with clients over the phone or via video chat because their communication with the supernatural is enacted through their own bodies, and not through the body of the clients; they can shorten the rituals to fit the pace of the urban lifestyle because they negotiate such changes with the spirits they venerate and receive their permission to do so; they can emigrate to places far from their ancestral burial grounds because the spirits of their ancestors are embodied within them. They still view their own physical materialization as a shrine for supernatural entities, and their clients hear that very same explanation when they ask about their beliefs and practices.

In their media appearances, the mudang explain this worldview using traditional terms and idioms because they feel needed in their communities, even when the grouping is no longer bound by geographic, national, or cultural boundaries. The fact that most venerated entities are Korean in origin is a result of the limited knowledge that mudang had about the world in premodern times. Thus, a contemporary mudang can venerate the American general MacArthur, who helped South Korea in the Korean

War, or Joan of Arc, if she appears in a mudang's dream. The musok pantheon is polytheistic, and among the thousands of venerated entities, there is room for all nationalities and cultures.

The vernacular is flexible in meaning and usage because institutions do not supervise it, and it is often an undocumented oral tradition, even when written down by the users, but not in canonized manuals. The vernacular is flexible because it stems from a personal interpretation of the religious experience (Primiano 1995, p. 43). Thus, when musok goes global, it is locally interpreted and transformed to fit the target audience.

This recent development does not mean that musok as a whole has become an international religion but, rather, that some of the practitioners have extended their work to various locations and cultures. The local mudang continue to pursue their traditions of spiritual practices—some even with distinct attention to local styles of practice. As emphasized by Hannerz (1990, p. 250), "there can be no cosmopolitans without locals." The mudang communicate with the supernatural in a nonverbal manner and, therefore, are not limited to spirits who speak the same tongue. Similarly, mudang can accommodate clients of every origin, but in this case, they might seek interpreters to bypass language gaps. So far, Google and Naver translation tools have not been very successful in translating musok terminology, but this is merely a technical hindrance. In their hearts, mudang believe that they can help everyone. They are truly cosmopolitan spirits.

References

Akamatsu, Chijo, and Takashi Akiba. 1938. *Chōsen Fuzuko no Kenkyū (Study of Korean Shamanism)*. Vol. 1, 2. Tokyo: Osakayago Shōten.

Augé, Marc. 1995. *Non-places: An Introduction to Anthropology of Supermodernity*. Translated by John Howe. London: Verso.

Bak, Gi-bok, dir. 2003. Mudang: Reconciliation Between the Living and the Dead (yoeongmae: sanja wa jugueunja eui hwahae). Seoul: M&FC – Production.

Bak, Chan-gyeong. 2014. *Mansin: Ten Thousand Spirits*. Seoul: BOL.

Baker, Don. 1994. Monks, Medicine, and Miracles: Health and Healing in the History of Korean Buddhism. *Korean Studies* 18:50–75. https://doi.org/10.1353/ks.1994.0011.

Blank, Trevor J. 2009. Toward a Conceptual Framework for the Study of Folklore and the Internet. In *Folklore and the Internet: Vernacular Expression in a Digital World*, 1–21. Logan, UT: Utah State University Press.

Bruno, Antonetta Lucia. 2002. *The Gate of Words: Language in the Rituals of Korean Shamans*. Leiden: University of Leiden Press.

Cho, Chin-gyu, dir. 2013. *Man on the Edge (baksu geondal)*. Seoul: Showbox.

Choe, Gil-seong. 1978. *Hanguk Musok eui Yeongu (Research of Korean Shamanism)*. Seoul: Asia Munhwasa.

Choi, Chungmoo. 1987. *The Competence of Korean Shamans as Performers of Folklore*. Ph.D. dissertation, Indiana University, Bloomington.

Creative, Denn. 2022, June 17. Euisim gadeuk han wegugini hanguk chegoeui mudangeul manandamyeon? (What If a Suspicious Foreigner Meets the Best Shaman in Korea?). https://www.youtube.com/watch?v=9_Q84zI6gCw. Accessed 25 January 2023.

Documentaries. 2019. Korean Film Page. http://koreanfilm.org/docs.html. Accessed 25 January 2023.

Elliott, Anthony, and Ross Boyd. 2018. Celebrity and Contemporary Culture: A Critical Analysis of Some Theoretical Accounts. In *Routledge Handbook of Celebrity Studies*, ed. Anthony Elliott, 3–25. New York: Routledge.

Giddens, Anthony. 2011. *Runaway World*. London: Profile Books.

Go, Jae-hyeon, dir. 2022. *Café Minamdang*. Seoul: KBS2.

Gottschalk, Simon. 2018. *The Terminal Self: Everyday Life in Hypermodern Times. Interactionist Currents*. New York: Routledge.

Grayson, James Huntley. 1998. Christianity and Korean Religions: Accommodation as an Aspect of the Emplantation of a World Religion. In *Korean Shamanism Revivals Survivals, and Change*, ed. Keith Howard, 133–152. Seoul: Seoul Press.

Guillemoz, Alexandre. 1992. Seoul, the Widow, and the Mudang: Transformations of Urban Korean Shamanism. *Diogenes* 158:115–127.

Hannerz, Ulf. 1990. Cosmopolitans and Locals in World Culture. *Theory, Culture & Society* 7:237–251. https://doi.org/10.1177/026327690007002014.

Hannerz, Ulf. 1991. *Cultural Complexity: Studies in the Organization of Meaning*. New Yok: Columbia University Press.

Harvey, Youngsook Kim. 1979. *Six Korean Women: The Socialization of Shamans*. St. Paul: West Publishers.

Hogarth, Hyun-key Kim. 1998. 'Trance' and 'Possession Trance' in the Perspective of Korean Shamanism. In *Korean Shamanism Revivals, Survivals, and Change*, ed. Keith Howard, 45–54. Seoul: Seoul Press.

Hong, Dae-han. 2006. *Hwanghae-do eui Muga (Shamanic Texts of Hwanghae-do Province)*. Seoul: Minsogweon.

Howard, Keith. 1998. Preserving the Spirits? Ritual, State Sponsorship, and Performance. In *Korean Shamanism Revivals, Survivals, and Change*, ed. Keith Howard, 187–217. Seoul: Seoul Press.

Janelli, Roger L., and Dawnhee Yim Janelli. 2002. Ancestor Rites and Capitalist Industrialization in a South Korean Village. *Korea Journal* 42:298–332.

Kalff, Andrea, and Iris Zachenhofer. 2022. *Die Schamanen-Therapie – Die Wissenschaft entdeckt die Heilkunst unserer Ahnen*. Vien: Gebundene Ausgabe.
Kendall, Laurel. 1988. *The Life and Hard Times of a Korean Shaman: of Tales and the Telling of Tales*. Honolulu: University of Hawaii Press.
Kendall, Laurel. 2008. Shamanic Nostalgia. In *Korea in the Middle: Korean Studies and Area Studies: Essays in Honour of Boudewijn Walraven*, ed. Remco E. Breuker, 144–176. Leiden: CNWS Publications.
Kendall, Laurel. 2021. Gods and Things: Is 'Animism' an Operable Concept in Korea? *Religions* 12:283. https://doi.org/10.3390/rel12040283.
Kim, Geum-hwa. 1995. *Kim Geum-hwa eui Mugajip: Gomunattae Mansin, Huina Baeksong eui Norae (Kim Geum-hwa Shamanic Texts and Songs)*. Seoul: Munumsa.
Kim, Seong-nae. 2003. Korean Shamanic Heritage in Cyber Culture. *Bibliotheca Shamanistica* 11:279–295.
Kim, Jin-yeong, dir. 2009. *Fortune Salon* (cheongdam bosal). Seoul: Next Entertainment World.
Kim, Jeong-uk, dir. 2013a. *The Silk Flower* (bidan kkotgil). Seoul: Mountain Pictures.
Kim, Kwang-ok. 2013b. Colonial Body Indigenous Soul: Religion as a Contested Terrain of Culture. In *Colonial Rule and Social Change in Korea 1910–1945*, ed. Hong-yung Lee, Yong-chool Ha, and Clark Sorensen, 264–313. Seattle: University of Washington Press.
Kim, Youna, ed. 2013c. *The Korean Wave: Korean Media Go Global*. London: Routledge.
Lee, Duhyun (I Du-hyeon). 1990. Korean Shamans: Role Playing Through Trance Possession. In *By Means of Performance: Intercultural Studies of Theatre and Ritual*. Edited by Richard Schechner and Willa Appel, pp. 149–166. New York: Cambridge University Press.
Mills, Simon. 2007. *Healing Rhythms: The World of South Korea's East Coast Hereditary Shamans*. Aldershot: Ashgate.
Natale, Simone. 2013. Spiritual Stars: Religion and Celebrity in the Careers of Spiritualist Mediums. *Celebrity Studies* 4:94–96.
Nisic, Natacha, dir. 2014. *Andrea's Sky* (Le Ciel D'andrea). Paris: Seconde Vague Productions. HD Video.
Oak, Sung-Deuk. 2010. Healing and Exorcism: Christian Encounters with Shamanism in Early Modern Korea. *Asian Ethnology* 69:95–128.
Park, Migyung [Bak Migyeong]. 2003. Korean Shaman Rituals Revisited: The Case of Chindo Ssikkim Kut (Cleansing Rituals). Ethnomusicology 47: 355–375.
Primiano, Leonard Norman. 1995. Vernacular Religion and the Search for Method in Religious Folklife. *Western Folklore* 54:37–56.
Ryang, Sonia. 1997. *North Koreans in Japan: Language, Ideology, and Identity*. Boulder, CO: Westview Press.

Sarfati, Liora. 2016. Shifting Agencies Through New Media: New Social Statuses for Female Korean Shamans. *Journal of Korean Studies* 21:179–212.

Sarfati, Liora. 2021. *Contemporary Korean Shamanism: From Ritual to Digital.* Bloomington: Indiana University Press.

Sarfati, Liora. 2023. The Cosmopolitan Vernacular: Korean Shamans (Mudang) in the Global Spirituality Market. *Religions* 14: 189.

Sarfati, Liora. 2024. From Rural Outcasts to Urban Cosmopolitans: Spiritual Healers in Seoul. *Urbanities-Journal of Urban Ethnography* 14 (1): 84–100.

Schmelzer, Thomas, dir. 2018. *Wiedegerburt* (Rebirth). Munich: Mystica GMBH. DVD.

Seo, Maria. 2002. *Hanyang Kut: Korean Shaman Ritual Music from Seoul.* New York: Routledge.

Thompson, Craig J., and Siok Kuan Tambyah. 1999. Trying to Be Cosmopolitan. *Journal of Consumer Research* 26 (3): 214–241.

Tvchosun, prod. 2012–2013. Job Stories (storyjobs). http://tv.chosun.com/enter/storyjobs/main/main.html. Accessed 16 March 2019.

Yang, Jongsung. 2004a. Korean Cultural Property Protection Law with Regard to Korean Intangible Heritage. *Museum International* 56:180–188.

Yang, Jongsung (Jong-seung). 2004b. Gangsinmu Seseupmu Yuhyeongrone Ttareun Musogyeongu Geomto (A Discourse of Korean Shamanism Studies Examining Possessed Shamans and Hereditary Shamans). Hanguk Musokhak (Korean Shamanism) 8: 9–34.

Yi, Chang-jae, dir. 2006. *Between* (sai-eseo). Seoul: DK Media.

Yun, Kyoim. 2019. *The Shaman's Wages: Trading in Ritual on Cheju Island.* Seattle: Washington University Press.

CHAPTER 8

Religious Disaffiliation and the Religious Identity of Koreans: Focusing on "Religious Nones" and "Meditation"

Hae-young Seong

1 Introduction

Contemporary society is undergoing a significant process of secularization, marked by a pervasive trend of religious disaffiliation. This phenomenon manifests in various forms, with the most prominent being the waning social influence of religion and a notable decline in the number of religious adherents. South Korea, a country historically recognized for its remarkably pluralistic religious landscape, is no exception to this development, as its religious population continues to diminish at an accelerated pace. According to a 2021 Gallup Korea survey, although Koreans continue to adhere to a wide array of Eastern and Western religious traditions, the proportion of individuals identifying as "religious nones" has surged from 46.5% in 2004 to an extraordinary 60% in 2022 (Gallup Korea).

H. Seong (✉)
Department of Religious Studies, Seoul National University,
Seoul, Republic of Korea
e-mail: lohela@snu.ac.kr

© The Author(s), under exclusive license to Springer Nature Singapore Pte Ltd. 2025

Y. Yoo, S. C. Lee (eds.), *Reimagining Korea*, Palgrave Series in Contemporary Korean Studies,
https://doi.org/10.1007/978-981-96-6990-5_8

The rapid growth in the share of religious nones in Korea has even sparked concerns about the potential extinction of traditional religions. Paradoxically, even amidst this weakening of religious influence and the accelerating trend of disaffiliation, an unexpected phenomenon has emerged. A significant number of people, regardless of their religious backgrounds—including those who identify as religious nones—are participating in Buddhist *Templestay* programs, which offer an opportunity to experience the life of a Buddhist monk. Furthermore, various forms of meditation, with "mindfulness" meditation at the forefront, are increasingly used in secular contexts such as higher education, healthcare, and psychological counseling, serving as therapeutic techniques for addressing modern mental health challenges. These developments are particularly noteworthy in that they involve the appropriation of religious places and contemplative practices, even in the absence of religious belief.

This trend is best analyzed through the conceptual structure of "identity," which has been explored through various lenses in philosophical, sociological, and psychological discourses, despite the inherent challenges in defining it (Breakwell 1986, 10; Deaux 1992, 10–15). This chapter primarily conceptualizes identity from a psychological perspective, viewing it as a multifaceted construct that encompasses a broad scope of personal characteristics, including personality, traits, ethnicity, and values. At its core, identity pertains to the way individuals define themselves and, by extension, how they articulate their sense of self in relational contexts. Furthermore, identity functions as a foundational system through which individuals establish long-term life purposes and translate these into concrete actions. The increasing popularity of *Templestay* and "meditation" can therefore be understood as an effort by non-religious Koreans to explore a new form of (religious) identity.

By focusing on the psychological aspect of personal identity and the pursuit of an expanded identity through religious experiences, William James' definition of religion provides an effective analytical approach. He treats "personal experience as the exclusive subject of his study," defining religion as "the feelings, acts and experiences of individual men in their solitude, so far as they apprehend themselves to stand in relation to whatever they may consider the divine" (James 1902, 36).

This chapter examines recent developments in Korea that transcend the traditional boundaries of institutional religion. As a preliminary step, it provides an analysis of Korea's religious landscape based on statistical data. It then examines the complex religious identities of individuals who self-identify as religious nones. Subsequently, the study investigates two illustrative cases of religiosity beyond traditional religious frameworks: Buddhist *Templestay* programs and university meditation courses. These cases reveal how some individuals in Korea are redefining their (religious) identities in distinct ways. Finally, I argue that these efforts involving new (religious) identities are likely to engender significant transformations, not only within traditional religious institutions but also across Korean society at large.

2 The Emergence of "Religious Nones"

In Korean, the terms *mujonggyoin* or *bijonggyoin* refer to individuals who do not identify with any religion, specifically those unaffiliated with organized religious institutions. This concept is commonly translated into English as "non-religious," "religious nones," or "religiously unaffiliated." This chapter primarily employs the term "religious nones," or more simply "nones."

The main factor contributing to the rise of nones is secularization, characterized by the diminishing societal influence of religion. Since the advent of modernity, religious values and norms have progressively lost their authoritative status, supplanted by human rationality as the dominant organizing principle of society (Berger 1967, 107; Wilson 1982, 148). This movement, originating in the West, has expanded globally. While debates continue regarding the degree and nature of secularization (Stark and Bainbridge 1985, 1–3; Hadden 1997, 597–607), it is undeniable that traditional authority of religion has weakened, resulting in a consistent decline in adherence to organized religious institutions.

This shift is also visible in South Korea, where the increasing proportion of nones reflects broader patterns of religious disaffiliation. Notably, the census conducted every five years by the *Korea Statistical Office* provides critical data due to its comprehensive sample size and high credibility. Religion was first included in the census in 1985, and data have been collected every decade since. According to the census, the percentage of nones was 57.4% in 1985, declined to 49.3% in 1995 and 46.9% in 2005, but surged to 56.1% in 2015, marking a nearly 10% increase over the decade (Korea Statistical Office 2015). The notably high figure of 57.4% in 1985 can be attributed to the inclusion of adherents of less formally institutionalized religious traditions, such as Confucianism, shamanism, and folk religion (Kang 1997, 91). Since 2005, the share of nones has risen by approximately 1% annually. In the same census, the largest religious group was Protestants (19.7%), followed by Buddhists (15.5%) and Catholics (7.9%).

Gallup Korea, which has conducted periodic surveys on religion since 1984, corroborates this tendency. In 2004, 46.5% of respondents described themselves as nones; by 2014, this figure had risen to 50%, closely aligning with the 56.1% recorded in the 2015 census. In 2021, Gallup reported that 60% of South Koreans identified as nones. The distribution of religious affiliation was similarly consistent: Protestants accounted for 17%, Buddhists 16%, and Catholics 6%.

A more recent survey conducted by the *Korean Christian Pastors Association* (KCPA) presents similar findings. Conducted every five years since 2012, the KCPA survey shows a rise in the proportion of nones from 44.9% in 2012 to 53.4% in 2017 and reaching a notable 62.9% in 2023. In 2023, the distribution of religious affiliation revealed that Protestants accounted for 16.6%, Buddhists 12.4%, and Catholics 7.8%. While all religious groups have seen a decline, the Protestant population has experienced the most significant reduction, decreasing from 22.5% in 2012 to 15% in 2022 (The Korean Christian Pastors Association 2023).

The aforementioned surveys concerning individuals who self-identify as nones are constrained by a methodological limitation: they do not provide a nuanced analysis of how respondents conceptualize the notion of religion nor do they elucidate the specific criteria underpinning their self-identification as nones. Despite these limitations, the statistical data reveal three defining characteristics of South Korea's non-religious population.

2.1 High Prevalence of Nones

According to Gallup Korea's 2021 survey, 60% of South Koreans identify as nones. This figure is strikingly high, excluding communist regimes, such as China, where 90% of the population identified as nones in 2018 (Pew Research Center 2023). In contrast, nones in the United States accounted for 26% of the population as of 2023 (The Public Religion Research Institute 2024), while the global average was 15.6% in 2020 (Pew Research Center 2022). The share of nones in South Korea is notably higher than that in Canada and Australia, countries that have been closely monitoring this phenomenon. In the case of Canada, the proportion increased from 10.5% in 1985 to 23.8% in 2010 (Wilkins-Laflamme 2015, 478), while in Australia, it grew from 16.6% in 1996 to 38.9% in

2021 (Possamai et al. 2024, 2). Given South Korea's status as a representative multi-religious society where both Eastern and Western religions actively coexist, the high prevalence of religious nones is particularly noteworthy.

2.2 *Rapid Growth of Nones*

The proportion of nones in South Korea increased from 46.9% in 2005 to 60% in 2021, according to Gallup Korea, reflecting an annual growth rate of approximately 1%. This rate is double that of the United States, where the share of nones increased by 5% over a decade (2013–2023). Furthermore, this rapid growth has coincided with a significant shift in societal perceptions of religion. Gallup Korea reports that the percentage of individuals who consider religion important to their personal lives declined from 68% in 1984 to 38% in 2021. Similarly, the KCPA survey indicates that 70% of respondents hold negative views of religion. For example, a survey by *the Christian Ethics Movement of Korea* found that only 9% of nones expressed trust in Christians, and just 10.6% had confidence in Korean churches (The Christian Ethics Movement ofKorea 2023).

2.3 *Generational Differences in Proportion of Nones*

Religious nones in South Korea are disproportionately concentrated among younger generations. According to Gallup Korea, 78% of individuals in their teens and 20s identified as non-religious in 2021, nearly double the 41% of those aged 60 and older. Younger generations also tend to exhibit more negative attitudes toward religion, particularly regarding its social significance and influence. This generational pattern, wherein the majority of younger Koreans identify as nones and hold critical views of religion, strongly suggests a bleak future for organized religion in Korea.

The high proportion of nones, the rapid growth of their population, and the generational divergence in attitudes toward religion are key to understanding the characteristics of Korea's non-religious population. These factors also underscore the pivotal role of nones in shaping Korea's evolving religious landscape. Notably, contrary to conventional assumptions, South Korea's nones are not a homogenous group, but rather exhibit complex and multifaceted religious identities.

3 The Complex Identities and Backgrounds of Nones

To date, no statistical survey has focused specifically on the religious identities of nones in South Korea. In existing surveys, nones have been uniformly categorized as a single residual group when determining religious affiliation. Nevertheless, Korean scholars who have examined this issue have recognized the varied identities of nones (Choi 2019, 14–17; Kang 1997, 107–113; Woo 2016, 43–46). In a similar vein, in the West, nones have introduced a range of non-religious categories—"atheists, agnostics, Spiritual but Not Religious (SBNR), secular humanists, or simply 'none'" (Cororan et al. 2021; Edgell et al. 2016; Sanders et al. 2020; Possamai et al. 2024).

In my assessment, nones in South Korea can be broadly classified into four distinct groups. The first comprises materialists who reject any supernatural dimension. The second group includes individuals who were once affiliated with religious institutions but no longer practice their faith. These individuals, such as "lapsed Catholics" or Protestant "*ganaan sindo* (Canaan believers),"[1] may still express a willingness to return to a particular religion and thus align with the concept of "believing without belonging" (Davie 1994, 74–91). The third group consists of those who, while not materialists, have no intention of affiliating with any organized religion. Some members of this group seek to embody forms of religiosity outside institutionalized frameworks, making them the primary focus of this chapter. It is important to acknowledge that a portion of this group may be categorized as "Spiritual but Not Religious (SBNR)." Nevertheless, some individuals within the SBNR category continue to retain a sense of affiliation with institutionalized religion, aligning more closely with the "Spiritual *and* Religious" classification, as observed in cases from the United States and Europe (Parsons 2022, 92). The fourth group includes individuals entirely indifferent to religion, representing the most ambiguous category in terms of religious identity. Given the absence of targeted statistical surveys, the precise proportions of these four groups remain

[1] The term *Ganaan Sindo* or "Cannan believers" refers to believers who refrain from attending church. This term is a creative wordplay on the Korean phrase *annaga* (meaning "not going"), reversed to form a meaningful designation. For a more comprehensive discussion on the "Canaan believers" in Korea, see Chong (2014).

unclear. However, several studies have highlighted the complex identities of religious nones in South Korea.

Existing statistical data indirectly confirm that nones are not a homogenous group. According to a 2021 Gallup Korea survey, 23% of non-religious respondents believed in the existence of the soul after death, while 45% accepted the possibility of supernatural miracles. Similarly, a 2021 survey conducted by *the Ministry of Culture, Sports, and Tourism* revealed that 24.4% of nones believed in an afterlife, and 34.9% acknowledged the existence of supernatural beings (the Ministry of Culture, Sports, and Tourism 2022). These findings show the presence of nones who accept supernatural dimensions, underscoring their incompatibility with a purely materialist classification.

Even in Western countries where theistic religions predominate, the multifaceted identities of nones are well acknowledged (Altemeyer 2009; Hout and Fisher 2002; Storm 2009). The systems of classification employed in these countries diverge from those in South Korea. In the United States, for instance, religious nones are categorized into three subgroups: atheists, agnostics, and those with "nothing in particular" (The Public Religion Research Institute 2024). This classification framework, however, fails to sufficiently account for individuals affiliated with atheistic religious traditions, such as Buddhism, as well as nones in South Korea who explicitly reject materialist worldviews.

Particular attention should be given to individuals who hold a non-materialistic worldview yet express no intention of adopting organized religion. This group is closely tied to emerging efforts in South Korea to explore new forms of religious identity. Unlike materialists, these individuals may eventually affiliate with specific religious institutions, thereby functioning as dynamic agents of change in the religious realm. Moreover, this group includes those who transcend traditional religious boundaries, seeking to embody religiosity in entirely novel ways. While there is broad scholarly consensus that accurately defining their identity is a complex task, in Western contexts, groups exhibiting such identities are typically categorized as SBNRs (Parsons 2022, 79–82).

Understanding the high proportion and complex identities of South Korea's nones requires considering not only the broader trend of secularization but also the distinctive characteristics of Korean religious culture. Unlike societies dominated by a single religion, Korea has historically fostered a heterogeneous religious environment. Moreover, religious traditions such as Confucianism and shamanism, which lack formal organizational structures, have exerted significant influence. According to the 1985 census—the first to include religion—57.4% of the population identified as non-religious. While the precise composition of this group remains unclear, it likely included many who identified with Confucian or shamanistic traditions (Kang 1997, 109–112). During the Japanese colonial period, Confucianism and shamanism were not classified as religions. Reflecting this shift, the 1985 census excluded shamanism from its religious categories. However, as organized religions such as Christianity and Buddhism expanded over the following two decades, the share of religious followers increased by approximately 10%, while the percentage of nones declined to 46.9% in 2005. Over the next decade, as believers left Christianity and Buddhism, the proportion of "genuine" nones—those without Confucian or shamanistic backgrounds—rose by approximately 10%.

Succinctly put, South Korea's high level of religious freedom and its pluralistic religious environment have significantly contributed to the rise of nones. In a society without a dominant religion, individuals experience minimal social pressure when changing or abandoning their faith. Except for a few insular new religious movements, Koreans generally face no significant barriers to joining or leaving religious organizations. This context has created a highly favorable environment for the growth of nones. Conversely, it has been documented that in societies where a particular religion predominates, non-religious individuals or atheists are at risk of experiencing moral condemnation or distrust (Yeatts et al. 2021).

Koreans exhibit a strong tendency to adopt religious doctrines, worldviews, and practices flexibly, irrespective of their formal religious affiliation. A representative example is the belief in reincarnation, as explored through the following question: "Do you believe that, after death, individuals are reborn in some form in this world?" According to a 2014 Gallup Korea survey, the percentage of respondents who accepted the concept of reincarnation was as follows: Buddhists (38%), Protestants (34%), Catholics (29%), and nones (21%) (Gallup Korea 2002).[2] Notably, reincarnation—while not a central tenet, but a component of the Buddhist worldview—was accepted by fewer than half of Buddhist respondents, a

[2]The acceptance rate of the doctrine of reincarnation among Buddhists was recorded at 29% in 1984, 37% in both 1997 and 2004, and 38% in 2014. For Catholics, the acceptance rate stood at 25% in 1984, 30% in 1997, peaked at 40% in 2004, and declined to 29% in 2014 (Gallup Korea 2002).

rate comparable to that of individuals from other religious traditions and nones. This suggests that Koreans readily adopt doctrines from multiple traditions, further underscoring the multilayered and complex nature of their religiosity (Baker 2008, 12–13).

The aforementioned characteristics, in conjunction with broader secularization trends, are essential for understanding the high proportion and nuanced identities of South Korea's nones. Unless there is a significant shift in current dynamics, nones are likely to continue reshaping South Korea's religious sphere. If their numbers continue to grow at the current rate, the possibility of religion's eventual decline—even within a historically multi-religious society—cannot be dismissed. However, the increasing popularity of religious services and programs such as *Templestay* and meditative practices suggests new and unexpected avenues for exploring religiosity within this increasingly secular context.

4 *Templestay* and Meditation and Practice Courses at University

Among various other examples, the *Templestay* program and university meditation courses stand out as particularly effective demonstrations of recent changes, supporting the critical points I highlighted earlier based on the provided statistical data. *Templestay* is an experiential initiative offered by Buddhist temples, designed to immerse participants in traditional Buddhist practices. The program includes a diverse range of activities, such as *Seon* (Zen) meditation, the 108 *bae* (108 prostrations), and tea ceremony with monks, thereby providing a glimpse into Buddhist culture. Typically conducted within temple precincts, *Templestay* programs are available as both single-day and overnight options, with participants covering the full cost. Initially launched in 2002 to accommodate foreign visitors during the Korea-Japan World Cup, the program aimed to introduce Korea's traditional culture while addressing accommodation shortages. Following its success, the "*Jogye* Order," the largest Buddhist sect in South Korea, expanded the initiative, leading to the establishment of a dedicated *Templestay Information Center* under the *Cultural Corps of Korean Buddhism*.[3]

[3] For detailed information on the *Templestay* program and the key initiatives of the Cultural Corps of Korean Buddhism and the Templestay Information Center, please refer to the following link: https://kbuddhism.com/

According to data from *the Ministry of Culture, Sports, and Tourism*, approximately 6.4 million individuals participated in *Templestay* programs between 2002 and 2023 (The Korean Culture Promotion Service 2022). Importantly, over half of the participants were non-Buddhists, highlighting the program's widespread appeal. Foreigners, in fact, accounted for roughly 10% of participants. Due to its remarkable success, *Templestay* was recognized in 2009 by the OECD as one of the "Top Five Successful Global Cultural Tourism Products" (The Korean Culture Promotion Service 2022). However, despite the success of the *Templestay* program, South Korea's Buddhist population declined by approximately three million between 2005 and 2015 (Jang 2018, 191–193). While public interest in Buddhist practices, particularly meditation, has surged, the number of Buddhist adherents has significantly decreased. This discrepancy, wherein *Templestay* flourishes while institutional Buddhism experiences a decline, calls for a nuanced interpretive analysis.

A related phenomenon, further blurring the boundaries between religion and secular practices, is the growing popularity of meditation across various societal sectors. In South Korea, meditation has increasingly been adopted in secular contexts, such as healthcare, education, and psychological counseling (Choe 2022, 117–119). A notable example is the *Meditation and Practice* course offered by the Department of Religious Studies at Seoul National University. This 15-week course introduces students to diverse meditative practices from various religious traditions and encourages them to develop their own personalized meditation techniques. The course curriculum blends theoretical lectures on the origins and development of meditative traditions with experiential practice sessions.

Originally introduced in the early 1980s to academically explore Buddhist doctrines and practices, the course gradually shifted its emphasis to meditation due to students' growing interest in *Seon* practice. Since 2016, when the course explicitly began focusing on the creation of personalized meditation methods, enrollment has consistently exceeded 100 students per semester. Participants, drawn from a wide range of academic disciplines, are predominantly non-religious, with over 80% identifying as such—a proportion that has steadily increased over time. This course exemplifies the secular adaptation of meditative practices, traditionally rooted in religious contexts, as therapeutic techniques in modern higher education. Similar courses are also offered at other institutions, such as *Wonkwang* University and *Dongguk* University, both of which were established by religious orders. However, although the course at Seoul National University has increasingly emphasized practice, it remains grounded in a comparative religious approach to teaching meditation, setting apart from those offered at the above-mentioned two universities with religious affiliations.

The central commonality between the *Templestay* program and the meditation courses offered at universities, as previously examined, lies in their focus on "meditation." This raises an important question: why has a religious practice like meditation gained such widespread popularity in a society where over 60% of the population identifies as nones? In the rapidly evolving social landscape of South Korea, individuals enjoy remarkable personal freedom but simultaneously bear immense responsibilities. The expansion of economic neoliberalism has intensified competition, weakened traditional family structures, and eroded long-standing values, leaving many Koreans feeling isolated. This newfound freedom, while offering greater autonomy, carries an implicit demand for total individual accountability, creating a sense of existential burden. As a result, many turn to meditation as a way to manage stress, anxiety, and other psychological challenges, often framing it within the context of "healing."

Simply put, Koreans connect with religious places, such as temples, and participate in religious practices, like meditation, as a means of seeking psychological comfort and exploring existential meaning. However, despite their engagement in these religious behaviors, they do not claim or adopt any formal religious affiliations. These individuals consciously engage with religious places and practices to confront deeper dimensions of existence and achieve personal healing, yet they reject affiliation with organized religion. In an attempt to comprehend such perplexing phenomena, new interpretative frameworks have been proposed.

In contemporary scholarship, spiritual aspirations traditionally realized within institutional frameworks are often categorized under "religiosity," whereas efforts to pursue these goals outside institutional boundaries are classified as "spirituality." As William James insightfully noted, the distinction between institutionalized religion and personal religion has been captured, particularly since the twentieth century, in the differentiation between religiosity and spirituality. "We are struck by one great partition which divides the religious field. On the one side of it lies institutional, on the other personal religion" (James 1902, 28). This distinct phenomenon corresponds to the conceptual framework of "*Spiritual but Not* Religious

(SBNR)" (Erlandson 2000; Fuller 2001, 5–7; Parsons 2022, 82–88).[4] Paradoxical concepts such as "the religion of no religion" (Kripal 2007, 8–11; Seong 2017, 1–2) and "religion beyond religion" (Choi 2005) further encapsulate this evolving trend.

As Parsons astutely observed, the spiritual pursuits of SBNRs are intricately aligned with therapeutic cultures, particularly with respect to "the need for wholeness, numinous experiences, and individuation" (Parsons 2022, 87–88). Within this paradigm, meditation assumes a foundational role in facilitating the construction of new (religious) identities. While these practices may not readily be classified as "religious" due to their detachment from traditional doctrines, their reliance on religious techniques and sacred places clearly situates them within a religious framework. This interplay between secular and spiritual dimensions underscores the evolving dynamics of religiosity and spirituality in contemporary South Korea (Choi 2012). Interestingly, these movements can be meaningfully interpreted within the context of Korea's religious culture.

5 Rediscovering an Ancient Future?

Two critical concepts for understanding the ongoing shifts in Korea are *the individual* and *identity*. Since the advent of modernity, the individual has emerged as the central agent of self-determination, a development that has profoundly influenced religious practices. People now exercise full autonomy, not only in deciding their religious affiliations but also in selectively adopting religious worldviews and practices irrespective of institutional membership. This transition is exemplified by *Templestay* programs and the growing social diffusion of meditation.

Moreover, the concept of individuality is inherently linked to identity. In Korea, many people are gradually moving beyond the confines of institutional religion in their search for an expanded sense of self. *Templestay*, for example, offers participants the opportunity to directly affirm their existential wholeness through Buddhist practices, facilitating personal

[4] Parsons asserts that the origins of the concept of SBNR (Spiritual but Not Religious) can be traced back to the mysticism of sixteenth- and seventeenth-century Europe, which emerged outside the framework of established religious traditions. He further argues that this notion evolved through the influence of William James, who emphasized the importance of individual mystical experiences, and can subsequently be observed among groups such as Theosophists, Transcendentalists, Quakers, Unitarians, and Spiritualists (Parsons 2022, 83–86).

healing and self-discovery. Similarly, students enrolled in the *Meditation and Practice* courses aim to enhance their adaptability to life by intuitively exploring previously unacknowledged dimensions of their being. In this context, meditation serves as a means for deconstructing and reconstructing constrained identities, enabling individuals to achieve an expanded self-awareness.

The roots of the demand for such transformative changes on self-discovery and identity can unexpectedly be traced back to Korea's religious history. Meditation has historically played a central role in shaping Korean religiosity (Baker 2008, 126–132). Most religious traditions in Korea—including Buddhism, Daoism, *Cheondo-gyo* (Cheondoism), and *Won Bulgyo* (*Won* Buddhism)—emphasize the transformative potential of intentional meditative practice, asserting that such practices can lead to extraordinary experiences that transcend the mundane. These traditions posit that through personal religious experiences, individuals gain profound insights into their identity and the interconnected nature of existence. Terms such as ***kkaedarum (enlightenment)***, ***dotong*** (***union with the Way***), ***innaechon*** (***Man is Heaven***), ***gyeonseong*** (***seeing one's true nature***), ***cheoninhapil*** (***unity of Heaven and Humanity***), and ***daeo*** (***great awakening***) attest to the possibility of achieving religious insight through experiential practice.

In other words, the current popularity of meditation in Korea should not be simplistically attributed to Western influences, such as secularization, despite the widespread adoption of "mindfulness" meditation techniques. Although mindfulness techniques were popularized in the United States, the significance of extraordinary experiences obtained through meditative practice has long been recognized in Korean religious traditions. Historically, Koreans have viewed such religious experiences as pivotal moments for deepening their understanding of self and the world. While the specific interpretations of these experiences have varied across religious traditions and historical periods, the emphasis on experiential insight remains a hallmark of Korean religious culture.

Additionally, Korea's pluralistic religious landscape has fostered a high degree of religious freedom, enabling individuals to selectively adopt and integrate doctrines and practices from various traditions. The contemporary movement of nones participating in religious places and practices based on personal needs reflects this pluralistic context. In a similar context, it has been observed that, compared to Westerners accustomed to theistic religions, Asians who identify with religious traditions such as

Buddhism, Confucianism, and Daoism tend to exhibit a greater affinity for multiple religious identities as well as for the identity of being unaffiliated with any particular religion (Cororan et al. 2021, 437). Today, many South Koreans, irrespective of their religious affiliation, engage in a variety of religious practices—such as meditation, *danjeon* breathing, yoga, and *gi (chi)* exercises—as a means of promoting personal well-being (Woo 2008, 36–44).

This historical receptiveness to diverse religious practices, coupled with a longstanding emphasis on profound religious experiences, serves as the foundation for the contemporary proliferation of meditation. The widespread appeal of *Templestay* and meditation signifies the individual's pursuit of affirming the inherent meaning and value of their existence. Arising from a demographic in which over 60% identify as non-religious, these practices symbolize attempts to rediscover and redefine personal identity. This significant phenomenon can thus be framed as both a psychological healing process and a search for an "expanded identity."

Given these dynamics, it would be overly simplistic to view South Korea's ongoing secularization and religious disaffiliation as indicators of religion's demise. While the rise in nones undoubtedly reflects the weakening of institutionalized religions, the growing popularity of *Templestay* and meditation suggests that we are not witnessing the collapse of religious worldviews. Religious nones in South Korea seeking to recognize dimensions beyond the self, either consciously or unconsciously, reject the label of "religious" or the concept of "religiosity" to describe these efforts. However, some of them selectively participate in various religious practices, including meditation, thereby expressing a personalized and eclectic form of religiosity (Chun 2016, 428–439; Kim 2018, 80–81). As Parsons suggests, "an unchurched, non-traditional, even anti-institutional orientation toward the divine" has emerged (Parsons 2022, 85). In other words, their efforts may be understood as an attempt to acknowledge and restore an integrative relationship with the transcendent reality. Consequently, the term "spirituality" has been adopted to encapsulate this trend.[5]

[5] While recognizing the inherent ambiguity and inclusiveness of the concept, numerous scholars have nevertheless endeavored to establish a consensus on its definition (Nolan et al. 2011; Norko 2018; Puchalski et al. 2014). Notably, the International Consensus Conference on Improving the Spiritual Dimension of Whole Person Care offers the following definition: "Spirituality is a dynamic and intrinsic aspect of humanity through which persons seek ultimate meaning, purpose, and transcendence, and experience relationship to self, family, others, community, society, nature, and the significance or sacred. Spirituality is expressed through beliefs, values, traditions, and practices" (Puchalski et al. 2014, 46).

Nonetheless, it would also be premature to conclusively interpret this trend as the appearance of an entirely new form of religiosity. This is because not all nones who interact with religious places and practices for the purpose of healing identify as religious, nor do they consider the meditation they practice to be religious. The majority of these individuals primarily seek psychological solace through *Templestay* and meditation (Song et al. 2014, 258–259). Therefore, these developments in South Korea suggests an ongoing exploration and potential reshaping of (religious) identity.

6 Conclusion: Religious Nones in Korea and the Future of Religion

Contemporary society is undergoing a significant transformation in various domains, including marriage, family, and career. These radical shifts exacerbate uncertainty, and the search for new identities inevitably leads to confusion and disorientation. Religion is not exempt from these dynamics. The conceptual differentiation between religiosity and spirituality, coupled with the increasing individualization of religious meaning, has importantly reshaped traditional understandings of "religion."

In South Korea, a complex and multifaceted religious spectrum has emerged, encompassing materialists, spiritual seekers unaffiliated with institutional religion, "*ganaan sindo* (Canaan believers)," lapsed adherents, and religious fundamentalists. At the center of these transformations lie nones, a group that is projected to continue growing in South Korea. According to a 2021 survey conducted by *the Ministry of Culture, Sports, and Tourism*, only 10.6% of religious nones expressed any intention of adopting a religion in the future (the Ministry of Culture, Sports, and Tourism 2022). Given the widespread indifference toward religion among younger generations, the expansion of nones appears inevitable. This trend is poised to serve as a critical factor in reshaping South Korea's religious landscape, potentially challenging the very survival of institutionalized religion.

The quest for (religious) identity among nones is likely to drive significant changes not only within the religious domain but also across broader societal contexts. South Korea, characterized by pervasive social conflicts and widespread psychological insecurity, ranks among the world's most conflict-prone nations, according to research conducted by the Policy Institute at King's College London (The Policy Institute at King's College London 2021). In this context, the increasing interest of non-religious Koreans in *Templestay* and meditation holds the potential to foster positive transformations in their lives. This growing trend is reflected in the sustained rise in the popularity of meditation. Moreover, the personal benefits gained from meditation may, and indeed should, inevitably extend to broader societal dimensions (Oh 2018, 247–255).[6] In particular, the pursuit of expanded personal identities—fueled by economic prosperity, high educational attainment, and a heightened sense of political rights—has already led to significant transformations in South Korea's religious sphere. Therefore, the efforts of nones to explore and construct (religious) identities deserve careful examination on multiple levels. These endeavors are not only personal attempts to derive meaning in life but also carry profound social implications.

Given their significance, the rising prevalence of nones in South Korea necessitates thorough academic investigation. Key areas of research could include the diverse composition of nones, the multifaceted nature of their identities, and the emerging forms and meanings of religiosity they may exhibit. Notably, future research on nones must prioritize the development of statistical methodologies that transcend dichotomous frameworks of religious affiliation or the exclusive selection of a single religious identity. Such methodologies could facilitate a more nuanced and comprehensive understanding of the increasingly complex, dynamic, and elusive nature of religious identities.

References

Altemeyer, Bob. 2009. Atheism and Secularity in North America. In *Atheism and Secularity*, ed. Phil Zuckerman, vol. 2, 1–21. Santa Barbara, CA: ABC-CLIO.

Baker, Don. 2008. *Korean Spirituality*. University of Hawaii Press.

Berger, Peter L. 1967. *The Sacred Canopy*. Garden City, NY: Doubleday.

Breakwell, G. 1986. *Coping with Threatened Identities*. London: Methuen.

[6] Oh critiques the tendency of meditation to remain confined to the domain of individual self-improvement, often neglecting structural societal issues. He argues that relational forms of meditation, which emphasize the practice of love and compassion, have the potential to transcend the limitations of introspective, self-centered meditation.

Choe, Yong-un. 2022. "Myeongsang Yeolpung-e Daehan Sahoehakjeok Gochal" (A Religious-Sociological Study on the Meditation Craze). *Jonggyoyeongu (the Journal of Religious Studies)* 82 (2): 115–135. [In Korean].

Choi, Joon-Sik. 2005. *Jonggyo-reul Neomeoseon Jonggyo (Religion Beyond Religion).* Seoul: Sagyejeol. [In Korean].

Choi, Hyun-Jong. 2012. "Jedohwadoen Yeongseong-gwa Hanguk Jonggyo Jihyeong-ui Byeonhwa" (Institutionalized Spirituality and Religious Change in South Korea: Focusing on Catholicism and Protestantism). *Jonggyo wa Munhwa (Religion and Culture)* 22:137–156. [In Korean].

Choi, Hyun-Jong. 2019. "Hanguk-ui Bijonggyoin-e Daehan Yeongu" (A Study on Non-religious People in Korea). *Jonggyo wa Munhwa (the Journal of Religion and Culture) 37:1–24.* [In Korean].

Chong, Chaeyong. 2014. "Jonggyo seokyukhwa-ui han cheukmyeon-euroseo sosok eomneun sinhwangindeul-e daehan yeongu" (A Research on 'Believing without Belonging' as an Aspect of Secularization). *Sinhak gwa Silcheon (Theology and Praxis)* 39:575–606. [In Korean].

Chun, Myung-soo. 2016. "Nyueiji undong-ui Hanguk suyong gwa poseuteu-modeonijeum" (Korean Reception ofNew Age Movement and Postmodernism). *Hangukhak Yeongu (The Journal of Korean Studies)* 25:415–444. [In Korean].

Cororan, Katie E., Christopher P. Scheitle, and Ellory Dabbs. 2021. Multiple (Non)Religious Identities Leads to Undercounting Religious Nones and Asian Religious Identities. *Journal for the Scientific Study of Religion* 60 (2): 424–441.

Davie, Grace. 1994. *Religion in Britain since 1945: Believing without Belonging.* Oxford: Basil Blackwell.

Deaux, Kay. 1992. Personalizing Identity and Socializing Self. In *Social Psychology of Identity and the Self Concept*, ed. G. M. Breakwell, 9–33. London: Surrey Univ Press.

Edgell, Penny, Douglas Hartmann, Evan Stewart, and Joseph Gerteis. 2016. Atheist and Other Cultural Outsiders: Moral Boundaries and the Non-religious in the United States. *Social Forces* 95 (2): 607–638.

Erlandson, Sven. 2000. *Spiritual but Not Religious: A Call to Religious Revolution in America.* New York: Iuniverse Inc.

Fuller, Robert C. 2001. *Spiritual but Not Religious: Understanding Unchurched America.* Oxford University Press.

Gallup Korea. 2002. *"Hangugin-ui Jonggyo 1984–2021 (1) Jonggyo Hyeonhwang" (Religions of Koreans, 1984–2021 (1): Religious Landscape).* Seoul: Gallup Korea Research Institute. [In Korean].

Gidoggyo Yulli Silcheon Undong (the Christian Ethics Movent of Korea. CEMK). 2023. "2023-nyeon Hanguk Gyohoeui Sahoejeok Silroedo Yeoronjosawa Gyeolgwa Jaryojip (Choejong)" (2023 Public Opinion Survey Report on the Social Credibility of Korean Churches (Final). [In Korean]

Hadden, Jeffrey K. 1997. Toward Desacralizing Secularization Theory. *Social Forces* 65 (3): 587–611.

Hanguk Gidoggyo Mokhoeja Hyeobuihoe (The Korean National Association of Christian Pastors, KACP). 2023. "Hangugin-ui Jonggyo Hyeonhwang" (*2023 Survey on the Religious Landscape of Koreans*). [In Korean] http://www.mhdata.or.kr/bbs/board.php?bo_table=gugnae&wr_id=108&page=3

Hanguk Munhwa Hongbowon (Korean Culture Promotion Service). 2022. "Tempeul Seutei 20-nyeongan Chamga Inwon 600man Myeong·Oegugin 11%" *(Temple Stay Attracts Over 6 Million Participants in 20 Years, 11% Foreigners*). October 25. [In Korean]

Hout, Michael, and Claude S. Fisher. 2002. Why More Americans Have No Religious Preference: Politics and Generations. *American Sociological Review* 67 (1): 165–190.

James, William. 1902. *The Varieties of Religious Experience*. Mineola, NY: Dover Publications.

Jang, Hyung-Chull. 2018. "2005-nyeon gwa 2015-nyeon Ingu Chongjosa Gyeolgwa Bigyo-reul Tonghaeseo Bon Bulgyo, Gaesingyo, Cheonjugyo Ingu Byeondong-ui Teukjing" (Characterizing the Change of Korean Religious Population [Buddhism, Protestantism, Catholicism] by Comparative Analysis of the Result of 2005 and 2015 Census). *Sinhak gwa Sahoe (Theology and Society)* 32 (1): 191–219. [In Korean].

Kang, In-Chul. 1997. "Hanguk Mujonggyoin-e Gwanhan Yeongu" (A Study on the Korean 'Religious Nones'). *Sahoe wa Yeoksa (Society and History)* 52:87–118.

Kim, Hyung-Rog (Ven. Inkyung). 2018. Socioreligious Meaning of Healing Culture in Korea. *Myeongsang simri sangdam (Journal of Meditation Based Psychological Counseling)* 19:77–82.

Korea Statistical Office (KOSTAT). "2015 Ingujutaekchongjosa Pyobonjipgyegyeolgwa Bodojaryo" (*2015 Population and Housing Census*). https://kostat.go.kr/board.es?mid=a10301020100&bid=203&tag=&act=view&list_no=358170&ref_bid= [In Korean]

Kripal, Jeffrey. 2007. *Esalen: The Religion of No Religion*. Chicago: University of Chicago.

Nolan, S., P. Saltmarsh, and C. Leget. 2011. Spiritual Care in Palliative Care: Working Towards an EAPC Task Force. *European Journal of Palliative Care* 18 (2): 86–89.

Norko, M. A. 2018. What Is Truth? The Spiritual Quest of Forensic Psychiatry. *The Journal of American Academy of Psychiatry and the Law* 46:10–22.

Oh, Yong-Suk. 2018. "Gyeongjaeng Sahoe-e Natanan Hilling Damnon Gochal" (A Study on the Self-Healing in a Competitive Society: Focusing on the Relational Insights of Buddhist Meditation). *Bulgyohak Yeongu (the Journal of Buddhist Studies)* 54:237–267. [In Korean].

Parsons, William B. 2022. Religion in the Twenty-First Century: Whither Being Spiritual but Not Religious. *The New Centennial Review* 22 (2): 79–110.

Pew Research Center. 2022. *Religious Composition by country, 2010–2050.*. https://www.pewresearch.org/religion/feature/religious-composition-by-country-2010-2050/?utm_source=chatgpt.com

Pew Research Center. 2023. *Measuring Religion in China.* https://www.pewresearch.org/religion/2023/08/30/measuring-religion-in-china/

Possamai, Adam, Alanna Kamp, and Rhys Gower. 2024. Overseas Born 'Religious Nones' in Australia. *Secularism & Nonreligion* 13 (5): 1–12.

Public Religion Research Institute (PRRI). 2024. *Religious Change in America.* https://www.prri.org/research/religious-change-in-america/

Puchalski, C. M., R. Vitillo, S. K. Hull, and N. Reller. 2014. Improving the Spiritual Dimension of Whole Person Care: Reaching National and International Consensus. *Journal of Palliative Medicine* 17:642–656.

Sanders, David, M. Norko, B. Fallon, J. Phillips, J. Nields, et al. 2020. Varieties of Religious (Non)Affiliation: A Primer for Mental Health Practitioners on the 'Spiritual but Not Religious' and the 'Nones'. *The Journal of Nervous and Mental Disease* 208 (5): 424–430.

Seong, Hae-young. 2017. "Mujonggyo-ui Jonggyo (Religion of No Religion) Gaenyeom-gwa Saeroun Jonggyoseong: Sesokjeok Sinbijuui-wa Simcheung Simrihak-ui Mannam-eul Jungsim-euro" (The Concept of 'Religion of No Religion' and Emerging Spiritualities: Focusing on Secular Mysticism and Depth Psychology). *Jonggyo wa Munhwa (Religion and Culture)* 32:1–28. [In Korean].

Song, Eun-Jung, Beom-Soo Han, and Kang-Wook Cho. 2014. "Tempeulstei chamyeo donggi wa cheheom chiyu wa ui gwangye-e gwanhan yeongu" (The Research on the Correlation between the Motivation for the Templestay Participation and the Healing Experience). *Gwangwanghak Yeongu (Journal of Tourism Science)* 38 (9): 239–263. [In Korean].

Stark, Rodney, and William S. Bainbridge. 1985. *The Future of Religion: Secularization, Revival and Cult Formation.* Berkeley: University of California Press.

Storm, Igrid. 2009. Halfway to Heaven: Four Types of Fuzzy Fidelity in Europe. *Journal for the Scientific Study of Religion* 48 (4): 702–718.

The Ministry of Culture, Sports, and Tourism. 2022. "Gukmin Jonggyo Munhwa Saenghwal Jipyo Gaebal mit Siltaejosa" (Development of Religious and Cultural Indicators and Survey on Actual Conditions). [In Korean]

The Policy Institute at King's College London. 2021. "Culture Wars Around the World: How Countries Perceive Divisions." https://kcl-pure.kcl.ac.uk/portal/en/publications/culture-wars-around-the-world-how-countries-perceive-divisions.

Wilkins-Laflamme, Sarah. 2015. How Unreligious are the Religious 'Nones'? Religious Dynamics of the Unaffiliated in Canada. *Canadian Journal of Sociology* 40 (4): 477–500.

Wilson, Bryan R. 1982. *Religion in Sociological Perspective*. Oxford: Oxford University Press.

Woo, Hairan. 2008. "Poseuteu Modeon-gwa Sinjonggyo: Poseuteu Modeon Sidae-ui Saeroun Jonggyo Hyeonsang - Hanguk-ui Yereul Jungsim-euro" (Postmodernity and New Religions: New Religious Phenomena in the Postmodern Era, Focusing on Korea). *Sinjonggyo Yeongu (Journal of New Religions)* 19:25–55. [In Korean].

Woo, Hairan. 2016. "Dongsidae Jonggyo Hyeonsang-eurosseo Yudongjeok Jonggyo (Fluid Religion)-e Daehan Nonui" ('Fluid Religion' as a Contemporary Religious Phenomenon). *Jonggyo wa Munhwa (Religion and Culture)* 30:33–65. [In Korean].

Yeatts, P. E., D. M. Abbott, and D. Mollen. 2021. Development and Evaluation of the Atheist Identity Concealment Scale (AICS). *Journal of Religion & Health*. https://doi.org/10.1007/s10943-021-01465-6.

CHAPTER 9

Samboilbae and Ochetuji in the 10.29 Itaewon Disaster Movement: Affirmations of the Value of Life and the Establishment of New Identity

Minah Kim

1 Introduction

On October 29, 2022, a crushing accident occurred in Itaewon, Seoul, where the Halloween festival was held, causing the death of 159 people. The victims were mainly young people in their 20s and 30s, and 26 of the victims were foreigners from countries like Iran, Russia, China, the United States, and Japan. At the time, many people had gathered in Itaewon for the upcoming Halloween, and the large crowd rushing through the narrow alley at the entrance of the Itaewon district led to a massive number of casualties. This accident was the deadliest disaster in South Korea since the 2003 Daegu Subway Fire, which claimed 192 lives, and the 2014 Sewol Ferry Sinking, which resulted in 304 fatalities. Compared to other

M. Kim (✉)
Incheon National University, Incheon, Republic of Korea
e-mail: kyu486@snu.ac.kr

© The Author(s), under exclusive license to Springer Nature Singapore Pte Ltd. 2025

Y. Yoo, S. C. Lee (eds.), *Reimagining Korea*, Palgrave Series in Contemporary Korean Studies,
https://doi.org/10.1007/978-981-96-6990-5_9

crowd crush incidents around the world, the Itaewon disaster had a higher death toll than the 1989 Hillsborough disaster in the United Kingdom (97 deaths) and the 2022 Kanjuruhan stadium disaster in Indonesia (132 deaths), and it was the ninth deadliest crowd crush incident in the twenty-first century globally.

The Itaewon disaster, which occurred in a public space in the heart of Seoul, shocked and saddened many people. Criticism quickly arose about the cause of the disaster and who was responsible. It was widely predicted that a large crowd would gather for the first Halloween festival after the COVID-19 social distancing guidelines were lifted, but the government failed to implement any crowd control system, leading to allegations that the disaster was the government's responsibility. One of the key debates around the responsibility and punishment for the crowd crush was the role of the police. The police, who were responsible for maintaining order at the event site, were criticized for failing to deploy sufficient personnel or respond appropriately. On the day of the accident, a considerable number of police personnel were dispatched for a task related to enhancing the security measures for President Yoon, and the number of police officers deployed at the scene was significantly lower than what was necessary given the scale of the event and the number of participants. This resulted in an uncontrollable and dangerous situation as the crowd packed into the narrow streets. Subsequent investigations revealed that the police authorities had failed to establish adequate plans and procedures for crowd management, and had also neglected training for such disaster response, which proved to be fatal, resulting in the loss of 159 lives.

The families, survivors, and citizens mourning the tragedy and engaging in the movement for uncovering the truth behind this disaster officially named it the "10.29 Itaewon Disaster." This reflects their determination to remember and commemorate the date and location of the disaster, and it signifies resistance to the South Korean government's initial attempt to diminish the social significance of the disaster by using the term "accident." While "accident" typically refers to an unfortunate event that happens unexpectedly and is attributed to the individual, "disaster" denotes a relatively large-scale and deadly event and implies attributing the handling the event, investigating the cause, and taking measures to prevent future recurrences to the responsibility of the government. In this context, South Korean civil society has retrospectively designated events such as the Seongsu Bridge collapse in 1994, the Sampoong Department Store collapse in 1995, the Hwaseong Sealand Youth Training Center fire in 1999, the Daegu subway fire in 2003, the officially acknowledged humidifier disinfectant crisis in 2006, the Sewol Ferry sinking in 2014, the Gwangju demolition building collapse in 2021, the Itaewon tragedy in 2022, and the Osong underground road flooding in 2023 as social disasters. By uncovering the truth behind these disasters and rigorously evaluating victim support measures in ways that are broadly understood and accepted by the pubic, civil society underscores the importance of ensuring comprehensive accountability and fostering systemic change to prevent future tragedies (Special Investigation Committee on Social Disasters 2020).

In the 10.29 Itaewon disaster movement, bereaved families and citizens demanded a thorough investigation to uncover the truth behind the disaster, the strict accountability of those responsible, a formal and sincere government apology, and the implementation of preventative measures. To support these efforts, they initiated the enactment of a "10.29 Itaewon Disaster Special Law" to establish a legal foundation for these objectives. Within this process, religious rituals rooted in Buddhism, such as Samboilbae (three-step one-bow) and Ochetugi (five-body prostration), were actively performed, garnering significant public attention. This chapter seeks to address why religious rituals were prominently utilized in the social disaster movement and to analyze their impact. I argue that while the overt religious connotations of these rituals are intentionally removed when repurposed as strategies for social movements, their ritual significance remains. This latent religious meaning is recontextualized and gains political resonance when aligned with the objectives of a specific civic movement. In the case of the Itaewon disaster, Buddhist-origin rituals such as Samboilbae and Ochetugi served as mechanisms for reaffirming the value of life and fostering a new collective identity within the social disaster movement.

The following discussion explores the theoretical foundations of rituals within social movements, laying the groundwork for the study. It also provides a brief historical overview of how Samboilbae and Ochetuji have been used in Korean social movements, with a particular emphasis on their role in the Itaewon disaster struggle. The discussion then examines the impacts of these rituals in the Itaewon disaster movement, analyzing how they help reaffirm the value of life and catalyze a transformation in the participants' identities through their embodied experience of the suffering of the victims and their families.

2 Religious Rituals and Social Movements

Traditional perspective on the relationship between rituals and beliefs posits that "beliefs are primary, with rituals merely giving public expression to these preexisting beliefs." However, within the Durkheimian tradition, ritual participation is considered socially significant in itself, as rituals produce bonds of solidarity without requiring uniformity of belief, that is, thought. Those who participate in rituals "live a life of emotion, not of thoughts" (Kertzer 1988: 67; Jung 2005: 8). In his analysis of primitive religion, Durkheim (1995) outlines the process through which religious beliefs concerning the sacred are elevated to collective consciousness via religious rituals, thereby reinforcing collective solidarity. During rituals, participants draw on shared emotional responses to collective values or ideas, symbolically renewing these values and deepening the moral and emotional bonds among them. Ultimately, the core function of rituals is to bring individuals together in a shared space, allowing them to deeply engage with values that, though commonly held, often remain dormant in everyday life. Through this experience, rituals help strengthen participants' identities and reinforce their mutual bonds, all centered around the values revived during the ritual (Park 1998: 38).

Durkheim's concept of rituals provides a compelling framework for understanding the creation and maintenance of solidarity, a core value of social movements. Social movements, as collective practices aimed at achieving shared goals, can be linked to the phenomenon of "co-presence," which Durkheim identifies as a fundamental attribute of rituals. Durkheim (1995) observes, "Once the individuals are gathered together, a sort of electricity is generated from their closeness and quickly launches them to an extraordinary height of exaltation. Every emotion expressed resonates..., each one echoing the others. The initial impulse is thereby amplified each time it is echoed, like an avalanche that grows as it goes along" (217–218). According to Durkheim (1995), collective fervor serves as a mechanism through which common beliefs, shared traditions, memories of revered ancestors, and collective ideals are reproduced and reinforced (352). Furthermore, this collective fervor facilitates the transformation of individuals from secular beings into self-transcendent moral agents. As collective emotions are more intensely expressed within social movements, participants become increasingly driven by ideological rather than material interests, fostering a stronger moral commitment to the ideals and values of the movement (Park 2007: 32).

However, Park highlights the limitations of Durkheim's concept of rituals in adequately explaining contemporary secular rituals within social movements. Primitive religious rituals are defined by their predetermined forms and content, compulsory participation, homogeneity among participants, and the absence of distinctions between participants and observers. In contrast, modern secular rituals are often characterized by amorphous processes and multilayered meanings. Furthermore, participation in these rituals is voluntary, and a clear differentiation exists between participants and observers (Kertzer 1988; Bell 1997: 199; Park 2007: 34–35). In addition, rather than generating a temporary collective effervescence or inducing emotional outbursts such as awe, euphoria, or catharsis, as Durkheim suggested, rituals in modern secular contexts are analyzed as being performed repeatedly in a calm and mundane manner. Through this process, they contribute to the formation of new social positions and identities, ultimately leading to changes in individuals and groups. In analyzing various forms of contemporary rituals, post-Durkheimian ritual scholars have emphasized performance as a highly stylized, attention-focusing, conventional, and repetitive act (Park 2007: 35). The concept of performance emphasizes the process through which participants in rituals are transformed into new social subjects by creating and redefining rituals with novel meanings. By introducing the concept of performance, scholars shift their focus from the traditional ritual theory, which prioritizes the maintenance and integration of the status quo, to examining how individuals actively construct rituals and reshape their worlds. Human actors are thus portrayed as dynamic agents of cultural continuity and change (Yoo 2005: 259–260). The bereaved families and citizens engaged in the Itaewon disaster movement who participated in Samboilbae and Ochetuji constituted a relatively homogeneous group, pursuing common ideals and performing rituals based on a largely predetermined structure. As Durkheim posits, their engagement in these rituals strengthens collective identity and reinforces their mutual bonds. However, rather than eliciting intense collective fervor or spontaneous emotional outbursts, these rituals are conducted in a composed and contemplative manner. Performed against the backdrop of urban noise from passing vehicles, they evoke the solemnity of temple ceremonies, accompanied by rhythmic chants and drumbeats led by the procession leader. Through the continuous and repetitive enactment of these rituals, participants symbolically reconfigure urban space, cultivating an alternative social atmosphere wherein transformations in identity and social order can be experienced and pursued.

Victor Turner (1982) conceptualizes rituals as performances, defining them as symbolic practices strategically designed to evoke extraordinary emotions, energy, and experiences distinct from everyday life. He viewed rituals as a form of social drama and asserted that performing is what makes a difference (79). Turner divided the ritual process into three stages: separation from everyday life, liminality, and reintegration, which signifies a return to everyday life—but as a fundamentally transformed being. Turner's primary focus lies in the liminal stage, characterized by its transitional nature. Liminality refers to a state of being "betwixt and between the positions assigned and arrayed by law, custom, convention, and ceremonial"—an anti-structure that temporarily suspends the social structures and hierarchies governing daily life (Turner 1969: 95). Turner argued that during this liminal phase, performances that symbolically and dramatically reproduce sacredness enable the emergence of new situational awareness, modes of thought, and social ideals. In this regard, he suggested that the potential for social transformation is embedded within the ritual itself. Through Samboilbae and Ochetuji, the bereaved families of the Itaewon disaster and the citizens in solidarity with them transcended their pre-disaster social status, as well as differences in residence, religion, and political orientation. They are reduced to mere beings consumed by endless sadness and despair, unable to protect their beloved family members or fellow citizens. In this ritual context, they came to recognize themselves in new ways: as families who lost loved ones in the disaster, as individuals who empathize with and stand in solidarity with their suffering, and even as survivors who narrowly escaped—acknowledging the possibility that they, too, could have been victims. This process gives rise to new identities. Furthermore, it fosters a renewed situational awareness of systemic safety issues in Korean society and cultivates a new social ideal centered on building a life-respecting society. While these identity transformations also emerge in daily interactions and other forms of social activism, it is within the ritual space that they are most vividly experienced and dramatically expressed. Insofar as it provides an opportunity to relinquish a prior identity and adopt a new one, while also serving as a site where the power of social reform is exercised, Turner's concept of liminality can be applied to Samboilbae and Ochetuji.

What is noteworthy here is that through the strategic arrangement of liminality, not only do the performers but also the audience focus their attention on the ritual, elevating their emotions and fostering a sense of connection. As both a dramatic and communicative medium, the ritual conveys the sacredness of the symbols and values it aims to represent, thereby forming a consensus and awakening the latent consciousness of sacred values among the audience. The dramatic effect of the ritual lies in its ability to captivate the audience by repeating the performance over a certain period, thereby drawing them into the drama and enabling them to assume roles that allow for the direct experience and expression of sacred values (Turner 1982). Applying this to social movements, performances such as singing, chanting, and waving flags or candles serve to focus the attention of both performers and the audience, deepening their emotional exchange and fostering a sense of transcendent community existence and unity among the participants. In the context of a social movement, this liminality becomes a spectacle in itself, dissolving the boundaries between movement performers and street audiences (Park 2007: 37–38). The audience of Samboilbae and Ochetuji consists of passersby who witness the performance in person, as well as those who observe it through real-time broadcasts or news media. Some later join the performances themselves, directly experiencing and expressing comfort, empathy, and solidarity. Others contribute to affirming the value of life and safety by endorsing the bereaved families' appeals to the government.

Meanwhile, Catherine Bell's concept of ritualization emphasizes the formation of new subjects and identities through ritual practices. Bell highlights the process of ritualization, which reconstructs sacredness through specific actions and enables it to be collectively experienced. Bell (1992) uses the concept of ritualization to refer to "a way of acting that is designed and orchestrated to distinguish and privilege what is being done in comparison to other, usually more quotidian, activities" (74). This demonstrates her recognition of ritual as a performance. According to Bell (1997), "ritual is more complex than the mere communication of meanings and values; it is a set of activities that construct particular types of meanings and values in specific ways" (82). Bell especially focuses on the interaction between participants' bodies and their environments in the ritual process of meaning-making. According to Bell, the gestures of ritual participants help create a ritual environment that normalizes certain values while simultaneously establishing a cyclical process through which participants engage with the environment using their bodies. As the body interacts cyclically with the environment, specific values and powers are produced. Humans perform various rituals employing diverse strategies and devices, unconsciously embodying specific values in the process. This ritualized body gives rise to a subject that internalizes these specific values

(Yoo 2005: 257). At this point, the ritual use of the body is intertwined with the formation of a new identity, which contributes to the creation of the subject of the social movement. Those who participate in Samboilbae and Ochetuji embody the fragility of human existence in the face of life and death by kneeling under the scorching sun, heavy rain, or on snowy fields. This practice can be understood as contributing to the collective ideal of building a society that prioritizes life and safety within the social disaster movement. Through this process, the subject of the social disaster movement is formed.

By synthesizing the aforementioned theoretical perspectives, this chapter will concretely demonstrate the role of religious rituals in reaffirming the meaning of death and the value of life, as well as in shaping the identity of new subjects within the context of the 10.29 Itaewon disaster movement. Samboilbae and Ochetuji cultivate a sense of collective consciousness essential for social movements by strengthening empathy and solidarity between bereaved families and citizens. Through the physical hardships endured in these rituals, participants awaken to the meaning of death and the value of life, forging a deep bond with the victims and bereaved families. This recognition compels them to pursue the shared ideal of respecting life and building a safer society. Moreover, these rituals serve as a transformative process in which participants relinquish their previous social status, values, and way of life, forming a new identity as subjects of the social disaster movement. The materiality and visibility of Samboilbae and Ochetuji as performative acts also enhance their effectiveness in public engagement and media representation, drawing the audience into the emotions and experiences of the participants and thereby fostering broader solidarity with the bereaved families' social appeals. This, in turn, led both participants and audiences to recognize the social disaster as their collective concern, ultimately forming a community of remembrance and shared memory to respond to it together.

3 Samboilbae and Ochetuji in the 10.29 Itaewon Disaster Movement

Following the Itaewon disaster on October 29, 2022, there was no investigation into the cause of the tragedy, no accountability for those responsible, nor any government apology. In response, the bereaved families initiated a campaign for the enactment of the 10.29 Itaewon Disaster

Special Act. They gathered 50,000 signatures through National Assembly petitions, toured across the country, and engaged in a hunger strike. However, when the National Assembly made little progress, Samboilbae and Ochetuji were invoked as a last resort, aiming to appeal to both the National Assembly and citizens.

From August 22 to 24, 2023, approximately 100 bereaved family members, members of religious communities, and citizens undertook a three-day Samboilbae march from the citizens' memorial altar in front of Seoul City Hall Square to the National Assembly. Despite scorching temperatures exceeding 30 degrees Celsius and heavy rain during the monsoon season, the participants marched approximately three kilometers each day, prostrating themselves on the ground as they progressed. Later, in December 2023, just before the National Assembly's session was set to close, they participated in another Ochetuji march along a snow-covered road in the freezing cold, with temperatures dropping to minus 10 degrees Celsius. Starting on December 18 and continuing daily until the Special Act was passed, participants circled the National Assembly every morning along a three-kilometer perimeter route by the surrounding wall. Approximately 100 bereaved families and citizens joined this march, leading to the National Assembly's passage of the Special Act on January 2, 2024. However, as President Yoon Suk-yeol considered vetoing the bill, the bereaved families and supporters launched another campaign on January 29, 2024, marching from Exit 1 of Itaewon Station, where the disaster had occurred, to the presidential office, urging the president to promulgate the Special Act.

Samboilbae is a Buddhist practice method aimed at enlightenment, involving the repetitive sequence of walking three steps, bowing deeply, and repeating the process. The tradition of "three steps" (sambo) is rooted in the Buddhist teaching of the "three poisons": greed(貪), hatred(嗔), and delusion(痴). According to Buddhist doctrine, no matter how diligently one practices, spiritual progress is unattainable without overcoming these three poisons. Consequently, the act of taking three steps symbolizes the renunciation of greed, hatred, and delusion, while the deep bow represents an expression of sincere penitence for these impediments. Though the practice of Samboilbae lacks canonical origins, it has been widely embraced as a popular form of spiritual practice within Korean Buddhism (Kang 2017; Park 2018: 384–385) (Fig. 9.1).

Recently, this Buddhist practice has been integrated into social movements aimed at addressing societal conflicts. One of the innovative forms

Fig. 9.1 Samboilbae in the summber of August 2023. (© Susanna Kim)

of protest in Korean society emerged during the 2003 movement opposing the Saemangeum reclamation project. Buddhist monk Sukyeong, a key leader of the movement, initiated the Samboilbae march in collaboration with a Catholic priest, a Protestant pastor, and a Won Buddhist clergy. These four religious leaders united in their conviction that the Saemangeum reclamation project would devastate marine ecosystems. From March 28 to the end of May 2003, they marched over 320 kilometers from the Haechang mudflat in Buan County, North Jeolla Province, to Seoul. Throughout the 65-day journey, the number of participants engaging in the act of bowing in protest ranged from dozens to 300. By the conclusion of the march in Seoul, more than 8,000 people had joined the religious leaders in solidarity. What is noteworthy is that the media consistently covered the Samboilbae march, generating various discussions around it. This sustained attention can be attributed to the fact that the method of protest, Samboilbae, represented an unfamiliar and distinctive form of social movement (Cho 2009: 1051–1054; Yoo 2013: 108).

Samboilbae, originally a practice at the individual level, gains political significance and reinforces a sense of community unity when appropriated within social movements. In the movement against the reclamation of Saemangeum, Samboilbae was used not only as a personal ritual of prayer or penance but also as a means of publicly affirming the legitimacy of the movement. Through this practice, the movement sought to create a visual impact and raise awareness among the broader public, while simultaneously performing an outward-facing role to engage those outside the movement. Furthermore, in the context of performing rituals in an ecological environment—where the sea, rocks, and life on the rocks are perceptible through the five senses—the environment is recognized not as an empty space but as a living habitat for various creatures such as fish, insects, and birds. This experience fosters a sense of interconnectedness, reminding participants that humans are part of a larger ecosystem (Lee 2004: 11; Yoo 2013: 113).

Following the 2014 Sewol Ferry disaster, bereaved families, religious groups, and citizens embarked on a 107-day Samboilbae pilgrimage from Paengmok Port in Jindo Island, South Jeolla Province, to Gwanghwamun in Seoul, advocating for the raising of the Sewol ferry's hull. Apart from its roots in Buddhism, the practice of enlightenment through pain was adopted by religious communities as part of the life ecology movement to save Saemangeum. This practice was subsequently embraced by citizens and reappropriated as a form of protest against social disasters, symbolizing the collective mourning and response to the tragic loss of many lives.

Ochetuji is a Buddhist practice in which five body parts—the two elbows, two knees, and forehead—are brought to the ground in a deep and humble bow. This is considered the most respectful form of worship in Buddhism, as it involves humbling oneself and showing reverence to the Three Jewels (the Buddha, the Dharma, and the Sangha). Tibetan Buddhists practice Ochetuji during pilgrimages to sacred sites such as the Jokhang Temple in Lhasa, believing that the physical challenge and pain of the journey purify their sins and lead to their transformation into new beings (Kim 2013: 6; Yoo 2021: 143–144) (Fig. 9.2).

While Samboilbae is widely practiced in Korea as both a form of spiritual discipline and a strategy within social movements, it lacks a canonical origin. In contrast, Ochetuji is recognized as one of the prominent practices of the Korean Buddhist tradition. Within this tradition, Ochetuji is typically performed in cycles of 108, 1080, or even 3000 prostrations as a rigorous spiritual practice. Prostration holds a unique significance in

Fig. 9.2 Ochetuji in the winter of December 2023. (© Susanna Kim)

Buddhism, as it simultaneously engages both body and mind, fostering humility and reverence for others (Kim 2020: 1). Samboilbae is well-suited for pilgrimage as it involves taking three steps before each prostration, whereas Ochetuji, like in Tibetan Buddhism, can be practiced as a form of pilgrimage or performed in a stationary setting. Its accessibility—requiring only a small space—allows not only Buddhist monks but also lay practitioners to engage in the practice. Bowing practices such as Ochetuji aim to transcend the self through humility, dissolve past karma through repentance, and ultimately attain enlightenment through the experience of self-effacement (Kim 2020: 1).

Ochetuji has been strategically employed in social movements in Korea, particularly by disabled individuals and workers, as it visually conveys intense emotions of desperation and suffering. Notably, environmental activists opposed the installation of cable cars on Seoraksan Mountain in 2015, with many citizens performing Ochetuji along the planned cable car route in protest. In 2016, Ochetuji was also employed by numerous citizens advocating for the impeachment of President Park Geun-hye. Since 2018, disability rights groups have engaged in annual Ochetuji protests, opposing welfare budget cuts and demanding the rights to mobility, education, and labor. In 2020, a protest was held in downtown Seoul, where participants performed Ochetuji to commemorate a labor struggle from 35 years earlier and to call for the reinstatement of a female shipyard worker who had been unjustly dismissed for joining a labor union. This practice, with its profound physical demands, serves as a powerful symbolic act to express grievances and demand attention to social injustices

4 The Effects of Samboilbae and Ochetuji in Social Disaster Movements

Rituals performed in public places are disseminated both directly by witnesses on the ground and secondarily through the media, leaving a powerful impression that contributes to the public visibility of social disaster movements. In the case of the 10.29 Itaewon disaster movement, the organizer of the Samboilbae and Ochetuji rituals, activist Kim Ji-ae (2024), stated that her aim was to harness the visual impact of these practices to demand the government's enactment of a special law and to rally citizens' support, even to the extent of crawling on the ground.

The effects were significant: as the organizer noted, city parades, hunger strikes, and the 159 bows performed at the civic altar in front of Seoul City Hall—108 being the traditional number of bows in Buddhist rituals, but adjusted to 159 to reflect the number of victims in the Itaewon disaster—received little attention from both civil society and the government. However, the three-day Samboilbae march from Seoul City Hall to the National Assembly garnered widespread media coverage and explosive support from citizens. Initially, the Samboilbae march was planned as an activity involving only the four religions: Protestantism, Catholicism, Buddhism, and Won Buddhism. This was due to the belief that the strong religious connotations of the Samboilbae ritual made it difficult to elicit a response from ordinary citizens. While the four major religions participated in the Samboilbae march, their involvement was limited to a small group of progressive and socially engaged individuals within each religion. The majority of religious followers, however, remained indifferent or passive toward the Itaewon disaster movement, including the Samboilbae march. However, upon realizing the massive impact it generated in just one day, civil society began to actively participate starting on the second day. Furthermore, when the Ochetuji ritual was performed around the National Assembly in the winter of 2023, the chairman of the National Assembly mentioned the Itaewon disaster special law during the plenary session for three consecutive days, strongly urging an agreement between the ruling and opposition parties on the issue (Jo 2023; Kim-Yoon 2023).

The exhibition of such painful rituals has a clear visual impact and serves to effectively convey the pain of the bereaved families to civil society. However, the effects of Samboilbae and Ochetuji cannot be solely explained by the exhibitionary aspects of the performance. By examining the changes in the values and identities of both the participants and the audience directly engaged in the ritual, its effects can be understood more comprehensively.

1. Reaffirmation of the Meaning of Death and the Value of Life

Samboilbae and Ochetuji can be interpreted as symbolic acts representing death and regeneration, moving beyond worship or personal expressions of faith. The physical act of lying on the ground may be seen as symbolizing the death of the past self, while rising again could be understood as embodying renewal into a new existence. Bereaved families participating in these rituals conveyed their despair over failing to protect their loved ones and the survivor's guilt through physical hardship. Yet, they rise again, reaffirming the value and meaning of life through a shared sense of solidarity and resilience, even in the face of death. This interpretation reflects the Buddhist symbolism inherent in Samboilbae and Ochetuji.

Focusing on the ascetic nature of Samboilbae and Ochetuji as rituals that inflict physical suffering serves to diminish their religious dimensions while amplifying their political and social significance. Regardless of religious affiliation or belief, participants engage in these rituals as a means of exploring the meaning of death and the value of life. Participants commemorate the lives lost in the disaster and reflect on what lies beyond death, what death means to humans, why we fail to recognize the finiteness of life, and the importance of respecting life as an absolute value. Additionally, the pain induced by Samboilbae and Ochetuji fosters contemplation of the fundamental question of human existence: the reflection on death. The intensity of physical strain deepens participants' embodied engagement with death, fostering critical contemplation of its meaning within the context of human mortality. One bereaved family member stated, "I am an atheist, but when I couldn't reach my daughter on the day of the disaster, I found myself praying to all gods, including God and Buddha. I participated in the Samboilbae with the hope that a divine being who would watch over my daughter in the heavens, offering incense as an act of prayer" (Bereaved Family Member 1, 3 2024). She confessed that it wasn't until she lost her daughter that she began to believe in a world beyond death, leading her to reflect on the idea that death is not the end. Moreover, the process of social healing through the experience of pain provides participants with opportunities to internalize new values for life. It is not uncommon for individuals who have lost loved ones to gradually become central figures in bereaved family movements, transforming their personal grief into collective action. For instance, participants in the three-day Samboilbae march described their motivation, stating, "We felt as though we had no choice but to do this. Our children are gone, and if we do nothing, we will feel unworthy as a parent in the face of this overwhelming grief" (10.29 Itaewon Disaster Writers' Documentation Group 2024). After losing their children, they reflected on the purpose their lives should serve, attempting to navigate the profound pain of loss while finding strength and purpose in their collective struggle.

Certainly, the religious significance of these rituals was considered when they were adopted for the Itaewon disaster movement. In particular, the organizer, who is also a Protestant preacher, believed that although Samboilbae and Ochetuji were not Protestant practices, they were suitable for addressing themes of death and life. These rituals symbolized the thorough death of the former self and the birth of a new being. The decision to perform Ochetuji around the National Assembly was particularly influenced by the biblical story of the fall of Jericho (Joshua 6) (Kim 2024). However, the organizers' intentions were not always directly understood or accepted by the ritual participants. For example, Protestant participants defended the rituals in response to a statement from the Korean Association of Church Communication, which criticized Samboilbae as an unbiblical ritual. They argue that the essence of the ritual lies not in its form but in empathizing with the suffering of the bereaved families and participating with heartfelt remembrance. This perspective was unrelated to the original religious significance of the ritual (Lim 2023).

Nevertheless, as the organizer emphasized, religious rituals hold significant meaning in social disaster movements that engage with the themes of death and life. This is because religion, irrespective of its tradition, has long been deeply concerned with these existential matters. Mircea Eliade (1987) asserts that the finite nature of human existence inherently evokes a transcendental longing to envision and aspire toward realms beyond these limitations—a trait he defines as the essence of *homo religiosus*. Death is the ultimate boundary of human existence, an inevitable reality underscored by its fundamental forcefulness. This inevitability compels religious individuals to reflect deeply on meanings that transcend death and to affirm the value of life as a counterpoint to mortality (Yoo 2021).

A social disaster represents a death imbued with social significance. The term "social" extends beyond the dimension of scale—where many societal members are affected or where the event profoundly impacts society as a whole—to encompass collective deaths arising from systemic and structural causes. These causes generate widespread pain that permeates the social fabric, leading to collective suffering. Consequently, addressing and healing this pain must occur at the societal level, encompassing measures such as "truth-seeking, indemnification, apologies, recurrence prevention, memorialization, support for practical stability and needs, reconciliation, and fostering social reintegration" (Shin 2020: 58).

Remembering a social disaster entails posing numerous questions about the tragedy and seeking answers to them: Why did the victims lose their lives? Who bears responsibility? What obligations does the community have to ensure a safe environment? What measures are necessary to prevent such tragedies from happening again? While these questions may initially appear to center on death, they are, in fact, fundamentally about life. They address the kind of life we should strive to lead and the transformations our society must undergo in the wake of disaster-induced loss (Lee 2023: 35). Religion has long carried the responsibility of addressing themes of life, death, and the beyond, offering hope in moments of profound pain, posing questions about the limitations of human existence beyond the distinction between victims and ordinary citizens, and seeking meaningful answers. This is where the relation between religion and social disasters becomes evident.

In fact, interfaith cooperation has been actively occurring in the context of social disaster movements. Protestantism, Catholicism, Won Buddhism, and Buddhism have actively supported the 10.29 Itaewon Disaster Bereaved Families' Council. Each religious group has established organizations dedicated to supporting the council and coordinating solidarity efforts. These include the Association of Christians Who Remember and Act on the 10.29 Itaewon Disaster; the Justice, Peace, and Environment Committee of Korean Catholic Men's/Women's Religious Orders; the Won Buddhism Civil Society Network; and the Jogye Order of Korean Buddhism Social and Labor Committee. While these groups cannot be said to represent each religion, and the number of religious individuals participating in the 10.29 Itaewon disaster movement is small, they unite across doctrinal differences with the shared goal of affirming the value of life and promoting safety. A bereaved family member shared that she initially perceived religions as conflicting but found it profoundly moving to witness four religions holding a joint memorial service and praying together for the victims' souls (Bereaved Family Member 1, 3 2024). This interfaith harmony extends to ritual practices. For instance, the 2024 winter Ochetuji march around the National Assembly integrated Buddhist ritual Ochetuji with the biblical narrative of the fall of Jericho, in which the city was encircled once daily.

Bereaved family members, whether religious or not, often turn to religious leaders during times of hardship or when seeking support. They particularly seek solace for their deceased loved ones or hope in the face of despair. Religious leaders are frequently asked to "pray for parents enduring pain and tears after losing their children" and to draw upon their longstanding traditions and practices to honor the memory of the disaster (Im 2024). Religious groups were also requested to carry the portraits of the victims during the process of setting up a memorial altar for the citizens. The procession through the city center with the portraits of the victims can be interpreted as a collective funeral. Bereaved family members request that religious leaders, when marching with the portraits, don traditional clerical attire indicative of their religious roles. Regardless of religious affiliation or the absence thereof, bereaved family members expect religious individuals to hold the portraits with respect and dignity. These expectations underscore the bereaved families' recognition of religious leaders as specialists in matters of life and death. By entrusting them with such responsibilities, the families seek to ensure that the deaths of their loved ones are treated with the solemnity and gravity they deserve.

Through the act of bowing, bereaved family members, religious figures, and citizens participating in Samboilbae and Ochetuji honor the spirits of the victims while acknowledging the value of their own lives as living beings. In enduring suffering, they express their guilt and remorse for the victims and, in doing so, reaffirm their commitment to a renewed life as bereaved individuals and fellow citizens. This illustrates that, although Samboilbae and Ochetuji have evolved beyond their traditional Buddhist connotations, they continue to uphold the spiritual responsibility inherent in a religion that addresses both death and life.

2. Establishment of a New Identity

Samboilbae and Ochetuji primarily serve as rituals to mourn the victims. Bereaved family members engage in these rituals to empathize with the suffering of the deceased and to honor their memory. One bereaved family member shared that during Samboilbae, she experienced shortness of breath from the intense heat and severe leg pain. In that moment, she felt as though she was reliving the death of her son alongside him (Bereaved Family Member 2 2023). Another bereaved family member recalled that each time he bowed, he was reminded of every moment he had spent with her deceased daughter and felt her presence. Yet, with each rise, he felt a deep sadness and anger that she was no longer with him (Bereaved Family Member 1, 3 2024). Jacques Derrida (2001) defines mourning as making "the completely other, dead, living in me" (42). In the city center, where the hustle of traffic and everyday lives of people continue, the ritual carves out a liminal space and time, providing bereaved families with an opportunity to meet and commemorate their lost loved ones. It fosters solidarity and empathy among the bereaved. They say that the grief and despair of losing a loved one are most profoundly understood and empathized with by fellow bereaved family members next to them. They find considerable comfort and support in sharing the ritual of suffering together (10.29 Itaewon Disaster Writers' Documentation Group 2024). Through Samboilbae and Ochetuji, the bereaved families not only forge a connection with their deceased loved ones but also establish a collective solidarity with one another.

Through rituals, citizens establish a physical connection with the disaster. In the silence of the Samboilbae and Ochetuji marches, people foster both physical and emotional solidarity. The rituals involve stylized, repetitive, and structured physical actions that generate an immediate and tangible sense of understanding. By providing an opportunity for the public to meet the bereaved, these rituals enable citizens to empathize with the pain and grief of the families. Furthermore, by embodying the pain of the victims, they come to internalize the social tragedy as their own suffering, rather that of others, and come to recognize their direct or indirect involvement and responsibility for the deaths. This recognition—that they are both victims of and responsible for the disaster—leads to the establishment of an identity as active participants and supporters in the social disaster movement. This understanding is rooted in the belief that social disasters can befall anyone. One participant stated that, being of the same age as the victims, she too could have been a victim (Participant 2023). By performing Ochetuji alongside the grieving families, she resolved to become more actively involved in the Itaewon disaster movement.

Through Samboilbae and Ochetuji, participants, including the bereaved families, are reborn as the subjects of the social disaster movement—not merely as victims' families, the injured, or those who have lost something precious, but as active agents who seek and protect the values of life and safety. Through Samboilbae and Ochetuji, the bereaved families transition from the identity of victims who have lost their loved ones in the disaster to the active subjects of a movement aimed at revealing the truth behind their families' deaths and using this as a stepping stone to create a safer society. In this process, they acquire a new identity—not simply as those who mourn their losses, but as agents of change who seek to redefine the meaning of their loved ones' deaths and pursue justice and societal transformation. Similarly, citizen participants, through their connection with the victims and bereaved families, transform from passive, guilt-ridden beings into active members of the social disaster movement, driven by a shared sense of purpose and solidarity.

Audiences witnessing the bereaved families and citizens performing Samboilbae and Ochetuji in the city center respond by mourning the victims' deaths and empathizing with the grief of the bereaved families. As members of the social system, they experience a sense of guilt and recognize their responsibility in creating a society that upholds life and ensures safety. This shift in awareness is reflected in the substantial outpouring of support from civil society following the Samboilbae and Ochetuji rituals. One participant confessed that it was only after engaging in Ochetuji that she was able to fully mourn and commemorate the victims, and she vowed not to remain a passive observer in the future struggles of the bereaved families (Participant 2023). The movement transcends solidarity with the victims, evolving into a collective effort to protect not only oneself but also others, fostering a renewed commitment to building safer communities and systems

In this way, the bereaved families and citizens emerge as active subjects of social disaster movements, forming communities centered around mourning and remembrance. Specifically, in the context of the Itaewon disaster, mourning itself became a social and political act. Many of the victims, young people celebrating Halloween, faced criticism and derogatory remarks from the Korean Protestant Church, which complicated the grieving process for their families and denied them the opportunity for proper mourning and solace. Additionally, the government's actions to suppress the families' voices were apparent from the onset of the tragedy: withholding the names of the victims, omitting their photographs and plaques from state-organized memorial events, and obstructing communication among the families, all aimed at silencing them. These efforts to erase the tragedy further hindered citizens' ability to mourn and mobilize as a movement. In this context, Samboilbae and Ochetuji became crucial spaces for mourning and sanctuary, offering the victims and their families protection from a social climate that insulted the victims and imposed a framework of victimhood on the bereaved. Given that mourning is both a victim's right and a form of support for victims, rituals that physically manifest the collective will to remember, alongside the moral awareness of citizens who witnessed injustice, serve as authentic acts of mourning that actively challenge social narratives surrounding victimhood.

Samboilbae and Ochetuji also offer some measure of relief to the bereaved families, who endure constant insecurity and fear as they fight for the truth of the disaster and seek accountability for those responsible. The rituals are often preceded by clashes with opposing citizens and police attempting to disrupt them, yet once they begin, the serene tone of voice, attire, language, and symbols create a distinctive and sacred atmosphere that sets the participants, including the bereaved families, apart from the ordinary world (Yoo 2014: 142).

The rituals of mourning serves as a process of social cohesion, imbuing the death of a victim with meaning and establishing the responsibility and commitment of those left behind to ensure that such unjust deaths are not repeated. Through the concept of collective effervescence, Durkheim

(1995) argues that rituals foster a profound experience of sacredness and unity through collective engagement, thus cultivating a shared sense of "we" and reinforcing common values and beliefs among participants. Religious rituals in social disaster movements offer a means to connect victims with the broader society, forging a collective memory that not only facilitates community reintegration but also plays a critical role in preventing the recurrence of such tragedies by rescuing collective memory from oblivion (Kim 2019: 167). In this context, Samboilbae and Ochetuji are integral to the "politics of mourning," which encompasses "the full spectrum of practical actions undertaken by the survivors of a social disaster to honor their fidelity to the dead, through appeals, demands, and pressures directed at the state and society to uncover the truth and pursue social justice" (Jung 2023: 56). This process unfolds as those who participate in or witness these rituals acquire their identities as active participants and agents within social disaster movements.

5 Conclusions

Rituals in social movements have been variously interpreted as expressions of faith and channels for the intervention of the sacred and supernatural, or alternatively, as mere spectacles—performances of power that utilize religious practices for secular ends. Undeniably, ritual as a form of social activism in the public sphere encompasses a dimension of visual performance. Samboilbae and Ochetuji exemplify such visual performances, characterized by their strong protest nature. These rituals functioned as a medium to express the profound grief of bereaved families who had lost their loved ones, while simultaneously demanding accountability and transparency regarding the causes of the disaster. Furthermore, they aimed to raise awareness and garner support from a broader audience for the movement's cause and objectives (Yoo 2014: 124, 131).

The rituals practiced within social disaster movements undeniably transcend the boundaries of religious tradition, serving broader purposes such as mourning, truth-seeking, and shaping public opinion. However, these rituals cannot be regarded as a complete departure from their religious roots. They continue to reflect religion's unique specialization in addressing the profound questions of death and life. The rituals embody a dimension in which participants, through physical suffering, connect with the grief of the bereaved, generate new meanings surrounding death, and affirm the values of life, safety, and solidarity that arise from it. This process fosters a transformation in participants' perceptions of self and the world. In the 10.29 Itaewon disaster movement, participation in Samboilbae and Ochetuji represents an act of full mourning for the victims. Through these rituals, participants consciously or unconsciously come to recognize the social disaster as a communal issue implicating society as a whole, including themselves, and position themselves as part of the collective response. In this way, rituals become a site where values are reaffirmed, and new identities are constructed, extending their significance into the broader social disaster movement.

Social disaster movements are often described as unwinnable struggles. Unlike social movements such as labor, women's, disability, or LGBTQ rights movements—aimed at achieving civil rights or rectifying injustice, discrimination, or hatred—social disaster movements confront the irrevocable reality that the dead cannot be brought back. Faced with the extreme limits of human existence, particularly in instances of mass deaths resulting from the failure of social safety systems, religious rituals emerge as integral to these movements. They are invoked not merely for their effectiveness as novel or attention-grabbing performances but to mourn the victims, seek truth, and confront the profound existential questions posed by such tragedies.

Modern civil society is generally understood to exhibit a non-religious characteristic and is often perceived as such. Jürgen Habermas (1991) contended that modernity is characterized by a process of secularization, through which civil society and the modern public sphere are formed by distancing themselves from religion (11). In contemporary South Korea, this dynamic is reflected in the negative perception of religious discourse and practices in the public sphere, with efforts to establish clear boundaries between the religious and secular realms. Nevertheless, religious values continue to play a role in addressing social issues, particularly in the context of social disasters. This is evident in the use of religious rituals such as Samboilbae and Ochetuji to convey desperation and resistance, as well as the reliance on religious experts in matters of death. Such practices affirm that religion's enduring association with death, its accompanying worldview, the meaning and purpose of life, and the experience of the sacred beyond secular concerns remain deeply embedded within contemporary civil society.

References

Bell, Catherine M. 1992. *Ritual Theory, Ritual Practice.* New York: Oxford University Press.

Bell, Catherine M. 1997. *Ritual: Perspectives and Dimensions.* New York: Oxford University Press.

Bereaved Family Member 1, 3. 2024. Interview on the Samboilbae and Ochetuji Rituals for the 10.29 Itaewon Disaster Movement. Interview by Minah Kim, 30 December.

Bereaved Family Member 2. 2023. Interview on the Samboilbae and Ochetuji Rituals for the 10.29 Itaewon Disaster Movement. Interview by Minah Kim, 22 August.

Cho, Seongyoon. 2009. *The Rebirth of Religious Rituals: Samboilbae as a New Form of Social Movement.* Proceedings of the Sociological Conference for the Korean Sociological Association; 18–19 December 2009, Seoul: Korean Sociological Association.

Derrida, Jacques. 2001. *The Work of Mourning.* Translated by P. Brault and M. Nass. The University of Chicago Press.

Durkheim, Emile. 1995 [1912]. *The Elementary Forms of Religious Life.* Translated by Karen E. Fields. New York: Free Press.

Eliade, Mircea. 1987 [1959]. *The Sacred and Profane: The Nature of Religion.* Translated by Willard R. Trask. New York: A Harvest Book.

Habermas, Jürgen. 1991 [1962]. *The Structural Transformation of the Public Sphere: An Inquiry into a Category of Bourgeois Society.* Translated by T. Burger. Cambridge, MA: MIT Press.

Im, Seokgyu. 2024. Christians Are the Ones Who Still Comfort the Grieving Families of the Itaewon Disaster. *Ohmynews*, 29 October. https://www.ohmynews.com/NWS_Web/View/at_pg.aspx?CNTN_CD=A0003074677. Accessed 23 December 2024.

Jo, Eunsol. 2023. Kim Jin-pyo, Chairman, Proposes a Mediation Plan for the Itaewon Special Law... "Let's Implement It After the General Election without a Special Investigation." *Daejonilbo*, 21 December. https://www.daejonilbo.com/news/articleView.html?idxno=2104235. Accessed 22 February 2025.

Jung, Keun-sik. 2005. The Ritual Representation of Uprising Memory: Focused on the May Events and the Eve Festival in Kwangju. *Journal of Democracy and Human Rights* 5 (1): 5–33.

Jung, Wonok. 2023. For Mourning: The 10.29 Itaewon Disaster. *Culture Moonhwagwahak* 113:43–66.

Kang, Jang-seok, Glenn D. Paige, and Chung-Si Ahn. 2017. *Nonkilling Korea: Six Culture Exploration.* Seoul: Seoul National University.

Kertzer, David I. 1988. *Ritual, Politics, and Power.* New Haven: Yale University Press.

Kim, Sun Keun. 2013. The Concept of Miraculous Prostration of Master JinBodhi as a Principle of Social Reconciliation. *Journal of Buddhist Professors in Korea* 21 (2): 5–31.

Kim, Myeonghee. 2019. Emotional Politics of Disaster and Sociology of Commemoration: For Social Healing Beyond the Medicalization of Emotions. *Emotion Studies* 19:145–178.

Kim, Bang Ryong. 2020. A Study on the Bow Practice of Korean Buddhism. *Institute for the Study of the Jogye Order Journal* 3:131–160.

Kim, Ji-ae. 2024. Interview on the Samboilbae and Ochetuji Rituals for the 10.29 Itaewon Disaster Movement. Interview by Minah Kim, 30 December.

Kim-Yoon, Nayong. 2023. Democratic Party and Justice Party: 'The Bereaved Families of the Disaster Perform Ochetuji … The Itaewon Special Law Should Be Passed by the End of the Year.' *The Kyunghyang Shinmun*, 20 December. https://www.khan.co.kr/article/202312201753001. Accessed 22 February 2025.

Lee, Sijae. 2004. Samboilbae (Three-Step-One-Bow) and Social Movements in Korea. *Catholic Journal of Social Science* 20:5–20.

Lee, Hee-Eun. 2023. Social Disaster and Death of Others: Why Was the Pain and Death of the Itaewon Disaster Excluded from Daily Life? *Cultural Studies* 11 (1): 23–41.

Lim, Hyeji. 2023. Protestant Participation in Itaewon Disaster's Samboilbae Sparks Debate: 'Contrary to Doctrine' vs. 'An Act of Remembrance.' *Cheonjiilbo*, 24 August. https://www.newscj.com/news/articleView.html?idxno=3056970. Accessed 15 October 2024.

Park, Sunwoong. 1998. Culture, Ritual and Political Change: The Democratic Transition in South Korea. *Korean Journal of Sociology* 32 (SPR): 29–61.

Park, Sunwoong. 2007. Ritual and Social Movement: Performance, Collective Effervescence and Solidarity in the June Uprisings. *Korean Journal of Sociology* 41 (1): 26–56.

Park, Chongdok C. H. 2018. The Power of the Samboilbae: The Korean Experience of Three Steps and One Bow. *The Journal of International Association of Buddhist Universities* 11 (3): 383–392.

Participant. 2023. Interview on the Samboilbae and Ochetuji Rituals for the 10.29 Itaewon Disaster Movement. *Interview by Minah Kim*, 26 December.

Shin, Jeongsik. 2020. Revisiting Spring: Reflections on Social Disasters and Healing. *Catholic Review* 45:54–61.

Special Investigation Committee on Social Disasters. 2020. Introduction to Special Investigation Committee on Social Disasters. Special Investigation Committee on Social Disasters Blog, 31 March. https://blog.naver.com/PostList.nhn?blogId=sdscsns&from=postList&categoryNo=1. Accessed 18 October 2024.

Turner, Victor. 1969. *The Ritual Process: Structure and Anti-Structure*. New York: Aldine Publishing Company.

Turner, Victor. 1982. *From Ritual to Theater: The Human Seriousness of Play*. New York: PAJ Publication.

Yoo, Ki Bbeum. 2005. The Ritual Dimension of Ecological Movements. *Studies in Religion* 40:245–269.

Yoo, Ki Bbeum. 2013. Eco-spirituality and Ritual in Contemporary Korean Religions: Focusing on the Ecological Sensibility to Non-human Animals. *Studies on Life and Culture* 29:91–126.

Yoo, Ki Bbeum. 2014. The Politics of the Senses in Eco-Ritual. *The Critical Review of Religion and Culture* 25:123–163.

Yoo, Yohan. 2021. *Understanding Religious Symbols*. Seoul: Sechang.

CHAPTER 10

New Mourning Spaces: Historical Reflections on Recent Youth Deaths in South Korea

Merose Hwang

1 Introduction

The South Korean public responds to mass death incidents in surprisingly varied ways and the nature of the response not only affects survivors' ability to heal from mass trauma, but it can also affect survivors' ability to integrate back into society, and society's ability to learn from their difficult past. In April 2024, I attended the 10th annual commemoration of the 4.16 Sewol Ferry Disaster in Ansan and awed at how bereaved families from older mass deaths across Korea reached out to the Sewol Disaster families, connecting their struggles and strategizing on ways to maintain public interest over their historical calamities. Special exhibitions and memory hall collaborations were made with the help of Jeju 4.3, Namyoung 12.14, and Gwangju 5.18 institutes. Two recent mass deaths show grieving families from 2014 passing the baton onto the grieving

M. Hwang (✉)
Department of History, Hiram College, Hiram, OH, USA
e-mail: hwangm@hiram.edu

© The Author(s), under exclusive license to Springer Nature Singapore Pte Ltd. 2025

Y. Yoo, S. C. Lee (eds.), *Reimagining Korea*, Palgrave Series in Contemporary Korean Studies,
https://doi.org/10.1007/978-981-96-6990-5_10

families that emerged in 2022, bringing to attention the state and society's ongoing failure to protect people's safety.

Narrowing my scope to compare these two recent tragedies can demonstrate how varied the general public's responses to mass youth deaths can be and how those responses can shape the culture of grief. On the morning of 16 April 2014, a ferry MV Sewol (that was en route from Incheon to Jeju City) sank near Byeongpung-do. Of the 476 passengers onboard, 304 died, including 250 students from Danwon High School in Ansan. On the evening of 29 October 2022, a crowd surge killed 159 people (mostly young women) and injured another 195 others down a steep, narrow, alleyway. The Sewol Disaster generated a sea of yellow-adorned protestors in Gwanghwamun Square and down Sejong-ro, in downtown Seoul helping to oust the country's President while the Itaewon Tragedy prompted a national week of mourning absent an official response or action plan.[1]

While both mass deaths prompted religious organizations to orchestrate large public rituals of mourning and commemoration, the survivors from both of these deadly events have shifted focus away from religious or spiritual consolation (Woo, H. 2024) toward other forms of care work. The Sewol Disaster bereaved families have successfully orchestrated several permanent memorials to be installed throughout Korea's eastern shoreline, meticulously featuring the names, pictures, and personal belongings of each "martyr" (Veritas, June 19, 2015). Meanwhile, Itaewon Tragedy activists hesitate to establish identifying markers of those killed. At the point when this chapter was written, Itaewon Tragedy activists only managed to maintain a temporary memorial tent near City Hall and a small bulletin in progress on the side of a building near subway Exit 1. While a public commemoration space continues to be postponed, these activists have raised makeshift memorial tents in front of City Hall that hold the funerary portraits and victims' names with incense for visitors to greet the dead, to offer their condolences, and to leave with purple ribboned keychains.

[1]There are many different terms used to refer to these two mass death incidents and they all have their justifications. Without claiming a position in that debate, from here on, I will use the terms most commonly used by survivors and bereaved: "Sewol Disaster" to refer to the "MV Sewol Ferry Disaster of 16 April 2014" and "Itaewon Tragedy" to refer to the mass death that occurred on 29 October 2022 in Itaewon, Seoul.

I see the normalizing of mass death in contemporary South Korea not only as drawing profit from social precarity (You and Park 2017) but also being enabled by state mnemocide where well foreseen risks (at the expense of vulnerable populations) are repeatedly taken, and then with every mass tragedy, knowledge of those risks erased in order to make each mass death appear accidental or incidental. To help make sense of this, I examine the 2014 and 2022 tragedies through rhetorical justifications that stem from two historical moments in Korea. The first discursive trope comes from a "negative eugenics" campaign as a remnant of Japanese colonial rule (1910–1945) and the second trope revolves around a "war rhetoric" that was prompted by the Korean War (1950–1953) and that continues to the present.

With these rhetorical legacies in mind, this chapter tries to understand trends in South Korea's public response to mass deaths by first examining the Sewol Ferry Disaster a bit more closely. This chapter explores the differences between how Korean death rituals deal with "good" versus "bad" deaths. As the Sewol Disaster epitomizes bad deaths, we consider how the victims' bereaved parents have dealt with their post-disaster roles as guardians of discontent child ghosts. It goes on to examine how those ghosts work alongside their grieving parents to educate the public about the disaster. This chapter also considers the burden that such consistent memorialization work might have on survivors as it shifts to the Itaewon Tragedy as a case in contrast that has generated ambivalence around "futile" or "self-imposed" deaths. It lists some of the ongoing issues where activists are blaming the government and industries while emphasizing the acute problem of victims' families and other survivors struggling to grieve their dead. The intense social shaming making it difficult for them to mourn the Itaewon Tragedy has caused "bystander-survivors" to take it upon themselves to provide alternative forms of care for people on the fringes of society in what I refer to as "queer youth space." Through this comparison, this chapter attempts to show how recent national tragedies have challenged traditional Korean collectivist values, how the erosion of trust in institutions is reshaping communal identity, how trauma has contributed to the rise of youth-driven political and social movements, and how repeated exposure to national disasters has fostered young populations to imagine new forms of mourning that reflect evolving techniques in community building while also transmitting the cultural tradition of deep, collective memory.

2 Historical Context

2.1 Negative Eugenics

The mnemocidal rhetoric that abound in the aftermath of the Itaewon Tragedy is not a new happening. Colonialist eugenics programs enabled the uneven valuation of human populations. This was evidenced in the wars and postwar developmentalist years of the twentieth century that saw an unprecedented loss of life, devastated ecosystems, and waves of migration. With nearly 123 million people killed during wartime and 80 million more during "peacetime" (White 2003), post-war governments locked their sites on socially engineering ways to repopulate their countries with state-driven eugenics agendas in laboratories and hospitals (Bashford and Levine 2010). Northeast Asia suffered the most depopulation from twentieth-century wars. In recent years, this region has suffered the most acute depopulation, but this time, under very different circumstances. South Korea ranks as having the lowest birth rate in the world. This is slightly offset by state-sponsored in-migration (Cho and Kim 2024), causing Koreans to panic that jobs are being stolen, that "social handicaps" (Kim, E. 2017: 139) are flooding their society, and that non-nationals are profiting from tax-payer handouts.

While shrinking populations may signal an advanced stage in Korea's compressed modernity (Chang, K. 2022), it could also be understood by comparing popular rhetoric on population issues of the past to the present. State-driven depopulation campaigns, emergency population supplants, and social xenophobia remind me of historical conditions that sprouted social engineering techniques employed under the Japanese colonial government in Korea from the late 1920s to 1945 and the post-war government of the 1980s. The colonial period was marked by military aggression, massive out-migration, and Western eugenics ("*woosaeng*," Shin, Y. 2006), while the post-war period was marked by an aggressive fertility sterilization program to meet the needs of a rapid export-led economy that required more female workers and less children (Moon 2005). Technocrats were tasked to engineer ways to expand depleted labor pools alongside print media propaganda campaigns to minimize unwieldy outcomes (Hwang 2012).

Currently, programs that follow the quotidian lives of desirable mixed-race families dominate television broadcasts. What they omit are certain undesirable couplings (i.e. with foreigners from Islamic traditions [Kim and Woo 2022], or offspring from absent, US military fathers Lee, J. 2010), rendering those types of children "invisible" and leading Koreans to embrace only certain kinds of ethnically distinctive babies as a signal of South Korea's global reach. These multiculturalism programs also blur the reality that Korean capitalists' have been poaching, shipping, detaining, and disposing of foreign laborers (Butler and Athanasiou 2013) with the help of conservative administrations and that poorer, sending countries are their targets. Those entertainment programs hush the ugly sides of the domestic lives, such as migrants' suffering higher levels of domestic violence, higher divorce rates, and unequal parental rights, to broader conditions surrounding their necropolitical labor, such as their spousal contingency to residency, lack of labor right representation, market liberalization, deregulation, and privatization under the current presidential administration (You and Park 2017; Yun, J. 2024a).

Even among ethnic Koreans, are some lives valued more than others? The media portrays Sewol Disaster children as the unsurmountable lost children who were dutifully attending a field trip while it treats Itaewon Tragedy youth as those who died while engaged in leisure, undervaluing the latter population as unwieldy excess and rendering them un-grievable. When there is such a shortage of births, the Sewol Disaster and Itaewon Tragedies should both remind us of the preciousness of all populations; and civil society should be outraged every time the state fails to protect youth in Korea. The valuation of group deaths based on posthumous mass character defamations also trumpet an ethic of proper parentage and individual responsibility, further enabling negative eugenics campaigns to negate certain people as collateral damage in the interest of the state. I fear that this kind of inhumanity during peacetime has as much a lasting effect as acute wartime distress and that it can manifest as intergenerational trauma.

2.2 *War Rhetoric*

A necropolitical use of social and political power can dictate how the dead are remembered or forgotten, and how well their survivors may thrive in the post-death world, revealing a neoliberal, neocolonial "deathworld" (Mbembe 2020). Achille Mbembe helps us appreciate the idea of "necropolitics" where contemporary state-sponsored deaths and social engineering campaigns endanger and extinguish people of color. Marina Gržinić and Šefik Tatlic (2016) take Mbembe's argument further by exploring global capitalist policies in the postcolonial world that essentially produce state surplus value from death. To make better sense of what the two tragedies in this study have in common, it may be useful to meditate on what Scott Knowles (2020) considers types of "slow disasters" where he notices how historical processes make large-scale disasters possible.

No matter the nature or date of a mass death, Cold War rhetoric abounds in Korea, compelling a closer look at the curious longevity of what Westerners consider antiquated, mid-century politics. Local historical conditions surrounding the Cold War as a long period of "hot war" may shed light on its ongoing currency. The end of Japanese colonialism and the Korean War caused twice more civilian than combatant deaths. The Cold War division of the country established a precedence where being called a communist or associated with one could put a person's life at risk in South Korea. Although the DMZ has kept families separated for over 70 years now, that radical, massive displacement from ancestral villages established an environment of "impossible citizenship" where dislocation remains one of the most enduring aspects of domestic politics (Kwon 2020: 37).

Some believe that South Korea has been cursed with corporate malpractices and government collusion since the early days of the Cold War (Jeju News 2023). The week after I attended the Sewol Disaster 10th anniversary commemoration, I visited a 4.16 Sewol Ferry Memorial Hall in Jeju and met with Director Dong-hoon Shin, who left his architect job on the mainland and relocated to the island to create a Jeju Peace Shelter and Memorial Hall. Just after he was released from jail, he shared with me how the police arrested him, initially suspecting him of violating the "national security act" (4.16 Yeondae Hwaldong 2023). They interrogated him, assuming that he was harboring communist insurgency organizers on the grounds of his 4.16 compound.

A month later, in May 2024, a meeting between the Sewol Disaster and Namyoung Ferry Disaster bereaved families was held at a Sewol Memorial Hall in Jeju Island. On 14 December 1970, a Namyoung Ferry left Busan for Jeju Island, sinking and killing 326 people. They compare the Namyoung Disaster to Sewol Disaster, calling these the "twin maritime disasters" (You and Park 2017), shedding light on how Park Geun-hye's mishandling of the Sewol Disaster resembled her father, Park Chung-hee's (1962–1979) mismanagement of the Namyoung incident. Scholars have compared the Sewol Disaster and Itaewon Tragedy to other major human-made disasters like the Sampoong Department Store collapse of 1995 and the Daegu subway bombing/fire of 2003 (Kim and Oh 2022; Kwon 2016).

As a country fastened to an eternal state of war, regimes of "crisis" force the broader public to bear hardship and humiliation without outrage or dissent. The crisis dictates that "there is no alternative." Limiting choices because of the potentiality of danger becomes the only rational and viable mode of governance where critical thinking and protest are treated as irrational, unpatriotic, or guerilla (Butler and Athanasiou 2013). The public shares responsibility for marginalizing certain disasters that render the people who protest the government or major corporations as political or social pariahs. This can be seen when conservative activists torment grieving families and their allies whenever they demand justice and government accountability, even when they simply gather to grieve. These ultra-right pile loudspeakers onto trucks, deface and tear event banners, and inch by mass tragedy commemorations to drown out survivors' voices. Their megaphones shriek that communists and pinkos have no place in their society. They treat anti-communism as an "East Asian value" to estrange and destroy certain people's right to publicly mourn (Bak 2015). In these ways, the mid-century fratricidal war and social political bifurcation continues to isolate, alienate, and estrange the mass bereaved.

3 The 04.16.2014 Sewol Ferry Disaster

3.1 Quality Send-Offs

Like any other rite of passage, funerals are meant to be highly social, communal affairs (Baker 2008). Those fortunate enough to die with "good endings" (with quality often contingent on the surviving family's material means, Lee and Kim 2018) may partake in palliative care to reduce the severity of pain and discomfort for the dying. Such families may witness a gentle death where they are able to offer or exchange soft farewells, sit by the dying one's bedside, holding their hand, consoling, and watching as the dying part with their last breath. They may follow prescribed customs to prepare for their death rituals, leaning on their friends and neighbors to help them move on with their own lives. To properly send off their loved ones and to induce a happy spiritual transfer, they may hold a three-day funeral at the hospital, cremate the body, bury the remaining bones in the family gravesite, perhaps conduct a 49-day mourning ceremony (especially for Buddhists), or even observe a three-year mourning period (for devout

Confucianists). Attending to the prescriptions of perfect happenings before, during, and after death are of utmost importance for the wellbeing of their survivors.

But loved ones left behind from mass deaths struggle to find order and move on. Depending on the trauma location volatility, post-incident time lapse, etc., it may be logistically impossible to retrieve the personal belongings of the deceased; their corpses may be missing or dismembered, otherwise unsuitable for proper preparation, processing, preservation, etc., and an ordinary funeral may be out of the question. Family members may not know the exact time of death or what the experience of dying was like for the dead. When the cause of death is shrouded by political cover ups and scandal, family members may be forced to conduct secret, makeshift funeral rites and grieve their kin in private (Kim and Hwang 2023). These deceased loved ones are marked by their socio-political aberration; their survivors are haunted by unsettled ghosts, their psychological restoration further compromised by their socio-cultural isolation (Somasundaram and Sivayokan 2013).

How long might grief last when deaths are due to "social disasters" (Kim and Oh 2022)? A year before the 10-year Sewol Ferry Disaster commemoration was due to happen, KBS Daegu broadcast a program that opened with this question on the lifespan of grief. The program marked the 20th anniversary of the day when an arsonist fire engulfed a six-car train and ravaged Jungangno Station in central Daegu on the morning of 18 February 2003, leaving 130 people dead. Camera crews followed Daegu bereaved family members last year as they visited the Sewol Disaster and Itaewon Tragedy memorials and mourned those losses as their own. Psychotherapist, Noda Masaki, touched on the question with, "Only when the people who remember the dead themselves die off can the dead truly die" (KBS Daegu 2023).

In the days and years that followed these terrible events, religious organizations throughout the country, and indeed, around the world, offered condolence prayers and memorial services to survivors and their communities. Immediately after the Sewol Ferry Disaster occurred, Catholic services were held in Gwanghwamun Plaza in the center of Seoul. Forty-six days after the disaster, intangible cultural asset shamans, featuring the famous Kim Geum-hwa, performed a *Jin-ogi gut* at the Incheon Coastal Pier Marine Plaza (Director Gwon 2018), then again at Paengmok Port, where the ferry sank. A few days later, Buddhist monks gathered on the 49th day to pray for the dead to ascend into heaven. *Jin-ogi gut* in commemoration of the Sewol victims continued to be performed throughout the year (Musok TV 2014). Whenever ritual specialists performed a parting ceremony, they paved the way to send the deceased to a good place and attendees departed with the knowledge that they would return to a similar commemoration again.

Although the institutionalization of memory spaces (Kim and Oh 2022) may prevent their disappearance, I am particularly interested in how Korea's shamanic tradition (the oldest but perhaps minor among many belief systems that exist in South Korea) handles "bad death" commemorations. Shamanic mass death rituals focus on processing the grief of survivors alongside the larger community as many other traditions do, but it also holds a unique space for the lamenting dead (ghosts speaking through shamans) to meet and engage in difficult, sometimes agonistic conversations with perpetrators, accomplices, neighbors, etc. The curative potential of the *gutdang* (shamanic ritual space) has made them types of "piacular rites" that are performed in times of crisis or tragedy, often to appease the sacred or restore harmony. Building off Emile Durkheim's argument, large, community *gut* for the mass dead has a psycho-social function (Jones, R. 1986; Oh, S. 2023). Ritual spaces may focus on the affects of collective memory when ritual specialists encourage participants to process unpleasant emotions like fear, anger, pity, resentment, helplessness, regret, and grief. Memories are corroborated with dead children/sibling ghosts; sometimes those ghosts detail and lament how they died alongside survivors' stories to recreate the time and conditions of death. The dead and the living are given an opportunity to process their feelings for one another, enabling emotional commiseration and consolation. Ultimately, survivors' relationship with their dead loved ones and neighbors is restored and some comfort is given to survivors as they promise their reunion at the next *gut* (Hwang 2023).

3.2 Custodians and Post-mortem Belongings[2]

Some Sewol Disaster survivors may be engaged in various religious commemoration activities while spiritual trauma appears conspicuously

[2] Thanks to Dr. Yohan Yoo (Seoul National University, Religious Studies Department) for encouraging me to pursue this project and for inviting me to submit this chapter. Special

missing from their museum and memorial spaces. But upon closer inspection, spiritual healing is being processed through their fight to resist the community's push for mnemocide. A point to consider is how bereaved parents have handled these battles with their neighbors in Danwon and throughout Ansan.[3] In the aftermath of the disaster, school parents, neighbors, and people from across the country visited Danwon High School in droves to show their support and grief. The busloads of condolence visitors so overwhelmed the school that they had to establish a unidirectional pathway through campus, greatly limiting queuing and visiting hours. Once the traffic died down, bereaved parents suggested that the school should designate the victims' six classrooms into permanent memorial rooms. Then, a nasty battle ensued with the Danwon High School administrators and other parents. Bereaved parents argued that other parents who they once considered friends began to push back, complaining that the school was already suffering from insufficient space. The school administration issued a public-facing response that the school needed to maintain its priority to use those rooms to address the space-shortage problem and to return them to teaching their existing students.

This political tussle points to the contemporaneousness of child ghosts as those tethered to their quotidian, physical locations, causing everyone in their proximity to manipulate the material world around them. Bereaved parents reasoned that they had a duty to take care of their dead kids who were still active members of Danwon High School and, just like any other student, they were demanding their right to keep their belongings in the school. If the school got rid of their classrooms, their kids would have nowhere else to go and would be hopelessly lost. Non-victim students complained to their own parents that they no longer felt comfortable going to school because the intense mourning was luring student ghosts into the building. Even though those students were only secondary witnesses to the 16 April incident, they were being newly traumatized by

thanks go to Jiseong Lee, director of the 4.16 Memory Archives, Director of the Memorial Hall management team of 4.16 Institute of Democratic Citizenship Education, and Memory of the 4.16 Memory Archives bereaved families committee and co-organizer, Dr. Scott Gabriel Knowles and Seulgi Lee of "Sewol Haggyo," and the Slow Disaster Lab at Korea Advanced Institute of Science and Technology (KAIST), Ansan, South Korea, April 2024; many thanks to Jaewoo Kim (Seoul National University, Religious Studies Department) for your great insights and advice on this work.

[3] I am grateful to Gyeongbin Im's mother, who shared personal stories about her neighbors. Danwon, Ansan, South Korea.

their dead classmates. Most of the parents' association vehemently rejected the bereaved parents' request, compelling the school principal at the time, Chu Kyo-yang, to tell bereaved families and mourning visitors to stop entering the school altogether.

After much push back, the school conceded to allow a small memorial space to be secured in a gymnasium that was planned for renovation. They later reneged on that offer, saying that the space had been sold off to an anonymous buyer for a private venture. At that point, the bereaved families' association had no choice but to tear down and rebuild their children's classrooms off site. Parents insisted that the new classrooms look exactly as they did on that fateful day. Alongside architects, engineers, tradespeople and many volunteers, every possible part of the six classrooms, from ceiling tiles and lighting fixtures, to windows, doors, cabinets, and every movable object in between was painstakingly disassembled, moved, and meticulously reassembled at a new 4.16 Institute. Finishing the relocated classroom memorial should have been a cause to celebrate but that was cut short once the bereaved families learned that the buyer of the high school's renovated gymnasium had waited for that moment to sell his building back to the school, leaving them feeling ever more estranged from their Danwon friends and neighbors.

3.3 Memory Classrooms as a Vanguard Place

The Sewol Disaster bereaved family's association has benefited from a wealth of survivors' techniques spanning back nearly 70 years. This association honors their elder traditions while inventing post-trauma spaces and experiences in ways that have never been seen before. 4.16 Memory Archives Director, Jiseong Lee argues that the process of preservation and sharing the history helps bereaved families with their sorrow. The institutional spaces of the 4.16 Foundation work as insurgent warehouses, spiritual solace spaces, and experiential classrooms. Volunteers at the Ansan Hwarang Park exchange small and heavy talk as they spend hours crafting hundreds of yellow ribbon keychains. One container at the park stores materials that the government has deemed classified. Their collection, catalog, and operation are made possible through generous private donations, acting as a kind of "mercenary" archive to aid people who are pursuing independent investigations. In the storeroom of the 4.16 central archives in Mirae Huimang Gwan (Future Hope Hall), the family association has bagged, tagged, and categorized a ton of seafloor mud that was excavated from the Sewol Ferry Disaster site, making them a part of the 4778 types of ephemera in their repository. Archive Director Jiseong Lee, gingerly caresses one of these bags as she tells us about missing children's corpses.[4] Ms. In-suk Jeon, who goes by the title, "Gyeongbin Im's Mother" leads a walking tour of Danwon's old residential neighborhood and walks us around a memorial walkway that encircles one half of the school grounds as she mutters bitterly about the school fight (Lee 2022). We stop under a tree next to Ansan Lake where she hears a splash and turns to spot a fish jumping out of the pond. She smiles, reflecting on how much her son loved fish and waves toward the water telling us that he might be coming up to greet us. Such momentary ruptures between temporal worlds suggest a pattern of grief metalepsis by demonstrating a narrative transgression or a coping mechanism where the speaker mixes the boundaries between the world IN which she tells and the world OF which she tells (Genette 1980).

Grief memory transgression spreads to random people working and speaking on behalf of these bereaved families. Unaffiliated parental guides and young content creators alike bear witness and dive into their bystander-survivors' guilt as they post newsletters and blogs and run book tours on their memoirs (Yu, G. 2023) and novels (Yun, Y. 2024b). A young performance artist creates a video montage with voiceovers from interviews with bereaved mothers as they meditate on their lost children. The artist shows videos of the victim children's performances and home movies. She then video records herself watching gallery attendees weeping as they watch these children's videos and listen to their mothers' voiceovers. Then, the artist records herself watching the gallery attendees and we hear her voiceover talking about her own daydream of birthing, loving, and then, tragically losing that child forever (Black Jaguar 2016; Jeong 2023).

Activists throughout the country, including in downtown Seoul, Suwon, and Bonggae-dong (in Jeju City), continue to work to ensure that society does not forget this tragedy. In April 2025, Sewol scholars are given a tour of South Korea's largest marine safety training center that recently opened in Pyeongtaek-si, Gyeonggi Province (the provincial government's initiative in response to the disaster). A privately funded 4.16 Sewol Disaster in Jeju Memorial Hall, down the street from the Jeju 4.3

[4] The 4.16 Institute reports to have 10,213 records in its public repository. Special thanks goes to Bereaved Father, Gwang-bae Kim for sharing his book and his stories with me at the 4.16 Sewol in Jeju Resting Place, 20 April 2024.

Peace Park, is run by progressively minded volunteers and students. Every month they switch out a portrait wall to celebrate each Sewol Disaster victim's birthday. Its Director Dong-hoon Shin solicits businesses in the vicinity to help him expand and maintain 4.16 display tables in storefronts, as a reminder for patrons to not forget the Sewol Disaster. Even if their content is disaggregated, the themes, characterizations, and public displays of intimacy among dead children, surviving families, visitors, grassroots activists and local governments can coalesce and cohere with one another.

The death of a child locks surviving loved ones outside of chrononormative life. A wrongful, violent, or unjust death of a child makes their post-death environment all the more precarious (even dangerous) to the living and those who continue to guard such death spaces may be seen as living in "queer time" (Samuels, E. and Freeman, E. 2021). Of all the places that work to preserve 4.16, the memory classrooms seem to most resemble a queer place between an unused child's bedroom and a publicly facing memorial. The 4.16 Memory classrooms are places for important grassroots work and experimental pedagogy. In one of these classrooms, Im Gyeongbin's mother asks a bunch of fifth graders to sit at the desks with the ghosts of their fallen upperclassmen, to notice the victims' names and portraits. She asks them to find Gyeongbin's desk. When one girl raises her hand, students gasp, and the air is momentarily sucked out of the room. One student asks, "Why is Gyeongbin's chair different from the others?" pointing at a bright yellow, crotched seat cover. His mom responds again in metalepsis, "I made that for him ... in case he might be cold." She utters, "my son would be 26 years old now" and then returns to the class, vividly accounting the moments of that nightmarish day. She urges each student to handle the victim's personal belongings, pictures, and photos that are resting at each desk. Then, she asks the children to write their own memories, hopes, and dreams into those dead children's memory books. She pauses throughout the lesson to encourage the children to not be afraid, assuring them that their dead seniors are happy and grateful for their visit. Daily, these mothers do this, running these experiential memory classrooms where they invoke their dead children to interact with junior student visitors, not only to help younger generations learn about structural dangers and public safety but also to communally interact with the dead in these vanguard memory places.

4 The 10.29.2022 Itaewon Tragedy

4.1 Skeletons in the Closet

The remainder of this chapter will look closely at the underexplored relationships between failed political movements to protect public spaces, the deterioration of bereaved family health, and the emergence of "queer youth space" memorials as strategies for bystander-survival. One might generalize that impartial, comprehensive investigations have not been conducted on these mass deaths and their outstanding issues are too numerous to discuss in this chapter. However, this section will touch on a few outstanding political matters to tie these two recent tragedies together. One line of questioning that municipal and national governments are shirking revolves around whether or not pre-existing, preventative measures could have averted these mass deaths? Related to Itaewon, Hamilton Hotel's Chief of Hotel, Mr. Lee, was post-facto fined a meagre $6200 for allowing the hotel's utility units to be illegally extended, jutting into the already narrow alleyway by 17.2 square meters and making it inaccessible to EMS vehicles (Park, B. 2023). The pitch of a handful of alleyways in that area were already too steep to meet normal foot traffic demands, all suggesting a disaster waiting to happen. That night in 2022, police and EMS forces—that were present in past years for the same Halloween festival – were mysteriously redirected to President Yoon's office in an order to prioritize his security during an anti-government protest rally. A meagre 137 officers remained in Itaewon, with 50 allocated to other tasks like operating undercover for a drug bust. Unlike previous years, on that evening of 29 October 2022, not only were security forces missing, routine festival foot traffic signs were not installed, safety barricades were not set up, and the main subway egress was not blocked to redistribute traffic to other stops. Several emergency calls were made to the police in the hours preceding the tragedy but to no avail.

In the days that followed, rather than issuing an emergency investigation into these issues, President Yoon abruptly enforced a period of mourning, silencing the social media frenzy around the tragedy (Peik, S. and Jo, M. 2023). In the spring of 2024, the Democratic Party requested a special council be created to conduct a fresh round of impartial investigations which the President stonewalled. Also that year, the South Korean court acquitted Seoul's former police chief, Gwang-ho Kim (who was indicted in January 2024), convicting just one lower ranking police officer of negligence, whereby sparing "senior government officials from blame" (Guinto 2024). When people push their issues aside and turn their attention to more recent political scandals, like Yoon's martial law decree, a presidential impeachment (Rashid, R. 2024), and yet another mass death with a Jeju Air plane crash that left 179 people dead (Kim, H. and Kim, T. 2024), preexisting bereaved families are retraumatized by new tragedies and by social pressures to forget their own fight or to move on.

Just as Jeju, Gwangju, and Namyoung, Sewol bereaved families, etc. have handed down political activism strategies to one another, such advice is also being passed onto the newest grieving families with special attention paid to parents' failing mental and bodily conditions. Despite a strong show of support between these networks, the latest longitudinal studies done on Sewol families suggest that parents, children, and siblings continue to have worsening health to the extent that some lose their vision, teeth, and hair. Some have knees, hands, arms, and backs falling apart, requiring ever more acute medical attention. Chronic health problems have caused Sewol families to organize and fight for government medical relief packages to be extended. Anti-demonstrators make sure to show up to each of their public events to disrupt their proceedings and hurl insults at them, calling them communists, freeloaders, and thieves stealing handouts from hardworking, taxpaying citizens (Lee, M. et al. 2022). While some bereaved mothers rise above the adversity, reinventing themselves into self-made curators and thanatologists, they also mutter concerns about how their husbands drink too much, ideate suicide, and even continue to take their own lives (Lee, S. et al. 2024).[5] Still, others continue to uproot themselves to new cities or countries in the hopes of finding more hospitable environments.

Officially bereaved parents may attempt to protect their children from being re-triggered by disallowing them from attending their peers' funerals. They encourage their children to pursue activities akin to privatized Western medical systems, such as closed-door talk therapy, drug

[5] One study found that the "potential risk of suicide has gradually decreased over time" (Lee et al. 2024). This may be the trend but Ms. Buja Jeong, a bereaved mother told us about family members' deteriorating health, that one father committed suicide in March and another in April of 2024. Meeting was held at the Ansan Hwarang Park on 15 April 2024.

prescriptions, art therapy, rest and relaxation activities, and volunteer work (Yu, G. 2023). Those families attend religious ceremonies, tragedy memorial day events throughout the country, and work to provide comfort to other officially counted victims' families and survivors (as described above). Online trolling happens with any mass death in South Korea, but it appears rather pervasive when it comes to the Itaewon Tragedy (Choi, H. and Seo, J. 2024; Peik, S. and Jo, M. 2023). Trolls posted rape jokes onto photos of girls who had died at the site, causing many to close their social media accounts. A grieving couple started facing "a torrent of online abuse that started when they joined a group calling for an investigation into why government officials failed to prevent the deadly Halloween incident" that killed their son. Their daughter said she heard insults for the first time, like "*siche pali handa* (you're selling corpses)!" as she was attempting to publicly honor the death of her brother (Tse and Vit 2023). Once the Itaewon Tragedy broke on social media and the news circuits picked it up, many parents felt compelled to go on record to insist that their dead children were good people, urging the public to recognize their innocence (Lee, H. 2023a). Without public buy-in, many bereaved Itaewon Tragedy families continue to hide their identities, fearing public humiliation, victim blaming, and re-traumatization (Lee, H. 2023b). They keep themselves closeted when they see degrading, misogynistic, and humiliating comments on social media.

4.2 *Bystander-Survivors*

Since the end of the Second World War and especially to understand the anomaly of the Holocaust, social scientists have explored a new category of "bystanders," how crowds can perpetrate negligence and even indirectly foster violence. This has come to be known as the "bystander effect" (De Juan et al. 2023). Utilizing this theory, mass apathy and ambivalence have also been widely explored. Considering the high online visibility of the two recent mass deaths in South Korea, one can assume that a great number of people were exposed to or even impacted by those events. While many Koreans became bystanders, we cannot simply consider them associated as culprits or victims to those events. And, far from apathy or ambivalence, those remote bystanders have responded very strongly to the extent that (and for instance) the Sewol Ferry disaster caused millions of people to take to the streets for several months in protest.

Beyond victims' and their bereaved families, there is a neglected population of young, remote bystanders who identify themselves as survivors of both the Sewol and Itaewon mass death incidents. To better understand the connection between the two, these self-named, remote survivors deserve some attention. Among them are the numerous youth activists who have been working on Sewol over these past 10 years and the 20-something youth who continue to carry the torch for these latest Itaewon Tragedy survivors. These survivors have turned their trauma into strength and can be found working in and contributing to public spaces. On the flip side, some young people with secondary trauma secretly grieve, struggle to sleep, eat, work, study, and support relationships. They admit having had nothing to do with these tragedies, and without organized support, they tussle with their attachments and mask their survivors' guilt.

These bystander survivors disassociate from older generations believing they are *the* "tragedy generation." This highlights their chronologically non-normative self-awareness; that they were the same age as their Sewol Ferry peers when they watched their peers drown over their phones. They say "*nae ga doel su isseosseum*" ("it could have been me," Peik, S. and Jo, M. 2023), whereby referring to themselves as the lucky ones who narrowly escaped that fateful disaster. Five years after Sewol, they came of age under the unusual isolation of the COVID-19 pandemic crisis. They had to wait three long years for the social distance regulation to be lifted. Rather than follow Korea Disease Control and Prevention Agency advice to maintain caution and "stay put," these newly legal adults wanted to get together, not for school or work, but to do what they've been waiting so long to do: simply hang out with their friends at their local bars, restaurants, and cafés. South Korea claimed to have led the world in conquering the pandemic so why not celebrate their sacrifice and success? That day was supposed to mark a new era for these 20-somethings in a post-tragedy world. But that hope was dashed within a few hours.[6] Some had plans to go to Itaewon that night but made sudden change of plans; some were in Itaewon the night before or had plans to go the next day and they just "survived by chance" (*"uyeonhi salanamassda,"* Peik, S. and Jo, M. 2023)

[6] This project would not have been possible without the artwork, activism, and insights into the Itaewon Tragedy shared by Sohyeon Peik (Seoul National University, Sociology Department). Thanks also goes to Nagyeong Im for organizing group conversations between their peers and I on the Itaewon tragedy. This research was made possible in part due to their assistance and generosity.

Among the reasons these survivors remain deeply closeted is that the Itaewon Tragedy has been shaped into a highly privatized, anomalous affair where most of the blame has been posthumously placed on the dead's individual, free choice. The media has characterized these victims as young adults who made bad decisions, engaging in sordid pleasures which led to their own demise, making them essentially responsible for their own death. By contrast, there is no question about the Sewol victims' innocence as obedient school children who were forced into their situations and killed by negligent adults. The messiness of the Itaewon Tragedy has caused grassroots activist communities to even neglect their grieving families. This was clearly the case when I attended the 2024 International Women's Day events. A diverse array of social justice issues was slated for the official program, but the Itaewon Tragedy was missing from the speaker's list, and their struggle was nowhere to be found among the rows of tents. A grieving mother had to demand off-stage to be added as a last-minute speaker, demonstrating how even recognized victim family members must work to uphold the good reputation of their dead, young adult children.

4.3 *Creating a Queer Space for Grief*

These bystander-survivors plead their stories not to be conflated or exploited for political gain, asking us to notice how ambivalent the public has become since they collectively fought for their peers for the past eleven years. There is the belief that South Korea's deeply bifurcated political parties have each usurped these tragedies for their own agenda and to maintain the status quo with the institutional stakeholders. Therefore, the common plea is for youth rights and safety to not be co-opted by society's elders, dislocating, discriminating, and disenfranchising these bystander-survivors because of ongoing practices of exclusion or denial. These "deathscapes" demonstrate an undemocratic historical present with the useless impeachment of President Geun-hye Park, Jae-in Moon's failed promises to establish a better government, yet another wasted impeachment of Suk-yeol Yoon's followed by Lee Jae-myung as the likely Democratic Party successor in June 2025, who will again make promises that he will not keep and capitalist interests will continue to be prioritized over people's safety.

These bystander-survivors retain a subcultural, sub-ethnic identity. Although they may be ethnically Korean, culturally, they are not quite

Korean, not quite foreign, but rather, a fringe, queer people. They have been rescuing the meaning of foreignness from Itaewon's historical reputation as an area of ill-repute; a neighborhood targeted for forced sterilization and clean-up campaigns (Moon 1997). The area once developed as a center for foreign residents since the US military established the Yongsan military base in the mid-twentieth century, with a huge sex trade industry that catered to American GIs (Lee, J. 2010; Kim, Y. 2024b) and queer sex work. The neighborhood was seen as dangerous, with its American extra-judicial crimes, overconsumption, and contamination, causing the media to pin the spread of AIDS in the 1980s and the coronavirus in 2020 to its visitors and residents.

Unlike residents surrounding other mass deaths, many of these bystander-survivors are creating art with hyper-localized, indigenous-level insights. They declared that the partygoers who flooded the Hamilton Hotel alleyway (and most of the crush victims) were not locals; they were foreign and domestic tourists. While many parts of Itaewon have historically housed migrant residences and small foreign businesses, developers on the hill behind Hamilton erected megaclubs and massive eateries, promoting a Bourbon Street-like vibe to attract foreign clientele and rich, domestic tourists. Some of those trapped on that hill may have been clandestine "first timers," emboldened behind their costumes. These bystander-survivors knew how to avoid that part of town but especially so when some 100,000 Halloween tourists might be tearing up the street. That night, they may have returned to their old stomping grounds surrounding the tragedy epicenter. They were far enough away to escape the chaos but near enough to run back, be first-in to witness, report, and document the crisis as it was unfolding in their social domicile.

Out of this tragedy, these young artists have been creating queer space communities between and beyond private or public spaces of mourning. The aura of artistic authenticity in their spaces is intentionally ephemeral, residing instantaneously with "cult" value, outside the technical sphere of mechanized reproduction. They see that socio-political pressures make caring for them impossible, so these youngsters take it upon themselves to take care of one another. They explore their trauma through the ordinary, everyday, and through spectacular, subversive celebrations. A good example of this is Flag Sidekick, a collective run by Eui-seok Seong, Su-min Lee, and Han-gyeol Joo; dedicated to artistically mourning the 10.29.2022 tragedy. The collective launched a zine series titled, "Kebab After Drink" to broach the question, "are other ways of mourning beyond political polarization possible"? They held experimental workshops, discussion sessions, dance parties, and solicited work from members of their "subculture" to document momentary ephemera in a microscopic history. These have become a kind of queer 10.29 record of an otherwise unknown indigeneity that the collective described as those things that could be "shared but could not be capitalized" (Flag Sidekick 2023).

From October 22 through November 02, 2024, this artist collective curated a modest retrospective titled "Mix Kebab Compilation 2022-2024" at a Human Resource Market in nearby Hannam-dong. The exhibition room and zine-making room ran in a small studio on a side street to overlap with and somewhat dismiss the politically charged second anniversary commemoration of the 10.29 tragedy that ran through the weekend on the main street of Itaewon.[7] Their studio displayed the liveliness of young people eating and chatting, posters promoting 10.29 anniversary raves, stamp and postering campaigns, a beefcake flashing his ass in a club, lesbians making out in a cramped bathroom, gay men having anal on a bunk bed, a "cry and dance" party, pictures of daily filth inside a lonely apartment, street garbage and stacked barricades, a row of kitchen timers from nearby shops, etc.—an archive of Korea's cultural underbelly in post-tragedy Itaewon. Documenting this non sequitur, impersonal, fringe existence was a radical expression of resistance. Recording their creative and banal activities has become a way to confront and defy the logics of South Korea's deathworld and their workshops where people ate foreign fast food, walked, and talked, explored authentic, anti-capitalist pathways to mourning.

Their queer spaces may be seen as a refuge if not temples that work against dominant ideologies and that transforms cultural logic from within, chastising vampiric systems of power. Through non sequitur celebrations of idleness, chaos, irony, hunger, and grief, this collective work to escape politicians' piracy of their unique expressions. They literally and metaphorically huddle around the kebab, highlighting a popular ritual of ending an all-nighter around a Turkish food stall. This fast food for Itaewon insomniacs symbolizes a hard night of werking or twerking in bars, brothels, or clubs. Such ritualized expressions of survival (Esteban Munoz, J. 1999) toys with and rejects the trolls that made the 10.29 victims worthless because they simply "died while playing

[7] More information can be found @flagsidekick or flagsidekick.com. Pumpkin lantern (@itaewonpumpkin) also provided their support for this exhibition.

(*nordaga jukeotda*)" (Peik, S. and Jo, M. 2023). They gather other bystander-survivors to take communion with street food, helping to rescue the fateful images of their "foolishly" expired peers as they play hard enough to skirt around their own deaths, perhaps to make peace with their own existential futility someday.

5 Afterthoughts

How might we understand mourning when one's adjacency to death is not an anomaly but is on repeat? South Korea's young bystander-survivors recognize the precarity and (for some) the miraculousness of their own survival. They recognize that life after mass death cannot be ordinary. It is no longer a presence without an existential crisis. Their post-death lives are a collection of memories that permeate present and future experiences. For these young, bystander-survivors, grief has become constitutive and pervasive, rather than an intermittent, feature of life and they no longer feel safe in mainstream society. Meanwhile, parents should not be left fighting to plea their communities to honor their dead children, left with few choices other than prescribing their surviving children to medicate or journal their pain away. No nation knows trauma better than Koreans, with every generation of the twentieth century marred by mass civilian tragedies. When so many young people died before their time, when they were not properly memorialized, what became of them after their loved ones passed away? If our devotion to our shared histories is what makes us human, what will become of us if our memories and mourning of mass youth deaths are politically apprehended and become a form of mnemocide?

I find inspiration in these new mourning spaces that have been created out of profound struggle and radical love for they suggest the nascence of a utopian place of a mourning community and a space for artistic authenticity (Peik, S. et al. 2023) in South Korea. They are preserving the undergrieved in places where strangers can come together with loved ones to listen or remember deeply, experiment with time, and co-exist. Such exercises to embrace others' pain as our own, recognize, ritualize, and pay witness to our collective spirit may reveal a different historical present; they may cause us to document the lives that we have lived, lost, and survived with each fateful day and signal a better way forward.

References

4.16 Yeondae Hwaldong. 2023. Gukga boanbeop gwa saekggalron-eul doetssuiwo: Jeju pyeonghwa swimteo Sin Dong-hun daepyo-rul gusokhan gukjeongwon gwa gongandangguk-eul gyutanhanda (We Condemn the National Intelligence Service and the Public Security Authorities for Arresting Jeju Peace Shelter Director Sin Dong-hun by imposing the National Security Act). https://416sewolfamily.org/notice/385. Accessed 29 December 2024.

Bak, S. 2015. "Dongasiajeok gachi"-ui munhwa cheolhakjeok ihae (Cultural and Philosophical Understanding of 'East Asian Values). *Dongseo Cheolhak Yeongu (East-West Philosophy Research)* 76:483–504.

Baker, D. 2008. *Korean Spirituality.* Honolulu, HI: University of Hawai'i Press.

Bashford, A., and P. Levine. 2010. *The Oxford Handbook of the History of Eugenics.* Oxford, UK: Oxford University Press.

Black Jaguar. 2016. VEGA, Video Installation. https://vimeo.com/328382294. Accessed 14 August 2024.

Butler, J., and A. Athanasiou. 2013. *Dispossession: The Performative in the Political.* Cambridge, UK: Polity Press.

Chang, K. 2022. *The Logic of Compressed Modernity.* Cambridge, MA: Polity Press.

Cho, M., and M. Kim. 2024. Foreign Residents in Korea Reach Record High of 2.46 Million as International Work Force Spikes. *Korea JoongAng Daily*, October 24.

Choi, H., and J. Seo. 2024. Victims of the Itaewon Crowd Crush Died Twice: The Role of Justice Beliefs (General vs. Personal) and Fatalism in Predicting Victim-Blaming. *Asian Journal of Social Psychology.*

De Juan, A., et al. 2023. The Political Effects of Witnessing State Atrocities: Evidence from the Nazi Death Marches. *Comparative Political Studies.* https://doi.org/10.1177/00104140231178736.

Director Gwon. 2018. Sewolho uiryeongje jinogigut – Kim Geumhwa (Sewol Ferry Memorial Service Jinogigut – Kim Geumhwa). Yeongchang Pilleum (Yeongchang Film) 140531. https://www.youtube.com/watch?v=ddQzhBwYCAI. Accessed 20 December 2024.

Esteban Munoz, J. 1999. *Disidentifications: Queers of Color and the Performance of Politics.* Minneapolis, MN: University of Minnesota Press.

Flag Sidekick. 2023. Kebab After Drink Vol. 1. https://flagsidekick.com/1%ED%98%B8. Accessed 20 December 2024.

Genette, G. 1980. *Narrative Discourse: An Essay in Method.* Ithaca, NY: Cornell University Press.

Gržinić, M., and S. Tatlic. 2016. *Necropolitics, Racialization, and Global Capitalism: Historicization of Biopolitics and Forensics of Politics, Art, and Life.* Lanham, MD: Lexington Books.

Guinto, J. 2024. Seoul Police Chief Acquitted Over Halloween Crush. *BBC*, October 17. https://www.bbc.com/news/articles/c4gql68dwxxo. Asccessed on 20 December 2024.

Hwang, M. 2012. Shamans and Superstitious Mothers: Modern Health Care Discourse in 1920s–30s Korea. *Asian Journal for Women's Studies* 18 (1): 30–61.

Hwang, M. 2023. Kut as Political Disobedience, Healing, and Resilience. In *A New Outlook at Atrocities*, ed. N. Carranza Ko, 177–198. Singapore: Springer Nature.

Jeju Sinmun. 2023. Eopmusang gwa silsasangjoe-ui teukbyeol cheobyeolbeop sicho (Today in History: Beginning of Special Punishment Law for Business-Related Negligence). Jeju Sinmun 2604, January 9. http://pdf.jejupress.co.kr/2604/260414.pdf. Accessed 20 December 2024.

Jeong, A. 2023. Performing Memory and Testimony After a National Disaster: The Sewol Mothers in *Talking about her* (2016), *VEGA* (2016), and *His and her closet* (2016). *Studies in Theatre and Performance* 44 (2): 286–305.

Jones, R. 1986. *Emile Durkheim: An Introduction to Four Major Works.* Beverly Hills, CA: Sage Publications.

KBS Daegu. 2023. Ajikdo: Daegu jihacheol chamsa 20jugi chumo dakyumenteori (Still: Daegu Subway Disaster 20th Anniversary Memorial Documentary) 230224. https://www.youtube.com/watch?v=RrLChcgbwO8. Accessed 20 December 2024.

Kim, E. 2017. *Curative Violence: Rehabilitating Disability, Gender, and Sexuality in Modern Korea.* Durham, NC and London: Duke University Press.

Kim, G. 2024a. *Chaekim-eul Mutda (Hold Responsible).* Seoul: Gut Peulreoseu Buk (Good Plus Book).

Kim, Y. 2024b. A Chronological Study of Discourse on Prostitution Policy, Anti-Prostitution Feminist Movements, and Sex Workers' Rights Movements in South Korea. PhD dissertation. York University, Toronto, ON.

Kim, S., and M. Hwang. 2023. *Enduring Violence and Commemoration: Korea's Cheju April 3 Incident*, 83–100. An International Journal: Violence.

Kim, H., and T. Kim. 2024. Jetliner Skids Off Runway and Bursts into Flames While Landing in South Korea, Killing 179. AP World, December 29. https://apnews.com/article/south-korea-plane-fire-68da9b0bd5196feed6e7d2db849f461a. Accessed 29 December 2024.

Kim, J., and S. Oh. 2022. Sahoejeok chamsa wa gieokgan-ui jedohwa sewolho chamsa wa daegu jihacheol chamsa bigyo bunseok (The Institutionalization of Memory Places for Social Disasters: Comparative Analysis of Sewol Ferry and Daegu Subway Fire). Bipanhoe Hakhoe Haksuldaehoe Jaryojip (Conference Proceedings of the Critical Sociological Association) 136: 148–198.

Kim, M., and H. Woo. 2022. *Redefining Multicultural Families in South Korea: Reflections and Future Directions.* New Brunswick, NJ: Rutgers University Press.

Knowles, S. 2020. Slow Disaster in the Anthropocene: A Historian Witnesses Climate Change on the Korean Peninsula. *Daedalus* 149 (4): 192–206.

Kwon, H. 2020. After the Korean War: An Intimate History. *Studies in the Social and cultural History of Modern Warfare*. Cambridge, UK: Cambridge University Press.

Kwon, S. 2016. Hanguk-ui wigi daeeung gwa jeongbu chaekimseong – sampung baekhwajeom, daegu jihacheol hwajae, sewolho chamsa reul jungsim-euro (Crisis Response and Government Responsibility in Korea – The Sampoong Department Store Collapse, Daegu Subway Fire, and Sewol Ferry Disaster). *Crisisonomy* 12 (2): 17–34.

Lee, J. 2010. *Service Economies: Militarism, Sex Work, and Migrant Labor in South Korea*. Minneapolis, MN: University of Minnesota.

Lee, C. 2022. Sojungham-eul Namgigo Gan Aideul (Children Who Left Behind Precious Memories). Ansan: 4.16 Memory Storage, 4.16 Institute of Democratic Citizenship Education.

Lee, H. 2023a. Geumgi-ga doen kanibal-gwa aedo-ui wigye: Uri-neun wae Itaewon Chamsa-reul aedohaji mothago inneunga (Taboo Carnival and Hierarchy of Mourning: Why We Cannot Mourn the Itaewon Tragedy). *Munhwa Gwahak (Literature Studies)* 113:84–107.

Lee, H. 2023b. Sahoejeok chamsa wa tain-ui jukeum: It'aewon chamsa-ui gotong gwa jukeumeun wa ilsang-uro buteo baeje doeeutna? (Social Disaster and Death of Others: Why Was the Pain and Death of the Itaewon Disaster Excluded from Daily Life?). *Korea Journal of Cultural Studies* 11 (1): 23–41.

Lee, P., and H. Kim. 2018. Jangrye munhwa insik gwa welending-ui silcheong-waje yeongu – Seoul teukbyeolsi-rul jungsim-euro. (Awareness of Funeral Culture and Well-Ending [웰엔딩] Policy Implications – Focusing on Seoul Metropolitan City). *Munhwa Gisul-ui Yunghap (Journal of the Convergence on Culture Technology)* 4 (4): 67–75.

Lee, M., H. Huh, J. Oh, and J. Chae. 2022. Comparative Analysis of the Psychosocial Symptoms and Experiences of Bereaved Parents and Parents of Children Who Survived the Sewol Ferry Accident After 5 Years: A Qualitative Interview Study. *Journal of Korean Medical Science* 39 (19): 1–17.

Lee, S., J. Noh, K. Kim, B. Shin, and J. Chae. 2024. Suicidality Among Bereaved Families After the Sewol Ferry Disaster: A Longitudinal Study. *Journal of Loss and Trauma* 30:1–16.

Mbembe, A. 2020. *Necropolitics*. Durham, NC: Duke University Press.

Moon, K. 1997. *Sex Among Allies: Military Prostitution in U.S.-Korea Relations*. New York: Columbia University Press.

Moon, S. 2005. *Militarized Modernity and Gendered Citizenship in South Korea*. Durham: Duke University Press.

Musok TV. 2014. Mandu daetakgut je10hoe jeonggi balpyo hwejung jinoguigut (*Mandu Daetak Ritual* 10th Annual Presentation of *Jinogui Ritual*). https://www.youtube.com/watch?v=iKcd-1G3zt4. Accessed 20 December 2024.

Oh, S. 2023. Uigi sahoe eseo-ui gut gongyeon: uirye eseo yeongeuk-euro geurigo dasi uirye-ro (Performing Gut in a Crisis Society: From Ritual to Theatre and Back). Geulrobeol Hangukhak gwa Minsok Munhwa (Global Korean Studies and Folk Culture). Conference Paper, Seoul National University, Seoul, Republic of Korea.

Park, B. 2023. Chief of Hotel Adjoining Itaewon Tragedy Site Fined for Illegal Extension. *Yonhap News*, November 29. https://en.yna.co.kr/view/AEN20231129004100315. Accessed 20 December 2024.

Peik, S., and M. Jo. 2023. 10.29 Itaewon chamsa wa aedo bulganeungseong: salanam-eun jadeul-ui iyagi (10.29 Itaewon Tragedy and the Impossibility of Mourning: Stories of the Survivors). *Munhwa wa Sahoe (Culture and Society)* 31 (3): 165–224.

Peik, S., S. Jang, J. Chang, S. Park, and M. Cho. 2023. Seoul 2022. *Streetnotes* 30:61–68.

Rashid, R. 2024. How South Korea's President Sealed His Own Downfall. *The Guardian*, December 14. https://www.theguardian.com/world/2024/dec/14/south-korea-president-yoon-suk-yeol-downfall-analysis. Accessed 20 December 2024.

Samuels, E., and E. Freeman. 2021. Introduction: Crip Temporalities. *Crip Temporalities, special issue of South Atlantic Quarterly* 1220 (2): 245–254.

Shin, Y. 2006. Sikminji Joseon-eseo usaengundong-ui jeongae wa seonggyeok: 1930 nyeondae "usaeng (優生)"-eul jungsim-euro. (The Purpose and Character of the Eugenic Movement in Colonial Korea: Through the 1930s Term *usaeng*). *Uisahak (Medical Science)* 15 (2): 133–155.

Somasundaram, D., and S. Sivayokan. 2013. Rebuilding Community Resilience in a Post-war Context: Developing Insight and Recommendations – A Qualitative Study in Northern Sri Lanka. *International Journal of Mental Health Systems* 7 (3): 1–24.

Tse, J., and J. Vit. 2023. Abuse Is 'a stab to the heart': Trolls Target Families of Seoul Halloween Stampede Victims. *South China Morning Post*, April 19. https://www.youtube.com/watch?v=odET43m116Y. Accessed 30 December 2024.

Veritas. 2015. Sewol Ferry victims Should Be Called Nameless Martyrs. Society Column. Veritas, June 19. https://veritas.kr/news/18346.

White, M. 2003. Historical Atlas of the Twentieth Century. Scout Report for Social Sciences and Humanities. http://users.erols.com/mwhite28/20centry.htm. Accessed 17 December 2024.

Woo, H. 2024. Jenan yeongu wa hanguk-eui jonggyohak: geu daehwa-eui pilyo-seong-e daehayeo (Disaster Research and Religious Studies in South Korea: The Need for Dialogue. https://www.dbpia.co.kr/Journal/articleDetail?nodeId=NODE11976687. Accessed 20 December 2024.

You, J., and Y. Park. 2017. The Legacies of State Corporatism in Korea: Regulatory Capture in the Sewol Ferry Tragedy. *Journal of East Asian Studies* 17:95–118.
Yu, G. 2023. *Baram-i Doe-eo Sara Naerge (I Will Live as the Wind)*. Seoul: Dareun.
Yun, J. 2024a. A New Neoliberal Offensive in South Korea: The Conservative Politics of Rollback and the Disciplining of Organized Labor. *Critical Asian Studies* 56 (3): 471–494.
Yun, Y. 2024b. *Eonni (Sister)*. Seoul: Libeureu Bukseu (Libre Books).

Index[1]

[1] Note: Page numbers followed by 'n' refer to notes.

© The Author(s), under exclusive license to Springer Nature Singapore Pte Ltd. 2025

Y. Yoo, S. C. Lee (eds.), *Reimagining Korea*, Palgrave Series in Contemporary Korean Studies,
https://doi.org/10.1007/978-981-96-6990-5

The manufacturer's authorised representative in the EU is Springer Nature Customer Service Centre GmbH, Europaplatz 3, 69115 Heidelberg, Germany. If you have any concerns regarding our products, please contact ProductSafety@springernature.com

Printed and bound by CPI Group (UK) Ltd, Croydon, CR0 4YY
01/10/2026
02225913-0001